Advance Praise for *Antisemitism: History and Myth*

"As the author of a book on antisemitism that has been in print for forty years, it should mean something when I say that I do not believe a more important book on antisemitism has ever been written. What Robert Spencer has achieved in *Antisemitism* in terms of information and breadth of subjects is unparalleled. Combine that with a passion for searching for truth and the courage to convey it to the world and you have a book that will be read for generations. But what is urgent is that this generation read it. It is the antidote to the greatest eruption of Jew-hatred since the Holocaust."

—Dennis Prager is coauthor of *Why the Jews: The Reason for Antisemitism, the Most Accurate Predictor of Human Evil* and nine other bestselling books. He is a nationally syndicated radio talk host of forty years and the co-founder of PragerU

"Robert Spencer has written the definitive book on anti-Semitism for our time. Through outstanding scholarship, he takes the reader on a journey of understanding this ancient hatred and its modern manifestations. A must-read for anyone who wants to understand not only what anti-Semitism is, but how this ancient prejudice is destroying Western culture."

—Rabbi Michael Barclay
author of Sacred Relationships: *Biblical Wisdom for Deepening Our Lives Together*

"Robert Spencer has an unmatched historical knowledge of antisemitism, this plague that is trying to destroy forever the Judeo-Christian values of human dignity, equality and freedom, and the impartiality of justice. Spencer illuminates the evil, terror and forces of hatred that today challenge the roots of our civilization."

—Bat Ye'or, author, *Islam and Dhimmitude*

"*Antisemitism* is a very important and powerful book that will contribute to our understanding of what we are up against in the war against Jew hatred. I applaud Robert Spencer for his continuous dedication in addressing Antisemitism. I urge you to read this book to understand the dangers we all face."

—Dov Hikind, former member of
New York State Assembly and founder
of Americans Against Antisemitism

"A timely, unique and urgently needed book. A giant in the field of the Arab/Islamic war against the Jews and the West, Robert Spencer has provided a thorough and engrossing historical survey of the roots of Jew-hatred within Christianity, Islam, and national and international socialism, as well as a thoughtful examination of some of the most damaging antisemitic claims that are circulating today. Some thought that antisemitism would end with the breathtaking Middle Ages lies of Jews killing

Christian children for their blood to make Matzoh or the Jews poisoning the wells of Europe and causing the Bubonic plague or that it would surely end with the German Nazis and other's merciless murder of 6 million innocent Jews. Wrong! This book is a towering achievement as an indispensable guide to the mindless Jew-hatred that has once again engulfed the world since the Oct. 7 Muslim/Arab jihad attacks against Israeli Jews. These modern-day Muslim jihadists are now also threatening the rest of the world's Jews and even the Christians. Spencer's insights are a powerful weapon against that relentless, never-ending irrational and violent hatred of the Jewish people and now against the Jewish State as well. Read it now whether you're Jewish or not. This onslaught may start with the Jews but never ends with the Jews. Mahmoud Al Zahar, cofounder of Hamas, has publicly promised us that the Christians are next. We have been warned."

—Morton A. Klein, national president,
Zionist Organization of America (ZOA)

"As Jew-hatred surges across the world, Robert Spencer explains how the contributions of Christianity, Islam, Marxism and national socialism have led to today's 'perfect storm.' Spencer, who may know more about Islamic anti-Semitism than anyone—and who has the courage to say what he knows—took up this task as a rejoinder to people he had respected who stunned him by reacting to Hamas' October 7th pogrom with 'open avowals of age-old antisemitic myths.' An important book for those confused about the sudden inversion of the situation of the world's Jews."

—Charles Jacobs, president of Americans for Peace and Tolerance (APT)

"After October 7, Robert Spencer learned that two people he 'respected and admired' had openly avowed age-old antisemitic myths about Jews controlling the media, international organizations, and the like. In response, as 'a matter of simple justice,' he wielded his well-known skills to document and explain this ancient, unique scourge. His scholarship, common sense, and goodwill render *Antisemitism* an extraordinary contribution to a tragic topic."

—Daniel Pipes, Middle East Forum

"Antisemitism has been described as the world's longest hatred, the world's most widespread hatred, and the world's most irrational hatred. In this critically important, extremely timely book, Robert Spencer documents the latest manifestation of this ancient, deadly hatred, one which has taken the world by storm in the aftermath of the mass slaughter of Jews in Israel on October 7, 2023. From pre-Christian times until today, Spencer takes you on an eye-opening journey that is as painful to read as it is seemingly impossible—and yet every word is true. Most importantly, Spencer puts his finger on the major players and ideologies that are fanning the flames of Jew-hatred today, also demolishing many of the most common myths surrounding antisemitism in general and vitriolic anti-Zionism in particular. We cannot afford to ignore the contents of this book."

—Dr. Michael L. Brown, Host of the *Line of Fire* radio broadcast and author of *Christian Antisemitism*

"The world is once again in debt to Robert Spencer, the genius loci of *Jihad Watch*, authoritative scourge of Islamic fundamentalism, and intrepid scholar who eschews cant for the sake of historical truth, no matter how politically incorrect. Spencer has now turned his sights on one of the world's hardiest ideological and moral blights: anti-Semitism. In this important new book, *Antisemitism: History and Myth*, Spencer brings encyclopedic historical knowledge and finely calibrated moral passion to anatomize this recurrent spiritual illness. In this post-October 7 world when anti-Semitism and anti-Israeli sentiment is once again on the rise, Spencer has done us all an invaluable service. His new book is both a revelation and an admonition. Everyone on the side of civilization should read it."

—Roger Kimball, Editor & Publisher, *The New Criterion*

"It's been shocking to witness the rise of vicious antisemitism in riots and demonstrations, some even showing support for the massacre of Jews on October 7 of 2023. Hating Jews is always irrational and illogical, but it's no longer confined to the ignorant and lowest educated. It now emanates from the highest levels of Ivy League education. Robert Spencer's vital new book reveals why this is neither new nor unexpected, but still it's disturbing that people would justify blind hatred of Jews in what should be an enlightened society."

—Mike Huckabee

"The hallmark of true evil—which at its core is a satanic hatred of God—is a hatred of what God loves. Thus we see the deeply perverse hatred of the Jews reasserting itself through the millennia. That we are now again witnessing a resurgence of this ancient evil makes Robert Spencer's book more important than ever. I thank God that he was written it."

—Eric Metaxas, Author of *Bonhoeffer: Pastor, Martyr, Prophet, Spy* and host of Socrates in the City

"The literature of ancient Jewish wisdom has been beaming incandescent clarity upon the phenomenon of antisemitism for over 2,000 years. I have never seen a book that tackles antisemitism just as compellingly until I read Robert Spencer's masterpiece. Seldom has a book been more timely. It is a bold and brilliant roadmap to reality solving most of the mysteries surrounding the scourge of antisemitism. It is urgent because since the age of antiquity, embracing antisemitism has been a reliable sign of a society's impending extinction. If you are hoping for America, and indeed western civilization, to recover their vitality and you seek the road to resurgence, I earnestly recommend this book."

—Rabbi Daniel Lapin, President of the
American Alliance of Jews and Christians

Also by Robert Spencer

Muhammad: A Critical Biography

Did Muhammad Exist: An Inquiry into Islam's Obscure Origins—Revised and Expanded Edition

Empire of God: How the Byzantines Saved Civilization

The Critical Qur'an: Explained from Key Islamic Commentaries and Contemporary Historical Research

The Sumter Gambit: How the Left Is Trying to Foment a Civil War

The Palestinian Delusion: The Catastrophic History of the Middle East Peace Process

Obama and Trump: Who Was Better for America?

Rating America's Presidents: An America-First Look at Who Is Best, Who Is Overrated, and Who Was An Absolute Disaster

The History of Jihad: From Muhammad to ISIS

Confessions of an Islamophobe

ANTISEMITISM

ANTISEMITISM
HISTORY & MYTH

ROBERT SPENCER

BOMBARDIER
BOOKS

Published by Bombardier Books
An Imprint of Post Hill Press
ISBN: 979-8-88845-644-6
ISBN (eBook): 979-8-88845-645-3

Antisemitism:
History and Myth
© 2025 by Robert Spencer
All Rights Reserved

Cover Design by Jim Villaflores

Post Hill Press
New York • Nashville
posthillpress.com

Published in the United States of America
1 2 3 4 5 6 7 8 9 10

Dedicated with love to all those who know that the line separating good and evil passes not between one group and another, but through every human heart.

Table of Contents

Introduction

THE RETURN OF
AN ANCIENT EVIL

It was Simchat Torah, a major Jewish holiday, and the Sabbath as well, when Hamas jihadis stormed into Israel and laid waste with a brutality and inhumanity that was reminiscent of the darkest days of National Socialist Germany.

The Hamas attack upon Israel on October 7, 2023, says the Center for Strategic & International Studies, "will go down as one of the worst terrorist attacks in history."[1] The unmitigated horror of that day makes those words seem like an inadequate summation.

The attackers gloried in their savagery and vied to outdo one another in cruelty. One survivor, a young man who had served in the IDF, recounted that on the fateful morning, he was asleep on a beach after a late-night party when he found himself in the middle of

---

[1] Daniel Byman, Riley McCabe, Alexander Palmer, Catrina Doxsee, Mackenzie Holtz, and Delaney Duff, "Hamas's October 7 Attack: Visualizing the Data," Center for Strategic & International Studies, December 19, 2023.

a war. "They fired hundreds of rockets at us within minutes."[2] Still, he and his friends thought it would soon be over, "until we saw the boats."[3] The jihadis in the boats "mounted the coast and started to slaughter everyone. Everyone. Fisherman who comes to that beach every Saturday for the last 30 years. Fathers and sons, friends, a couple of soldiers, we [were] the night before sitting together playing backgammon and having fun, and even two 17-year-old kids that came to sleep at the beach with a tent…. They murdered everyone."[4]

Later, this young man and several others managed to get in a car and tried to flee. But the nightmare was only beginning: "30m from the cars we saw a dead body, all dressed up in black, similar to the police uniforms. It wasn't a dead body, and he was not a cop. The dead body suddenly woke up and started shooting at us, at the same time his squad started shooting at us from the side. It was hell."[5] Several of those in the car were hit.

Another woman also tried to drive away, but by this time, the roads were blocked. "They found her and slaughtered her. Right on the spot. Like it was nothing. And they continued to murder people. We found her body a couple of days later."[6]

At the Kibbutz Kfar Aza, just two miles from the Gaza border, one family was preparing for a birthday party. A mother of three recounted: "We had a birthday cake. There was shooting all around us."[7] Another mother whose husband was murdered defending the kibbutz said of her six-year-old daughter: "My daughter is crushed. She understands that she doesn't have a father anymore. My son…a

2   "Oct. 7 Survivor Ariel Ein-Gal Tells His Story to Hollywood Community: A Guest Column on Nightmarish Day in Israel," *Deadline*, November 20, 2023.

3   Ibid.

4   Ibid.

5   Ibid.

6   Ibid.

7   Danielle Campoamor, "Their Kibbutz Was Attacked on Oct. 7. They're Determined to Rebuild," *Time Magazine*, November 21, 2023.

3-year-old can't understand. The first week he would cry, 'Daddy, daddy, daddy.' It was heartbreaking."[8]

To counter claims that the whole thing had been fabricated, Israeli authorities began to show journalists videos that the jihad terrorists themselves had taken of their murders and that had been recovered from jihadis who had been killed. One scene "showed a father and his two sons, aged approximately seven and nine, running in their underwear to what appeared to be a bomb shelter. A Hamas attacker threw a grenade, killing the man. The boys emerge bloodied and run. 'Dad's dead, it wasn't a prank,' one shouts. 'I know, I saw it,' replies his brother, later screaming: 'Why am I alive?'"[9]

The jihadis were happy with their work: in another scene, a jihadi "with an agricultural tool hacking at the head of a man lying on the ground, gunmen killing wounded female Israeli soldiers and a jubilant Hamas fighter calling his family: 'I killed 10 Jews with my own hands. I'm using the dead Jewish woman's phone to call you now.'"[10]

Then there were the mass rapes. The *New York Times* reported that it had "viewed photographs of one woman's corpse that emergency responders discovered in the rubble of a besieged kibbutz with dozens of nails driven into her thighs and groin. The *Times* also viewed a video, provided by the Israeli military, showing two dead Israeli soldiers at a base near Gaza who appeared to have been shot directly in their vaginas."[11]

An Israeli army reservist recounted: "Women were shot many times in the face... Their mouths were in grimaces, their eyes were open, their fists were clenched. They were shot so many times in

---

8   Ibid.

9   Rory Carroll, "Israel Shows Footage of Hamas Killings 'to Counter Denial of Atrocities,'" *Guardian*, October 23, 2023.

10   Ibid.

11   Jeffrey Gettleman, Anat Schwartz, and Adam Sella, "'Screams Without Words': How Hamas Weaponized Sexual Violence on Oct. 7," *New York Times*, December 28, 2023.

the head, in many cases it was like there was purposeful obliteration of women's faces. Our team has seen women shot in the crotch, in the genitals. Women were shot in the breast… Our team saw this. Women had legs cut off. It seemed like there was a systematic genital mutilation of women in the women we saw."[12]

In 1945, revelations of German viciousness led to worldwide revulsion and a massive display of sympathy and solidarity with Jews the world over.

In 2023 and 2024, the reaction was strikingly different.

Despite, or perhaps because of, the sickening brutality of the October 7 massacre, that attack unleashed expressions of hatred for Jews that, like the attack itself, had not been seen since the demise of Adolf Hitler's Thousand-Year Reich.

The hatred began almost immediately. The day after the massacre, with Israel and the world still reeling from the unfolding horror of what Hamas had done, conservative journalist Elijah Schaffer wrote: "1. What Hamas did was evil 2. What Israel is doing to the Palestinians is evil 3. Both think each other are the terrorists 4. One is in an open air prison."[13] Schaffer was just one of many who immediately tried to shift the focus and portray the Palestinian Arabs of Gaza as victims and Israel as the aggressor against whom virtually any action was justified.

The results of this shift of focus were unmistakable. On October 25, 2023, Reuters reported that "antisemitic incidents in the United States rose by about 400% in slightly over two weeks since war broke out in the Middle East."[14] That was just the beginning; the incitement

---

[12] "Women's Genitals 'Systemically Mutilated' in Hamas Attack, Says Israeli Reservist Who Dealt with Bodies," *Sky News*, February 1, 2024.

[13] Elijah Schaffer, X, October 8, 2023, https://twitter.com/ElijahSchaffer/status/1710990879790629080.

[14] Kanishka Singh, "US Antisemitic Incidents up about 400% since Israel-Hamas War Began, Report Says," Reuters, October 25, 2023.

continued. In mid-November, an imam in California, Dr. Sayed Moustafa al-Qazwini, declared that the Jews were "the first people to disbelieve, to disbelieve their own book."[15] After accusing them of murdering their own prophets, he concluded: "This is the result of racism. The result of racism is to see yourself have the sense of entitlement to do anything. And you are not binded [sic] by any law; you are above the law. This is the result of racism."[16] He added: "We pray that Allah will descend his victory, his aid, and his support, upon the people of Gaza, inshallah, and defeats their enemies, because they are the enemies of mankind, the enemies of humanity."[17]

Taher Herzallah, associate director of American Muslims for Palestine, stated in a similar vein that "anybody who…identifies themselves [sic] as a Jewish person or as a Christian Zionist…are [sic] enemy number one."[18]

Another prominent imam, Canada's Sheikh Younus Kathrada, went farther, praying: "Oh, Allah, bring annihilation upon the plundering and criminal Jews. Oh, Allah, annihilate them because they are no match for you. Oh, Allah, show us the black day that you inflict upon them. Oh, Allah, make their plots backfire on them. Oh, Allah, shake the ground under their feet."[19] Kathrada wanted the deity to grant him not just the annihilation of the Zionists, but of the Jews.

Numerous others besides Kathrada wanted to see at least some Jews annihilated. In Times Square, a young Muslim girl told a

---

[15]   "California Imam Dr. Sayed Moustafa Al-Qazwini: The Jews Killed Their Prophets, Have a Sense of Entitlement, Are Liars; the Enemies of Gaza Are the Enemies of Mankind, Humanity," MEMRI, November 17, 2023.

[16]   Ibid.

[17]   Ibid.

[18]   Canary Mission, X, December 9, 2023, https://twitter.com/canarymission/status/1733535753496330295.

[19]   "Canadian Imam Sheikh Younus Kathrada: Israel Has the Right to Defend Herself? Seriously? Anyone with an Ounce of Logic Will See How Wrong That Is; Oh Allah, Bring Annihilation upon the Plundering and Criminal Jews," MEMRI, November 24, 2023.

famous rabbi to kill himself because he was a Jew.[20] Others apparently wouldn't have minded if Jews were annihilated, and some gave this view legitimacy: in early December 2023, the presidents of MIT, Harvard, and the University of Pennsylvania all refused to say that open calls for a genocide of the Jews on their campuses would violate any university regulations.[21]

When pro-Hamas "encampments" sprang up at universities all over the United States in April 2024, the result of this cowardice became all too clear. At George Washington University, a protester carried a sign calling for a "Final Solution," the term that the National Socialists of Germany used in the 1940s to refer to their genocide of the Jews.[22] The leader of the Columbia University encampment, a student named Khymani James, published a video of himself saying: "Be glad—be grateful—that I'm not just going out and murdering Zionists. I've never murdered anyone in my life, and I hope to keep it that way."[23] Supporters of Israel, James said, "don't deserve to live."[24] When this video circulated widely and caused a firestorm, Columbia expelled James; it quickly came to light, however, that he had said much the same thing to university officials in January 2024, and they had done nothing.[25]

20 Rabbi Shmuley Boteach, X, December 27, 2023, https://twitter.com/RabbiShmuley/status/1739884958259269911.
21 Andrew Bernard, "House Committee Probes University Presidents on Campus Antisemitism," *JNS*, December 5, 2023.
22 Megan Palin, "Horror as GWU Protester Carries Sign with Nazi 'Final Solution' Call for Extermination of Jews," *New York Post*, April 26, 2024.
23 Guy Benson, X, April 25, 2024, https://twitter.com/guypbenson/status/1783643422680592687.
24 Ibid.
25 "Columbia Expels Protester Who Said 'Zionists Don't Deserve to Live' – Reports," *i24News*, April 27, 2024; Daniel Greenfield, "Columbia U Allowed Student Who Talked about Killing Jews to Remain on Campus for Months," *FrontPage Magazine*, April 28, 2024.

James wasn't the only one wishing death on Jews. In mid-December 2023, synagogues all over the US received bomb threats.[26] In Munich, of all places, a Muslim gang set upon a man who was recognizable as a Jew because of his yarmulke and beat and kicked him.[27] In New York City, three thugs, one of whom screamed "Free Palestine!," set upon three Jews, including a teenage boy, and beat and kicked them in separate attacks.[28] In London, two women beat a Jewish woman until she lost consciousness as passersby casually went on their way.[29]

In Paris, a knife-wielding man entered a Jewish daycare center and said to its female director: "You're a Jew, you're a Zionist. Five of us are going to rape you, cut you up like they did in Gaza."[30] Also in Paris, another man brandished a knife while screaming "Allahu akbar" on a busy street.[31] He asked a women who was passing by if she was Jewish; when she answered that she wasn't, he exclaimed: "You're lucky; otherwise, you would have taken it," that is, the knife, "in the gut!"[32] In Washington, DC, two supporters of Hamas stood outside a Hanukkah event at the Israeli Embassy and screamed at those leaving the event: "We will kill you all!"[33]

---

[26]   Pat Pratt and Jon Kipper, "Creve Coeur Police Conduct Bomb Search at 3 Synagogues Sunday Following Emailed Threat," *KMOV*, December 17, 2023; "Jewish Temple Was Searched by Police after a Bomb Threat Was Called In, Rabbi Says," *WMTW*, December 17, 2023; Tony Garcia and Dryden Quigley, "Nashville Jewish Organization Reports Email Threat," *WSMV*, December 17, 2023; "Police Investigating Threat Made against Congregation in East Lansing," *WILX*, December 17, 2023.

[27]   "Gruppe aus Syrern und Eritreern prügelt auf Juden ein," *Apollo News*, December 16, 2023.

[28]   Rocco Parascandola, "Bigoted Trio Beats Up 3 Jewish Strangers, Including 15-Year-Old Boy, in 40-Minute Brooklyn Hate Crime Spree," *New York Daily News*, November 30, 2023.

[29]   Shomrim (Stanford Hill), X, December 8, 2023, https://twitter.com/Shomrim/status/1733133750853136542.

[30]   Ben Cohen, "'Zionist, We Are Going to Rape You!' Knife Wielding Intruder Threatens Director of Jewish Daycare Center Near Paris," *Algemeiner*, December 14, 2023.

[31]   Guillaume Poingt, "Paris: au cri d'«Allah Akbar», un homme muni d'un couteau menace une femme et lui demande si elle est juive," *Le Figaro*, December 12, 2023.

[32]   Ibid.

[33]   "Watch: Protesters Threaten to Kill Jews Leaving Israeli Embassy in D.C.," *The Yeshiva World*, December 13, 2023.

Even when Jews were not physically attacked or threatened, they were menaced. In one incident that was uncomfortably reminiscent of Kristallnacht, when Jewish-owned businesses, as well as synagogues and other establishments, were attacked and destroyed all over Germany on the night of November 9, 1938, pro-Palestinian protesters gathered in front of a Philadelphia falafel shop, Goldie, on December 3, 2023, and chanted: "Goldie, Goldie, you can't hide. We charge you with genocide."[34] The owner of the shop, Michael Solomonov, was not only Jewish, but Israeli.

The menacing of Goldie was far enough over the line to draw a rebuke even from the White House. Biden administration spokesman Andrew Bates stated: "It is antisemitic and completely unjustifiable to target restaurants that serve Israeli food over disagreements with Israeli policy."[35] Yet much the same thing happened in Detroit on December 16. Israel-haters gathered in front of Townhouse Detroit, another Jewish-owned restaurant, and taunted its owner, Jeremy Sasson: "Jeremy, Jeremy, what do you say? How many kids did you kill today?"[36] It was shocking enough when protesters against the Vietnam War chanted this at President Lyndon B. Johnson in the 1960s, but he was the president, and the US was embroiled in a quagmire in Vietnam. Jeremy Sasson was a restaurant owner, not a head of state.

In Toronto, New York City, and elsewhere, protesters chanted the slogan, "From the river to the sea, Palestine will be free."[37] If Israel were indeed erased from the Jordan River to the Mediterranean Sea,

---

34   Jordan Van Glish, X, December 3, 2023, https://twitter.com/thatJVG/status/17314401583 63222485.

35   Daniel Arkin, "White House Blasts Protest of Israeli Restaurant in Philadelphia as 'Unjustifiable,'" *NBC News*, December 4, 2023.

36   Adar Rubin, X, December 16, 2023, https://twitter.com/rubin_a1/status/1736175585120 883185.

37   Visegrád 24, X, December 3, 2023, https://twitter.com/visegrad24/status/1731434020301 332850; Era Gigman, X, December 31, 2023, https://twitter.com/idan_bg/status/174 1640289163354496.

it would mean certain death for millions of Jews. In Maryland, a teachers' union official compiled a list of wealthy Jews, to whom she referred as "gluttons and thieves."[38]

At Farley's East coffee house in Oakland, California, employees refused to allow a Jewish woman to use the restroom, which was emblazoned with graffiti reading "Zionism = fascism" and "Neutrality helps genocide in Gaza."[39] In mid-December, a poll showed that 67 percent of young people between the ages of eighteen and twenty-four agreed with the claim that "Jews as a class are oppressors and should be treated as oppressors."[40]

In New Jersey, a contractor named Melquisedec Francis announced that "he would not provide services to Jewish patrons in at least three online communications in violation of the New Jersey Law Against Discrimination."[41] In one of these, Francis stated flatly: "I am currently not offering my services to the Jewish community."[42] British Airways, meanwhile, shelved plans to offer a Jewish sitcom, *Hapless*, on its flights over a concern that doing so might give the impression that the airline had decided to "take sides" in the Hamas-Israel war. The series had nothing to do with the war or with the Israeli-Palestinian conflict.[43]

All this, and there was much more of it, was accompanied by the reappearance of claims about Jewish power and control over world events that had circulated for decades, sometimes even longer, but

[38] Luke Rosiak, "Teachers Union Official Compiled List of Nearby Wealthy Jews, Calling Them 'Gluttons and Thieves,'" *The Daily Wire*, December 4, 2023.

[39] Visegrád 24, X, December 7, 2023, https://twitter.com/visegrad24/status/17326917676175 81102.

[40] Harvard Caps Harris Poll, December 13–14, 2023, https://harvardharrispoll.com/wp-content/uploads/2023/12/HHP_Dec23_KeyResults.pdf.

[41] "Decrying Man Who Won't Work for Jews, New Jersey AG Cites Islamophobia," *JNS*, December 1, 2023.

[42] Ibid.

[43] Adam Mawardi, "Jewish Sitcom 'Paused' from Airline's Inflight Entertainment," *Telegraph*, December 15, 2023.

had not appeared in mainstream public discourse since before World War II. October 7 led to a large-scale reappearance of attacks on Jews and assertions that Jews secretly controlled various nations (most notably, of course, the United States), institutions, and industries, all with nefarious intent.

All this was not new. It was something the world has seen many, many times before. The hatred of Jews has been with us almost as long as there have been Jews.

There are about fifteen million Jews worldwide today, two or three million more than there are Zulus, and constituting less than two-tenths of one percent of the global population. Israel ranks ninety-third among the countries of the world in population, more populous than Honduras but less so than Portugal, Papua New Guinea, and the Dominican Republic. It ranks 149th in size among the world's nations, larger than Eswatini but smaller than Djibouti and Belize.

There are numerous peoples that are greater in number than the Jews, and nations of the earth that are larger and more populated than Israel, and yet receive a fraction of the attention that is accorded to the Jewish state and to Jews around the world. Jews and Israel occupy an outsize portion of the world's attention, and a very great deal of that attention is negative.

After the October 7 massacres, I myself encountered this recrudescence of anti-Jewish false claims and conspiracy theories. People whom I had previously trusted and respected took issue with my support for Israel against Hamas, claiming that the two sides were equivalent human rights abusers. Christians warned me that ancient prophecies held that the Antichrist would arise from modern-day Israel. Fervent and articulate opponents of globalism and socialism began sending me articles in which globalists and socialists rehearsed all the alleged evils and misdeeds of Israel. Vociferous critics of the

United Nations began citing its figures on civilian deaths in Gaza as if they were 100 percent reliable, despite coming straight from Hamas. Critics of jihad violence began invoking jihad apologists in the West to buttress their claims that Israel was a rogue state, unworthy of support from decent people.

I am not Israeli. I am not even Jewish. I am, however, aware of the German pastor Martin Niemöller's famous statement about the German failure to stand up to the National Socialists: "First they came for the socialists, and I did not speak out—because I was not a socialist. Then they came for the trade unionists, and I did not speak out—because I was not a trade unionist. Then they came for the Jews, and I did not speak out—because I was not a Jew. Then they came for me—and there was no one left to speak for me."

Jews are not perfect or sinless people any more than any other group is. It is easy to find stories of Jewish murderers and child molesters and rapists, just as it is easy to find stories of Roman Catholic murderers and child molesters and rapists, other Christian murderers and child molesters and rapists, Islamic murderers and child molesters and rapists, and so on. The question at hand is whether Judaism actually teaches and condones such behavior, and whether Jews have really engaged in it on a large scale in order to further shadowy goals of conquest and world domination that they have done their best to conceal but that non-Jews have nevertheless discovered.

Undertaking this investigation, for me, has been a matter of simple justice. In the aftermath of October 7, Jews have been targeted as they have not been since World War II. And claims that they are enemies of humanity and of all that is good have become mainstream as they have not been since Adolf Hitler put a bullet in his brain. The record needed to be set straight for anyone who was willing to see the truth.

As I began this investigation, one of these former friends accused me of inconsistency. He noted that as a longtime foe of jihad violence and Sharia oppression, I had been unafraid to look into Islamic texts and teachings and to track the connections between them and contemporary jihad activity but claimed that I was now too afraid of disapproval from Jewish friends and patrons to perform the same investigation of Judaism. If I did carry out such an investigation, one longtime associate insisted, I would see that what I was dismissing as antisemitism was justified and reasonable suspicion and that to dismiss it as such was tantamount to dismissing concern about jihad as "Islamophobia."

Very well. Here, old friend, is that investigation.

PART I

THE WELLSPRINGS

"Oh the Protestants hate the Catholics
And the Catholics hate the Protestants
And the Hindus hate the Muslims
And everybody hates the Jews... "[44]

When the secular Jewish humorist Tom Lehrer sang this song in 1965, "And everybody hates the Jews" was a punchline, a bit of dark humor twenty years after the end of the Holocaust. When Lehrer sang this song, "National Brotherhood Week," the general perception was that human civilization had moved on from all that. The hatred of Jews, justified in so many and various ways, had been taken to its ultimate conclusion in Europe under the domination of National Socialism. The world had seen the camps, the crematoria, and the stacks of dead bodies and recoiled in horror.

---

[44]   Tom Lehrer, "National Brotherhood Week," 1965.

Twenty years later, the iconoclastic Lehrer dared to joke about it precisely because of the widespread view that it was a thing of the past. This allowed people to perceive some distance between the state of the world at that time and what the Jews of Europe had experienced. It was all over now.

Of course, it wasn't. Not only was the hatred of Jews still very much present in the world, but Lehrer's song touched on another consistent aspect of it: it came from "everybody," or at the very least, the pretexts for it always shifted, while the hatred remained constant.

There have been four principal sources for this hatred; charges against the Jews that originated with each are still circulating worldwide today.

Chapter One

PRE-CHRISTIAN JEW-HATRED

MANETHO'S REVISIONIST EXODUS

The hatred of Jews, like the great foundational story of the liberation of the Jews, begins in Egypt.

A book of Jewish scripture, Exodus, which dates from around 1300 to 1450 BCE, recounts that the Israelites were enslaved in Egypt, oppressed by the Pharaoh, who rebuffed all efforts of the prophet Moses to allow them to go free. Pharaoh may have been the first to belittle the Jews with antisemitic characterizations, saying: "They are idle… Let heavier work be laid upon the men that they may labor at it and pay no regard to lying words."[45] To the Jews themselves, he said: "You are idle, you are idle; therefore you say, 'Let us

---

[45]   Exodus 5:8–9.

3

go and sacrifice to the LORD.'"[46] He may also have been the first to accuse the Jews of nefarious secret activities: "Look, you have some evil purpose in mind."[47]

After a series of plagues, Pharaoh allowed the Israelites to leave, but then changed his mind and pursued them. God miraculously parts the Red Sea to allow the Israelites to walk out of Egypt; when Pharaoh and his men pursue the escaping slaves in their chariots, the sea crashes back in on them.

This is the central story of Judaism, recalled every year at Passover and constituting a promise for Jews who have been enslaved and oppressed throughout history that God would someday once again liberate them from their enemies. According to Flavius Josephus, a Jewish historian in the first century CE, it also became the occasion for one of the first anti-Jewish polemics in history, the Egyptian historian Manetho. Manetho flourished in the third century BCE; most of Manetho's writings have been lost, but some fragments survive, and Josephus summarizes more.

Josephus profoundly disapproves of Manetho and accuses him of numerous inaccuracies. Working from Manetho's writings, Josephus states that Amenophis, the king of Egypt, "conceived a desire to behold the gods," and that a prophet told him that he could do so "if he cleansed the whole land of lepers and other polluted persons."[48] The king accordingly sent eighty thousand "into the stone-quarries to the east of the Nile, there to work segregated from the rest of the Egyptians," but then was overcome with remorse at how he had mistreated these people.[49] Josephus continues with what he says is a direct quote from Manetho: "When the men in the stone-quarries

---

[46] Exodus 5:17.
[47] Exodus 10:10.
[48] Flavius Josephus, *Of the Antiquities of the Jews, Against Apion*, I.26, https://penelope. uchicago.edu/Thayer/E/Roman/Texts/Manetho/History_of_Egypt/2*.html.
[49] Ibid.

had suffered hardships for a considerable time, they begged the king to assign to them as a dwelling-place and a refuge the deserted city of the Shepherds, Auaris, and he consented."[50]

Once there, according to Manetho, the lepers began a revolt and "appointed as their leader one of the priests of Heliopolis called Osarseph, and took an oath of obedience to him in everything."[51] Osarseph "made it a law that they should neither worship the gods nor refrain from any of the animals prescribed as especially sacred in Egypt, but should sacrifice and consume all alike, and that they should have intercourse with none save those of their own confederacy."[52]

Osarseph was not just a lawgiver. Manetho continues: "After framing a great number of laws like these, completely opposed to Egyptian custom, he ordered them with their multitude of hands, to repair the walls of the city and make ready for war against King Amenophis."[53] He sent emissaries to a group of shepherds in Jerusalem, asking them to join him and his fellow lepers in attacking Egypt. The shepherds agreed. Faced with a significant force arrayed against him, Amenophis fled to Ethiopia, whereupon the shepherds and the lepers attacked the people of Egypt and treated them "impiously and savagely."[54] They "set towns and villages on fire, pillaging the temples and mutilating images of the gods without restraint."[55] They even "made a practice of using the sanctuaries as kitchens to roast the sacred animals which the people worshipped: and they would compel the priests and prophets to sacrifice and butcher the beasts, afterwards casting the men forth naked."[56]

---

[50]   Ibid.
[51]   Ibid.
[52]   Ibid.
[53]   Ibid.
[54]   Ibid.
[55]   Ibid.
[56]   Ibid.

After telling this story, Manetho makes his big revelation: "It is said that the priest who framed their constitution and their laws was a native of Heliopolis, named Osarseph after the god Osiris, worshipped at Heliopolis; but when he joined this people, he changed his name and was called Moses."[57] Josephus concludes by noting that Manetho records the return of Amenophis from Ethiopia "with a large army."[58] This time, he took up the fight against the shepherds from Jerusalem and the Egyptian lepers led by Moses "and defeated them, killing many and pursuing the others to the frontiers of Syria."[59]

Josephus then states that he believes Manetho's account to be "manifest lies and nonsense," and it very well may be. There is even some question as to whether it originally referred to Moses and the Exodus at all. Some historians have concluded that the identification of Osarseph with Moses was not made by Manetho, but was a later interpolation, and that Manetho isn't talking about the Exodus, but the expulsion of the Hyksos, foreign rulers who were expelled from Egypt in the seventeenth century BCE, two centuries before the Exodus.

This was a common confusion. The expulsion of the Hyksos and the Exodus were conflated together even in some official Egyptian records. Whatever Manetho originally wrote, negative stereotypes of the Jews took hold and began to spread. In Josephus's version of Manetho's account, Moses is not a prophet or a hero, but a leper and an enemy of the gods. The ruler of Egypt is not a cruel oppressor, but someone who showed kindness to the lepers (who are the Israelites in his telling), only to be repaid with their rebellion. The Israelites are not miraculously rescued from Egypt, but are driven out by a king who had had his fill of their misdeeds.

---

[57] Ibid.
[58] Flavius Josephus, *Of the Antiquities of the Jews, Against Apion,* I.27, https://penelope. uchicago.edu/Thayer/E/Roman/Texts/Manetho/History_of_Egypt/2*.html.
[59] Ibid.

Manetho himself, if Josephus's version of his writings is accurate, may have been motivated by a desire to present a more positive view of the Egyptians than appears in the Exodus account. Whatever his motivations may have been, however, his upside-down version of the Israelites' Exodus from Egypt was extremely influential, to the extent that Josephus thought it necessary to rebut it four hundred years after Manetho lived.

In the ancient world, revisionist versions of the accounts in the Jewish scriptures became a cottage industry. The modern-day philologist Pieter van der Horst observes that Josephus/Manetho's "'anti-Jewish version of Exodus' sets the tone for a series of such retellings of the biblical story by subsequent writers in the second and first centuries BCE and later. One can only speculate why this motif begins to circulate at that time. It coincides more or less with the appearance of the Septuaginta, the first Greek translation of the Jewish Bible in Alexandria at the beginning of the third century BCE. We can guess that as the Exodus story became available in Greek, Manetho and other Egyptian intellectuals became familiar with it and were infuriated by Egypt's negative image in the Book of Exodus."[60]

Van der Horst did not actually assume that Josephus's quotations of Manetho were accurate. He identifies another writer Josephus quotes, the grammarian Lysimachus of Alexandria, as the first to turn "the Jews into enemies of humankind as a whole…and adversaries of religion and piety. It is from this writer [Lysimachus] onwards that the image of the Jews as misanthropes and atheists becomes a stock element in the anti-Jewish propaganda of pagan antiquity."[61]

---

[60] "The Egyptian Beginning of Anti-Semitism's Long History," Jerusalem Center for Public Affairs, October 10, 2007.

[61] Pieter W. van der Horst, *Studies in Ancient Judaism and Early Christianity (Ancient Judaism and Early Christianity, 87)* (Leiden: Brill, 2014), 390.

Lysimachus, according to Josephus, wrote this:

> The people of the Jews being leprous and scabby, and subject to certain other kinds of distempers, in the days of Bocchoris, king of Egypt, they fled to the temples, and got their food there by begging: and as the numbers were very great that were fallen under these diseases, there arose a scarcity in Egypt. Hereupon Bocehoris, the king of Egypt, sent some to consult the oracle of [Jupiter] Hammon about his scarcity. The god's answer was this, that he must purge his temples of impure and impious men, by expelling them out of those temples into desert places; but as to the scabby and leprous people, he must drown them, and purge his temples, the sun having an indignation at these men being suffered to live; and by this means the land will bring forth its fruits.

> Upon Bocchoris's having received these oracles, he called for their priests, and the attendants upon their altars, and ordered them to make a collection of the impure people, and to deliver them to the soldiers, to carry them away into the desert; but to take the leprous people, and wrap them in sheets of lead, and let them down into the sea.

> Hereupon the scabby and leprous people were drowned, and the rest were gotten together, and sent into desert places, in order to be exposed to destruction. In this case they assembled themselves together, and took counsel what they should do, and determined that, as the night was coming on, they should kindle fires and lamps, and keep watch; that

they also should fast the next night, and propitiate the gods, in order to obtain deliverance from them.

That on the next day there was one Moses, who advised them that they should venture upon a journey, and go along one road till they should come to places fit for habitation: that he charged them to have no kind regards for any man, nor give good counsel to any, but always to advise them for the worst; and to overturn all those temples and altars of the gods they should meet with: that the rest commended what he had said with one consent, and did what they had resolved on, and so traveled over the desert. But that the difficulties of the journey being over, they came to a country inhabited, and that there they abused the men, and plundered and burnt their temples; and then came into that land which is called Judea, and there they built a city, and dwelt therein, and that their city was named *Hierosyla* ["City of Temple-Robbers"], from this their robbing of the temples; but that still, upon the success they had afterwards, they in time changed its denomination, that it might not be a reproach to them, and called the city *Hierosolyma* ["City of Peace," Jerusalem"], and themselves *Hierosolymites*.[62]

This revisionism also became a kind of paradigm for anti-Jewish polemic throughout history. Josephus's Manetho and Lysimachus were the first in a long line of writers who believe themselves to be far too intelligent and insightful to believe the "official story" and who

---

[62] Flavius Josephus, *Against Apion*, I.34, http://www.earlyjewishwritings.com/text/josephus/apion1.html.

fashion a version of the events at hand that is more to their liking—one that blames the Jews.

"THEIR LAWS ARE DIFFERENT FROM THOSE OF EVERY OTHER PEOPLE"

Also in the Hebrew scriptures is the Book of Esther, which states that Haman the Agagite, a top official of the Persian King Ahasuerus, conceived a hatred of the Jews when one of the Jews, who were at that time in exile in Persia, refused to accord him what he considered to be proper respect. When "all the king's servants who were at the king's gate bowed down and did obeisance to Haman," the lone Jew, Mordecai, "did not bow down or do obeisance."[63]

Haman was "filled with fury," and not just at Mordecai alone: he "sought to destroy all the Jews, the people of Mordecai, throughout the whole kingdom of Ahasuerus."[64]

Haman told Ahasuerus: "There is a certain people scattered abroad and dispersed among the peoples in all the provinces of your kingdom; their laws are different from those of every other people, and they do not keep the king's laws, so that it is not for the king's profit to tolerate them. If it please the king, let it be decreed that they be destroyed, and I will pay ten thousand talents of silver into the hands of those who have charge of the king's business, that they may put it into the king's treasuries."[65]

Haman's plot comes to naught, and he himself meets a bad end. But in his words to Ahasuerus, he articulated what many a ruler would

---

[63]   Esther 3:2.
[64]   Esther 3:6.
[65]   Esther 3:8–9.

complain about the Jews throughout history: their laws are different, they do not assimilate, and consequently, they must be destroyed.

This in itself constitutes one of the fundamental reasons why the Jews have been persecuted throughout history: while there have always been some who went along, and even some who became leaders of movements that would have erased them as a distinct people, as a whole, they have resisted attempts at incorporation into the larger society. As a result, in the twenty-first century, while their ancient enemies in the Hebrew scriptures, the Canaanites, the Amorites, the Girgashites, the Hittites, the Hivites, the Jebusites, and the Perizzites, have long since vanished from the scene, absorbed into other peoples, the Jews remain, despite numerous attempts to eradicate them.

AN ASS'S HEAD IN THE TEMPLE

In the year 168 BCE, says the Second Book of Maccabees, the Seleucid King Antiochus IV Epiphanes was enraged that the Jews had rejected his choice for High Priest. He seized the opportunity to demonstrate his overlordship and contempt for the Jews by entering and profaning the temple:

> When news of what had happened reached the king, he took it to mean that Judea was in revolt. So, raging inwardly, he left Egypt and took the city by storm. And he commanded his soldiers to cut down relentlessly everyone they met and to slay those who went into the houses. Then there was killing of young and old, destruction of boys, women, and children, and slaughter of virgins and infants. Within the total of three days eighty thousand were destroyed, forty thousand in hand-to-hand fighting; and as many were

11

sold into slavery as were slain. Not content with this, Antiochus dared to enter the most holy temple in all the world, guided by Menelaus, who had become a traitor both to the laws and to his country. He took the holy vessels with his polluted hands, and swept away with profane hands the votive offerings which other kings had made to enhance the glory and honor of the place.[66]

Antiochus could not tolerate the idea that this recalcitrant people was not entirely under his control and could not be bent to his will. He would by no means be the last ruler to regard the Jews in this way.

As this episode retreated into history, it was amplified. The Greek historian Diodorus of Sicily, writing in the first century BCE, asserts that inside the temple, Antiochus encountered "the image of a man with a long beard, carved in stone sitting upon an ass."[67] This was unbelievable on its face, as Judaism forbade statues of human beings. The king understood this to be Moses, who, says Diodorus, "built Jerusalem and brought the nation together, and who established by law all their wicked customs and practices, abounding in hatred and enmity to all other men."[68] In his hostility to the Jews' refusal to assimilate, Antiochus performed calculated expressions of contempt for the Jews' beliefs before this statue, and at the altar:

> Antiochus, therefore, abhorring their antagonism to all other people, tried his utmost to abolish their laws. To that end he sacrificed a great swine at the image of Moses, and at the altar of God that stood in the outward court, and sprinkled them with the

---

[66]   2 Maccabees 5:11–16.
[67]   Diodorus Siculus, Books 34 & 35, 1, http://attalus.org/translate/diodorus34.html.
[68]   Ibid.

blood of the sacrifice. He commanded likewise that the books, by which they were taught to hate all other nations, should be sprinkled with the broth made of the swine's flesh. And he put out the lamp (called by them immortal) which burns continually in the temple. Lastly he forced the high priest and the other Jews to eat swine's flesh.[69]

The Egyptian Hellene Apion, who wrote a century later, says that inside the temple, Antiochus saw horrors that justified his profanation, as well as the burning of the Jewish books that supposedly taught them to "hate all other nations." Josephus laments that critics of the Jews "accuse us for not worshipping the same gods whom others worship," they "think themselves not guilty of impiety when they tell lies of us; and frame absurd and reproachful stories about our temple."[70] Apion's work is lost, but Josephus quotes him asserting that the Jews preceded Antiochus's profanation of the temple with one of their own: "The Jews placed an ass's head in their holy place."[71]

This was a curious charge. Why would the Jews, who forbade images, profane their own holy place with an image of an ass? It is, however, similar to charges that have reverberated throughout history: the Jews offered one image to the world but had all manner of secret beliefs and practices that were shrouded in darkness because even those who subscribed to them and acted upon them knew that they were evil.

And so Apion goes on, quoted by Josephus: "This was discovered when Antiochus Epiphanes spoiled our temple; and found that ass's head there made of gold; and worth a great deal of money."[72] The

---

[69] Ibid.
[70] Josephus, Against Apion, II.7, https://penelope.uchicago.edu/josephus/apion-2.html.
[71] Ibid., language modernized for clarity.
[72] Ibid., language modernized for clarity.

value of the thing indicated indirectly the depth of Jews' evil: not only had they profaned their own holy of holies with an ass's head, but they had devoted considerable expense to doing so. This was, apparently, an important priority for them.

Josephus then offers several points in rebuttal to this story: First, he says, it is the Egyptians, not the Jews, who worship asses and other "contemptible animals" as gods.[73] "As for us Jews," says Josephus, "we ascribe no honor, nor power to asses; as do the Egyptians to crocodiles, and asps; when they esteem such as are seized upon by the former, or bitten by the latter to be happy persons; and persons worthy of God."[74]

Josephus also marvels that "Apion does not understand this to be no other than a palpable lie," for, he points out, "we Jews are always governed by the same laws; in which we constantly persevere," and none of the other non-Jewish rulers who entered the temple, including the Romans Pompey, Crassus, and Titus, ever said that they had seen such a thing inside it.[75] Josephus adds that other writers who took note of Antiochus's entering the temple don't mention that he saw any such thing.

Nor did they mention another horror that, according to Apion, Antiochus found inside the temple. Josephus quotes Apion saying that "Antiochus found in our temple a bed, and a man lying upon it; with a small table before him, full of dainties; from the sea, and the fowls of the dry land. That this man was amazed at these dainties thus set before him."[76] When this man saw Antiochus, he jumped off his bed and approached him and "begged to be released."[77] Antiochus,

---

[73] Ibid.
[74] Ibid.
[75] Ibid.
[76] Josephus, Against Apion, II.8.
[77] Ibid.

intrigued, asked him to tell his story: what was he doing apparently living in the temple, and why was he surrounded by sumptuous food?

At that, this man "made a lamentable complaint, and with sighs, and tears in his eyes, gave him this account of the distress he was in." He explained that he was a Greek who had been kidnapped and imprisoned in the temple. There, he "was seen by no body, but was fattened by these curious provisions thus set before him."[78] He was overjoyed at first at his apparent good fortune. However, overcome by curiosity, he asked the servants who brought him his food why he was being held and treated so well. They told him that "it was in order to the fulfilling a law of the Jews, which they must not tell him, that he was thus fed: and that they did the same at a set time every year. That they used to catch a Greek foreigner, and fat him thus up every year; and then lead him to a certain wood, and kill him, and sacrifice with their accustomed solemnities, and taste of his entrails, and take an oath upon this sacrificing a Greek, that they would ever be at enmity with the Greeks. And that then they threw the remaining parts of the miserable wretch into a certain pit."[79] Apion says that this fellow told Antiochus that he had only a few days before he was to be sacrificed and begged the king to save him from the Jews.

Josephus accuses Apion of fabricating this story, which is likely in light of the fact that there is no indication that the Jews performed human sacrifice, which Judaism actually forbids.[80] Yet the story proved to be only the first of many such allegations, which proved to be the precursor to blood libel charges that became a feature of the persecution of Jews in medieval Europe: the Jews were accused, generally with little or no evidence that wasn't fabricated or coerced,

---

[78]   Ibid.

[79]   Ibid.

[80]   Rabbi Jonathan Sacks, "Does Judaism Believe in Human Sacrifice?," Chabad.org, n.d., https://www.chabad.org/parshah/article_cdo/aid/2740773/jewish/Does-Judaism-Believe-in-Human-Sacrifice.htm.

of carrying out a heinous act that was contrary to their stated beliefs. This was presented as evidence both of their evil and of the Jews' secrecy: what they *really* believed, those who propagated these stories insisted, differed sharply from what they *said* they believed.

The claim that the Jews kept an ass's head in the temple and practiced human sacrifice there persisted at least until the tenth century CE, when it appears in a massive encyclopedia produced in the Roman Empire, the *Souda*. Under the entry for Damocritus, a historian who wrote around 100 BCE, the *Souda* states: "Historian. [He wrote] Tactics in 2 books, [and] On the Jews; in which [latter] he says that they used to bow down to the golden head of an ass, and every seven years hunted a stranger and attacked him and tore his flesh into thin strips and thus killed him."[81] The entry for "Judah," meanwhile, says: "Concerning the Jews, the historian Damocritus says that they used to worship the golden head of an ass, and every three years they hunted and attacked a stranger. They tore his flesh into thin strips and in this manner they killed him."[82]

It's noteworthy that the *Souda* repeats Apion's charge about an ass's head in the temple and ascribes it to a much earlier authority, but the encyclopedia also contradicts itself. Did the Jews sacrifice a foreigner every three years or every seven? Or did they do it annually, as Apion states? Jew-haters will wave away these divergences of detail and insist on the commonality of the testimony. Yet it is striking that the compilers of the *Souda* couldn't state accurately what Damocritus actually claimed, and even odder that, if the Jews really were engaging in human sacrifice on a regular basis, the only testimony of it would

81 "Damocritus," *Suda* On Line, Jennifer Benedict, trans., https://www.cs.uky.edu/~raphael/sol/sol-cgi-bin/search.cgi?login=guest&enlogin=guest&db=REAL&field=adlerhw_gr&searchstr=delta,49.

82 "Judah," *Suda* On Line, Kristen Bentley, trans., https://www.cs.uky.edu/~raphael/sol/sol-cgi-bin/search.cgi?login=guest&enlogin=guest&db=REAL&field=adlerhw_gr&searchstr=iota,429.

be two claims published eight hundred years apart, with one written by someone who was manifestly hostile to the Jews. Did the hostility motivate the charge, or did the charge lead to the hostility? There is no way to tell at this point, but since the charge goes against all that is known of Jewish law and practice, it is much more likely that the hostility led to the charge and not the other way around. People don't always act in accordance with their stated principles by any means, but the fact that these charges violate so much of actual Jewish teaching makes it likely that if an ass's head had actually been set up in the temple and human sacrifices performed, there would have been protests within the Jewish community itself.

For many who have hated Jews throughout history, however, mere accusations were essentially proof of guilt. Yet ironically, the same kinds of charges were leveled against another group when it was small, despised, and a target of suspicion, engaging in rites that were little known among those outside the group, and thus fertile ground for rumormongering.

AN ASS'S HEAD IN THE CHURCH

The Christian writer Tertullian, who died around 220 CE, complains that wild accusations were being made against the Christians, who were then a small, outlawed, and despised sect in the Roman Empire, and that they weren't being allowed to rebut them. "Christians alone," he complained, "are forbidden to say anything in exculpation of themselves, in defense of the truth, to help the judge to a righteous decision; all that is cared about is having what the public hatred demands."[83] Tertullian says that in ordinary criminal cases, there is an investigation conducted in order to determine the facts of the matter, but "nothing like this is done in our case, though the falsehoods disseminated about us ought to have the same sifting, that it might be found how many murdered children each of us had tasted; how many incests each of us had shrouded in darkness; what cooks, what dogs had been witness of our deeds. Oh, how great the glory of the ruler who should bring to light some Christian who had devoured a hundred infants! But instead of that, we find that even inquiry in regard to our case is forbidden."[84]

Tertullian may have heard these charges against the Christians from a non-Christian named Octavius. Early in the third century, another Christian writer, Marcus Minucius Felix, engaged in a dialogue with Octavius, who accused the Christians of all manner of the bizarre and repulsive practices Tertullian mentioned. Octavius charged that the Christians know one another by secret marks and insignia, and they love one another almost before they know one another."[85] Christianity, he said, was a "religion of lust," and noted with disgust that "they call one another promiscuously brothers and sisters."[86]

Echoing Apion's report about the dark deeds that were being done inside the Jewish temple, Octavius continued: "I hear that they adore the head of an ass, that basest of creatures, consecrated by I know

---

[83]   Tertullian, Apology, 2, S. Thelwall, trans. From *Ante-Nicene Fathers*, Vol. 3. Alexander Roberts, James Donaldson, and A. Cleveland Coxe, eds. (Buffalo, NY: Christian Literature Publishing Co., 1885.) Revised and edited for New Advent by Kevin Knight, http://www.newadvent.org/fathers/0301.htm.

[84]   Ibid.

[85]   Marcus Minucius Felix, *Octavius*, 9, Robert Ernest Wallis, trans. From *Ante-Nicene Fathers*, Vol. 4. Alexander Roberts, James Donaldson, and A. Cleveland Coxe, eds. (Buffalo, NY: Christian Literature Publishing Co., 1885). Revised and edited for New Advent by Kevin Knight, http://www.newadvent.org/fathers/0410.htm.

[86]   Ibid.

not what silly persuasion—a worthy and appropriate religion for such manners."[87] Others, however, asserted that the Christians "worship the *virilia*," that is, the male member, "of their pontiff and priest, and adore the nature, as it were, of their common parent."[88] Octavius says that he doesn't know whether or not these claims are true. But he adds that "certainly suspicion is applicable to secret and nocturnal rites" and ascribes it all to the fact that Christians worship a convicted criminal: "he who explains their ceremonies by reference to a man punished by extreme suffering for his wickedness, and to the deadly wood of the cross, appropriates fitting altars for reprobate and wicked men, that they may worship what they deserve."[89]

Octavius even claims that "the initiation of young novices" involves the coating of an infant with meal; "this infant is slain by the young pupil, who has been urged on as if to harmless blows on the surface of the meal, with dark and secret wounds."[90] Once the deed is done, the assembled Christians move in: "Thirstily—O horror!—they lick up its blood; eagerly they divide its limbs."[91] Their common participation in this tremendous evil seals their loyalty to the group: "By this victim they are pledged together; with this consciousness of wickedness they are covenanted to mutual silence."[92]

All this thoroughly disgusts Octavius, who concludes: "Such sacred rites as these are more foul than any sacrileges."[93] He asserts that this is common knowledge regarding Christians: "And of their banqueting it is well known all men speak of it everywhere; even the speech of our Cirtensian testifies to it."[94] "Our Cirtensian" was

---

[87]   Ibid.
[88]   Ibid.
[89]   Ibid.
[90]   Ibid.
[91]   Ibid.
[92]   Ibid.
[93]   Ibid.
[94]   Ibid.

Marcus Cornelius Fronto, a Roman grammarian in Cirta of North Africa in the second century CE, who had apparently issued similar accusations against the Christians.

Octavius continued with a lurid account of the Christians' incestuous orgies, carried out under the cover of darkness after a mistreated dog puts out the light:

> On a solemn day, they assemble at the feast, with all their children, sisters, mothers, people of every sex and of every age. There, after much feasting, when the fellowship has grown warm, and the fervor of incestuous lust has grown hot with drunkenness, a dog that has been tied to the chandelier is provoked, by throwing a small piece of offal beyond the length of a line by which he is bound, to rush and spring; and thus the conscious light being overturned and extinguished in the shameless darkness, the connections of abominable lust involve them in the uncertainty of fate. Although not all in fact, yet in consciousness all are alike incestuous, since by the desire of all of them everything is sought for which can happen in the act of each individual.[95]

Octavius compares the Christians unfavorably to the Jews because of the Christians' secrecy: "The lonely and miserable nationality of the Jews worshipped one God, and one peculiar to itself," he says, "but they worshipped him openly, with temples, with altars, with victims, and with ceremonies."[96] By contrast, of the Christians, Octavius says, "He who is their God…they can neither show nor behold."[97]

---

[95] Ibid.
[96] Ibid., 10.
[97] Ibid.

Octavius doesn't have a firm grasp of either Judaism or Christianity. He asserts that the God of the Jews "has so little force or power that he is enslaved, with his own special nation, to the Roman deities."[98] And besides his claims, there is no indication that the early Christians sacrificed and ate a baby during their worship services, much less that they engaged in incest and promiscuous sex. Nor did their churches feature the head of an ass as an object of worship.

Minucius Felix rebuts all of Octavius's charges, but it is nevertheless illuminating to consider what non-Christians might have thought of Christians throughout the ages if they had remained a minority that was regarded with suspicion and hostility and that carried out rites with which the wider society was unfamiliar. It is likely that in that case, Octavius and Fronto would not have been among the only people to claim that the Christians behaved this way, and many people would consider that in the presence of so many accusations of this kind, there must be some truth to them. This is how numerous antisemitic myths have flourished and continue to spread.

AN EARLY POGROM

The Hellenistic Jewish philosopher Philo of Alexandria records another early pogrom, this one at the hands of Flaccus Avillius, the Roman governor of Egypt from 33 to 38 CE. Flaccus, according to Philo, "inflicted the most intolerable evils on all who came within his reach."[99] Philo charges Flaccus with attacking the Jews wherever he could: "though in appearance he only attacked a portion of the

---

[98] Ibid.

[99] Philo Judaeus, "A Treatise Against Flaccus," in *The Works of Philo Judaeus*, C. D. Yonge, trans. (London: Henry G. Bohn, 1855), vol. IV, I.1, https://penelope.uchicago.edu/Thayer/E/Roman/Texts/Philo/in_Flaccum*.html.

nation, in point of fact he directed his aims against all whom he could find anywhere."[100]

Flaccus had been a favorite of the Emperor Tiberius, but when Tiberius died and Gaius, commonly known as Caligula, succeeded him, his position was suddenly vulnerable. A group of powerful men of Alexandria came to Flaccus and told him that they would advocate on his behalf before Caligula if he began "abandoning and denouncing all the Jews."[101] Flaccus took their advice. Shortly thereafter, Caligula appointed Herod Agrippa the king of Judea and advised him to travel to his new domains by way of Alexandria. Flaccus's Alexandrian advisers told him that this was a provocation: "The arrival of this man to take upon him his government is equivalent to a deposition of yourself."[102] They argued that when Caligula had told him to go to Judea by way of Alexandria, Agrippa should have earnestly requested to be allowed to avoid Egypt, "in order that the real governor of it might not be brought into disrepute and appear to have his authority lessened by being apparently disregarded."[103]

Convinced that Agrippa was out for his throne and that the Jews of his kingdom had dual loyalty, to Agrippa as well as to himself as their rightful ruler, Flaccus began "destroying the synagogues, and not leaving even their name."[104] Philo adds that the enraged governor also began stripping the Jews of their rights.

> He proceeded onwards to another exploit, namely,
> the utter destruction of our constitution, that when
> all those things to which alone our life was anchored
> were cut away, namely, our national customs and our

---

[100]   Ibid.
[101]   Ibid., IV.21.
[102]   Ibid., V.30.
[103]   Ibid.
[104]   Ibid., VIII.53.

lawful political rights and social privileges, we might be exposed to the very extremity of calamity, without having any stay left to which we could cling for safety, for a few days afterwards he issued a notice in which he called us all foreigners and aliens, without giving us an opportunity of being heard in our own defense, but condemning us without a trial; and what command can be more full of tyranny than this?[105]

Having thus condemned the Jews and deprived them of their rights, Flaccus even went so far as to allow "anyone who was inclined to proceed to exterminate the Jews as prisoners of war."[106] The people of Alexandria then "drove the Jews entirely out of four quarters" of the city and "crammed them all into a very small portion of one."[107] The Jews were "deprived of all their property; while the populace, overrunning their desolate houses, turned to plunder, and divided the booty among themselves as if they had obtained it in war."[108] The rioters also broke into the Jews' shops and carried away everything they found inside. The Jews of Alexandria were "stripped of everything in one day, and also from the circumstance of their no longer being able to earn money by their customary occupations."[109]

The Jews, deprived of all means of supporting themselves, were reduced to begging. However, even the beggars in their misery were set upon:

And then, being immediately seized by those who had excited the seditious multitude against them, they were treacherously put to death, and then were

---

[105] Ibid., VIII.53–4.
[106] Ibid., VIII.54.
[107] Ibid., VIII.55.
[108] Ibid., VIII.56.
[109] Ibid., VIII.57.

dragged along and trampled under foot by the whole city, and completely destroyed, without the least portion of them being left which could possibly receive burial; and in this way their enemies, who in their savage madness had become transformed into the nature of wild beasts, slew them and thousands of others with all kinds of agony and tortures, and newly invented cruelties, for wherever they met with or caught sight of a Jew, they stoned him, or beat him with sticks, not at once delivering their blows upon mortal parts, lest they should die speedily, and so speedily escape from the sufferings which it was their design to inflict upon them.[110]

Others, including entire families, were burned to death. Still others were tortured in the cruelest of ways. Not content with terrorizing the Jewish population, Flaccus "arrested thirty-eight members of our council of elders" and subjected them to public torture and humiliation: he "commanded them all to stand in front of their enemies, who were sitting down, to make their disgrace the more conspicuous, and ordered them all to be stripped of their clothes and scourged with stripes, in a way that only the most wicked of malefactors are usually treated, and they were flogged with such severity that some of them the moment they were carried out died of their wounds, while others were rendered so ill for a long time that their recovery was despaired of."[111] He had some of the Jews crucified and others tortured and executed in other ways, "and after this beautiful exhibition," notes Philo acidly, "came the dancers, and the buffoons, and the flute-players, and all the other diversions of the theatrical contests."[112]

---

[110] Ibid., VIII.65–6.
[111] Ibid., X.75.
[112] Ibid., X.85.

All this happened because the Jews were suspected of not being loyal to the empire. The suspicions of disloyalty revolved around the fact that they did not worship the gods of the other people within the imperial domains. Caligula resolved to remedy that. Philo recounts that he was part of a delegation to visit the emperor to plead for justice for the Jews and permission to rebuild the synagogues Flaccus had destroyed. While they were waiting to see the emperor, however, "a man arrived, with bloodshot eyes, and looking very much troubled, out of breath and palpitating, and leading us away to a little distance from the rest (for there were several persons near), he said, 'Have you heard the news?' And then when he was about to tell us what it was he stopped, because of the abundance of tears that rose up to choke his utterance."[113]

Finally, Philo and his companions were able to calm the messenger sufficiently to hear what had made him so upset: "And he with difficulty, sobbing aloud, and in a broken voice, spoke as follows: 'Our temple is destroyed! Gaius has ordered a colossal statue of himself to be erected in the holy of holies, having his own name inscribed upon it with the title of Jupiter!'"[114]

The delegation that was waiting to see Gaius Caligula was immediately as grieved and horrified as the messenger: "And while we were all struck dumb with astonishment and terror at what he had told us, and stood still deprived of all motion (for we stood there mute and in despair, ready to fall to the ground with fear and sorrow, the very muscles of our bodies being deprived of all strength by the news which we had heard); others arrived bearing the same sad tale."[115]

They realized it was useless to appeal to Caligula: "Will it be allowed to us to approach him or to open our mouth on the subject

---

[113] Philo Judaeus, "On the Embassy to Gaius," Charles Duke Yonge, trans., XXIX.186, https://en.wikisource.org/wiki/On_the_Embassy_to_Gaius#XXX.
[114] Ibid., XXIX.188.
[115] Ibid., XXIX.189.

of the synagogues before this insulter of our holy and glorious temple? For it is quite evident that he will pay no regard whatever to things of less importance and which are held in inferior estimation, when he behaves with insolence and contempt towards our most beautiful and renowned temple, which is respected by all the east and by all the west, and regarded like the sun which shines everywhere. And even if we were allowed free access to him, what else could we expect but an inexorable sentence of death?"[116]

When the delegation asked the messengers why Caligula would conceive of doing such a thing, they replied: "He desires to be considered a god; and he conceives that the Jews alone are likely to be disobedient; and that therefore he cannot possibly inflict a greater evil or injury upon them than by defacing and insulting the holy dignity of their temple."[117]

Caligula was right. The pagan Romans had room in their pantheon for an infinite number of gods and had no problem in principle with the deification, or even the self-deification, of emperors. The Jews, however, were monotheists and would admit of no compromise on that issue. They would never accept a statue of Caligula, or anyone or anything else, inside their temple and would resist such a desecration to the death.

This led to ongoing tensions with non-Jews. Large numbers of Jews were killed in Alexandria once again in 66 CE. The conflict began, according to Flavius Josephus, when "the Alexandrines had once organized a public assembly to deliberate about an embassy to Nero," who was emperor by this time, "and a great number of Jews came flocking to the amphitheater."[118] Jews in Alexandria at that time had equal rights with the Greeks, but nonetheless, their loyalties

---

[116] Ibid., XXIX.192.
[117] Ibid., XXX.198.
[118] Flavius Josephus, *Jewish War*, trans. anon., 2.490, https://www.livius.org/sources/content/pogrom-in-alexandria/.

were here again suspected: "When their adversaries saw them, they immediately cried out, and called them their enemies, and said they came as spies."[119] The violence began quickly: "Then they rushed out, and laid violent hands upon the Jews, and as for the rest, they were slain as they ran away. There were three men whom they caught and hauled along, to burn them alive."[120]

Ultimately, the Romans set upon the Jewish community and "showed no mercy to the infants, had no regard for the aged, and went on in the slaughter of persons of every age, until all the place was overflowed with blood, and 50,000 Jews lay dead. And the remainder would have perished as well, had they not put themselves at the mercy of Alexander," the Roman governor of the city.[121] "He felt pity and gave orders to the legionaries to retire. Being accustomed to obey orders, the soldiers left off killing immediately." The rage of the people, however, was not so easily calmed: "But the populace of Alexandria bore such hatred to the Jews, that it was difficult to recall them, especially since they did not want to leave the bodies of their dead."[122]

The enmity of the people of Alexandria was directly related to the Jews' tendency to set themselves apart. They wouldn't sacrifice to the gods of the Alexandrians. They wouldn't intermarry with them. They stubbornly maintained their separate customs and traditions, forming a subculture in Alexandrian society and even appearing to pose a challenge to the survival of that society, for at that time, Jews proselytized and were making numerous converts. Their stubborn distinctiveness was a standing critique of the customs and mores of the Alexandrians.

---

[119]   Ibid., 2.491.
[120]   Ibid.
[121]   Ibid., 2.497.
[122]   Ibid., 2.498.

PARADIGMS ESTABLISHED

Some of the central paradigms for Jew-hatred throughout the ages were thus largely set in pagan antiquity. Like Manetho, opponents of the Jews would challenge the veracity of their accounts of their own history and related events and turn those accounts on their heads so that the Jews were the villains even on occasions when they had been victimized. The Jews would be characterized as enemies of the state and society solely for the crime of maintaining their own practices in the face of heavy pressure to assimilate. They would be accused of dual loyalty and of trying to subvert the established order, often simply for maintaining their distinct identity in a conformist atmosphere.

These characterizations would recur in numerous other contexts throughout the ages.

And around the time Philo was writing, all this would be compounded by charges that were far more sweeping and serious.

Chapter Two

CHRIST-KILLERS

TWO JEWISH COMMUNITIES

In 66 CE, the same year in which fifty thousand Jews were killed in Alexandria, the Jews began a large-scale revolt against Rome. Four years later, in 70 CE, the Roman Emperor Vespasian's Titus conquered Jerusalem and, fed up with the Jews' constant rebellions against Roman authority, destroyed the Jewish Temple. Six decades after that, they completed the action after another revolt of the Jews, led by a messianic claimant named Simon Bar Kokhba. When the putative messiah had been killed and the revolt finally put down in 134 CE, the Romans ordered that the Jews be expelled from the region (although many remained, from that time up to the present day) and, as a final insult, renamed Judea after the biblical enemies of the Jews, the Philistines, who had long since disappeared from the earth. As the Romans pronounced it, this became "Palestine."

That act would have profound and lasting repercussions, as would the earlier destruction of the temple. The temple had been the center of Jewish life. The Jewish scriptures contain elaborate details about how sacrifices and other observances were to be correctly carried out in the temple. Without the temple, there could be no sacrifices at all, and large elements of the Jewish religion as it was detailed in the scriptures simply could not be carried out.

It was at this time that the rabbis, the religious teachers of the community, faced with the destruction of their people now that a central foundation of its identity and unity had been destroyed, began a massive reevaluation and reinterpretation of Judaism as a whole. Their discussions and debates went on for several centuries and ultimately resulted in the creation of what is known today as Rabbinic Judaism, based on the teachings of the rabbis as set forth in the massive compendium known as the Talmud ("teaching").

There was, however, another form of Judaism that survived all the way from antiquity into the modern era. Several decades before the temple was destroyed, Jesus, a Jewish rabbi from Nazareth in Galilee, north of Judea, began preaching his own radical reinterpretation of Judaism. His followers maintained that he was the anointed one, the Messiah (or in Greek, "Christ"). In Jewish tradition, the Messiah was envisioned as a human king who would save the Jewish nation; the followers of Jesus, however, saw him as not only the Messiah but one who was unfathomably greater: God himself, they declared, had in Jesus assumed a human nature so as to take on the sins of human beings. They stated that Jesus had confirmed this by rising from the dead after he had been crucified as "the king of the Jews," for the Romans saw him as another challenger to their authority.

Other Jews disagreed. They disputed the new faction's use of the Jewish scriptures to show that Jesus was indeed the Messiah. It had been prophesied, they maintained, that the Messiah would set up an earthly kingdom. Jesus, however, had said that his kingdom was not of this world. The coming of the Messiah, they added, would also herald the dawning of a new age, in which the conflicts that marked all earthly endeavors would melt away, and the lion would lie down with the lamb. Yet the world was as full of strife, injustice, and sin after Jesus's coming as it had been before he came. His followers maintained that Jesus's sacrifice on the cross and his resurrection had opened the way for human beings to enjoy that Messianic age and that it would come to full fruition when he returned to earth a second time.

The biggest difference between what were initially two factions of Jews, however, was that the followers of Jesus, who quickly came to be known as Christians, allowed non-Jews to become full and equal members of their new community without undertaking any obligation to follow Jewish law.

At issue wasn't the acceptance of converts in itself, as the Jews at this time were proselytizing, as were the Christians. The point of controversy was that the non-Jews would not be following Jewish law, and neither would the Jewish Christians themselves, for the Christians said that Jesus's sacrifice had fulfilled the law and thus put an end to it as a necessary aspect of their religious observance. The Jews who did not accept Jesus as the Messiah realized that if they did, they would quickly disappear as a distinct people. To many who had seen the Jews maintain their loyalty to their God and his laws even to the point of shedding blood and had absorbed and taken to heart the lessons of scriptural accounts of Jews keeping their faith to the death, this was unacceptable.

And so, the two communities, initially two factions of the same community, grew increasingly apart and increasingly antagonistic.

"YOU ARE OF YOUR FATHER THE DEVIL"

This antagonism is apparent within the Christian scriptures. Yet the passages that have been used throughout the history of Christianity as pretexts for the persecution of Jews never sanction any violence against them; nor do they even necessarily refer to Jews in the aggregate.

In the Gospel according to Matthew, Jesus enters the temple and tells "the chief priests and the elders of the people" a parable about tenants of a householder who mistreat the householder's servants and finally kill his son.[123] The implication of this is unmistakable: The Jewish leaders have rejected the prophets, and now they are rejecting the Son of God himself. And so, "the kingdom of God will be taken away from you and given to a nation producing the fruits of it."[124] In case the point had eluded anyone, the Gospel adds: "When the chief priests and the Pharisees heard his parables, they perceived that he was speaking about them."[125] Yet in the traditional Christian understanding, Matthew was Jewish, as were the other apostles. This was a dispute not between Jews and non-Jews, but between certain Jewish leaders and a new faction that had arisen within the Jewish community.

Non-Jews, however, were involved. The apostle Paul, whose writings form a major part of the New Testament and are foundational for Christian theology, reminds the non-Jewish Christians in Thessalonica that "you suffered the same things from your own countrymen as they did from the Jews, who killed both the Lord Jesus and the prophets, and drove us out, and displease God and oppose all men by hindering us from speaking to the Gentiles that they may

---

[123] Matthew 21:23.
[124] Matthew 21:43.
[125] Matthew 21:45.

be saved—so as always to fill up the measure of their sins. But God's wrath has come upon them at last!"[126]

This states straightforwardly that "the Jews" killed Jesus. Jesus himself speaks more specifically, saying that while "the chief priests and scribes" will "condemn him to death," they will "deliver him to the Gentiles to be mocked and scourged and crucified, and he will be raised on the third day."[127]

The Gospel of John depicts Jesus in a dispute with "the Jews who had believed in him," but who are regarding what he says with pronounced skepticism.[128] When they say, "Abraham is our father," he responds: "If you were Abraham's children, you would do what Abraham did, but now you seek to kill me, a man who has told you the truth which I heard from God; this is not what Abraham did.... You are of your father the devil, and your will is to do your father's desires. He was a murderer from the beginning, and has nothing to do with the truth, because there is no truth in him. When he lies, he speaks according to his own nature, for he is a liar and the father of lies."[129]

In the apocalyptic Revelation to John, which contains a vision John the Evangelist received when he was "in the spirit on the Lord's day," there is a passage that has been widely taken to be another attack on the Jews, put into the mouth of Jesus himself: "And to the angel of the church in Smyrna write: 'The words of the first and the last, who died and came to life. I know your tribulation and your poverty (but you are rich) and the slander of those who say that they are Jews and are not, but are a synagogue of Satan."[130] And again: "Behold, I will make those of the synagogue of Satan who say that they are Jews

---

[126]   I Thessalonians 2:14–16.
[127]   Matthew 20:19.
[128]   John 8:31.
[129]   John 8:39–40, 44.
[130]   Revelation 1:10, 2:8–9.

and are not, but lie—behold, I will make them come and bow down before your feet, and learn that I have loved you."[131]

Who exactly are the people who say they are Jews and are not? Many Christians throughout history have assumed them to be the Jews who do not accept Jesus as the Messiah, although some have suggested that they are rather Christians who adopted Jewish practices while the mainstream Christian tradition was that the sacrifice of Christ had fulfilled the Mosaic Law and relieved Christians of the obligation to adhere to it. Yet despite the uncertainty of the reference, throughout the centuries, many Christians took these passages and others like them as indications that the Jews were the foremost foes not only of the Church, but of God himself. They had killed their Messiah, the Savior of the world, persecuted the apostles, and thereby displeased God to the extent that they were not the children of God, much less his chosen people (a role that had been taken over by the Church), but were instead enemies of God and children of the devil.

Less often noted, however, was the fact that the traditional authors of these passages, Paul the apostle and John the evangelist, were themselves Jews. Paul describes himself before his dramatic conversion to Christianity as "circumcised on the eighth day, of the people of Israel, of the tribe of Benjamin, a Hebrew born of Hebrews; as to the law a Pharisee, as to zeal a persecutor of the church, as to righteousness under the law blameless."[132] In one of his letters to the Galatians, the congregants of the church he established in Galatia, he refers to the Christian community as "we ourselves, who are Jews by birth and not Gentile sinners."[133]

The New Testament was not written when the Church was a huge and powerful force in European society, and the Jews a small,

---

[131] Revelation 3:9.
[132] Philippians 3:5–6.
[133] Galatians 2:15.

despised, and vulnerable minority. It was written at a time when the Christian community, which was made up of a large number of Jews, and the Jews who had not become Christians were competing within the Jewish community. At the same time, they were competing as well as within the larger marketplace of ideas in which both the Jews who believed in Jesus and the Jews who did not were active in the first century CE. These passages were not written in a context in which they could be used as pretexts to demonize, marginalize, and even kill Jews; rather, they were polemical writings of an internecine dispute between two factions of the same community.

THE CURIOUS CHARGE OF DEICIDE

They would, however, soon enough be used to bring about and justify exactly that marginalization. Abetting this was another passage: Pontius Pilate, the Roman procurator of Judea, is depicted in the Gospel according to Matthew as facing the Jewish mob that is demanding the execution of Jesus and washing his hands, saying: "I am innocent of this man's blood; see to it yourselves."[134] The crowd cries out in response: "His blood be on us and on our children!"[135]

It was largely on the basis of this passage, as well as the one in which Paul says that "the Jews...killed both the Lord Jesus and the prophets," that the charge began that the Jews in the aggregate, or at least those who had rejected the claim that Jesus was the Messiah, were nothing less than murderers, and not just murderers of the Messiah, but in view of the divinity of Christ, murderers of God himself.

The charge of deicide became the central and most enduring Christian indictment of the Jews and the basis for countless pogroms

---

[134]   Matthew 27:24.
[135]   Ibid.

throughout history. Yet of all the charges that haters of the Jews levy against them, this core allegation is one of the strangest, weakest, and most curious of all.

It is basic Christian theology that the death of Christ was the result of the sins of mankind. The apostle Peter says: "He himself bore our sins in his body on the tree, that we might die to sin and live to righteousness."[136] Christ's death was sacrificial, as he bore the weight of all human sin on the cross. Because of that, and in light of his resurrection, his crucifixion is not the tragedy that it would have been if he had been just an ordinary human being. It is, rather, the basis for the redemption of the world. Every human being who lives now and has ever lived, from this perspective, can say that he or she is responsible for the crucifixion of Christ, for were it not for human sin, there would have been no warrant for his incarnation and sacrifice.

In light of that, however, it is extremely strange to single out one group of people, the Jews, as responsible for his death, or more responsible than any other group. If the Jews killed Christ, and that was an act of supreme criminality, then how can it simultaneously be affirmed that he died as the result of the sins of all people and in order to renew and redeem them? The Roman Catholic mass for Holy Saturday contains the exclamation: "O happy fault, O necessary sin of Adam, which gained for us so great a Redeemer!"[137] Yet all too many who have prayed these words or heard them sung on Holy Saturday throughout history have gone out and behaved toward Jews they encountered as if it were anything but a "happy fault" and a "necessary sin," and that their own sins had nothing whatsoever to do with it.

---

[136] I Peter 2:24.
[137] Exsultet from *The Roman Missal: The Order of Mass, Holy Saturday.*

The passage in Matthew does depict the Jews who are calling for the crucifixion of Christ as saying, "His blood be on us and on our children," and this epitomizes the strangeness of the charge of deicide. This passage has been interpreted as meaning that the Jews bear a unique responsibility for the death of Christ, and that this responsibility extends not just to those who were present when Jesus was condemned to death and crucified, but to all Jews thereafter, the children of those who betrayed their own redeemer. Yet at the same time, the last book of the New Testament, the Revelation to John, depicts those redeemed in Christ as wearing white robes. "One of the elders" explains to John: "These are they who have come out of the great tribulation; they have washed their robes and made them white in the blood of the Lamb."[138] John refers to Christ as the one "who loves us and has freed us from our sins by his blood."[139]

The same apostle John says that "the blood of Jesus his Son cleanses us from all sin."[140] The letter to the Hebrews, which was traditionally attributed to Paul, says that "the blood of Christ" will "purify your conscience from dead works to serve the living God."[141] If one is to demand consistency, then to say, "His blood be on us and on our children," is to say that one is particularly blessed and redeemed. Yet for centuries, the phrase was instead primarily understood as the Jews incriminating themselves.

The idea that the Jews were primarily or singularly responsible for the death of Christ persists to this day. On May 1, 2024, as the House of Representatives was preparing to vote on a bill restricting various expressions of antisemitism, despite the fact that restrictions on the freedom of speech often begin with good intentions and end up enabling tyranny, Rep. Marjorie Taylor Greene (R-Georgia)

---

138   Revelation 7:13–4.
139   Revelation 1:5.
140   I John 1:7.
141   Hebrews 9:22.

announced: "Antisemitism is wrong, but I will not be voting for the Antisemitism Awareness Act of 2023 (H.R. 6090) today that could convict Christians of antisemitism for believing the Gospel that says Jesus was handed over to Herod to be crucified by the Jews."[142] The bill would restrict "using the symbols and images associated with classic antisemitism (e.g., claims of Jews killing Jesus or blood libel) to characterize Israel or Israelis."[143] Rep. Matt Gaetz (R-Florida) agreed: "The Gospel itself would meet the definition of antisemitism under the terms of this bill!"[144]

KILLER OF CHRIST, HATERS OF ALL THAT IS GOOD

By the second century CE, the Jews and the Christians were not in any sense a single community, and the antagonism between the two had grown bitter. In his mid-second century *Dialogue with Trypho the Jew*, which is designed to show that the Christian interpretation of the Hebrew scriptures is right and that of the Jews is wrong, the Christian apologist Justin Martyr invokes a passage from Isaiah and then adds: "This same law [of God] you have despised, and His new holy covenant you have slighted; and now you neither receive it, nor repent of your evil deeds."[145]

Late in the second century, the bishop Irenaeus of Lyon wrote that the prophet Jeremiah had prophesied the origin of the Antichrist. Jeremiah, according to Irenaeus, "does not merely point out his sudden coming, but he even indicates the tribe from which he shall come,

---

[142] Ron Kampeas, "Taylor Greene: Antisemitism Bill Rejects 'Gospel' That Jews Handed Jesus to Executioners," *JTA*, May 2, 2024.

[143] Ibid.

[144] Ibid.

[145] Justin Martyr, "Dialogue with Trypho," in "The Apostolic Fathers with Justin Martyr and Irenaeus," in Alexander Roberts and James Donaldson, eds., *The Ante-Nicene Fathers*, Vol. I (Grand Rapids, MI: Eerdmans, 1986), 200.

where he says, 'We shall hear the voice of his swift horses from Dan; the whole earth shall be moved by the voice of the neighing of his galloping horses: he shall also come and devour the earth, and the fullness thereof, the city also, and they that dwell therein.'"[146]

Irenaeus added that "this, too, is the reason that this tribe is not reckoned in the Apocalypse along with those which are saved."[147] Irenaeus was referring to a passage in the Revelation to John in which John sees in heaven thousands from each tribe of Israel, which he names, but the tribe of Dan is left out. This gave rise to the idea that the Antichrist would arise from the tribe of Dan and to the modern view among some Christians that this supernatural enemy of the faithful would be a Jew from the state of Israel.

Two centuries later, toward the end of the fourth century, one of the greatest influences on early (and subsequent) Christian theology in the Western Church, Augustine of Hippo (354–430), had a quite similar view of the Jews, calling them nothing less than the enemies of the Christian Church: "God has shown the Church in her enemies the Jews the grace of His compassion, since, as says the apostle, their offense is the salvation of the Gentiles."[148]

The Jews, in their misery, bore witness to the truth of Christianity: "But the Jews who slew Him, and would not believe in Him, because it behooved Him to die and rise again, were yet more miserably wasted by the Romans, and utterly rooted out from their kingdom, where aliens had already ruled over them, and were dispersed through the lands (so that indeed there is no place where they are

---

[146]   Jeremiah 8:16; Irenaeus of Lyon, "Against the Heresies," Alexander Roberts and William Rambaut, trans., From *Ante-Nicene Fathers*, Vol. 1. Alexander Roberts, James Donaldson, and A. Cleveland Coxe, eds. (Buffalo, NY: Christian Literature Publishing Co., 1885), 2.

[147]   Ibid.

[148]   Augustine, *City of God*, 18.46, Marcus Dods, trans. From *Nicene and Post-Nicene Fathers, First Series*, Vol. 2, Philip Schaff, ed. (Buffalo, NY: Christian Literature Publishing Co., 1887.) Revised and edited for New Advent by Kevin Knight, http://www.newadvent.org/fathers/120118.htm.

not), and are thus by their own Scriptures a testimony to us that we have not forged the prophecies about Christ."[149]

This was why God had not eradicated them from the earth: "And therefore He has not slain them, that is, He has not let the knowledge that they are Jews be lost in them, although they have been conquered by the Romans, lest they should forget the law of God."[150] That they had lost their homeland and been dispersed throughout the world was a matter of divine providence, so that they would bring the prophecies of Christ everywhere, and in their misery show forth the consequences of rejecting him: "But it was not enough that he should say, Slay them not, lest they should at last forget Your law, unless he had also added, Disperse them; because if they had only been in their own land with that testimony of the Scriptures, and not everywhere, certainly the Church which is everywhere could not have had them as witnesses among all nations to the prophecies which were sent before concerning Christ."[151]

This idea that the Jews bore witness to Christ may have contributed in no small measure to their being allowed to live, despite all manner of persecutions, in Christian lands throughout the medieval period and thereafter. They were, however, witnesses in spite of themselves, used by God without even being aware that they were being thus used. In his "Treatise against the Jews," Augustine refers to "Christ whom you, in your parents, led to death."[152] He also asserts that the Jews are suffering from "madness" and chides them for saying, "We are the house of Jacob," by challenging them to affirm that the scriptures apply to them when they say such things as, "Blind the heart of this people, and make their ears heavy, and shut their eyes,"

[149] Ibid.
[150] Ibid.
[151] Ibid.
[152] Augustine, "Treatise against the Jews," 7.10, https://www.roger-pearse.com/weblog/2015/06/11/augustines-treatise-against-the-jews/.

and, "I have spread forth my hands all the day to an unbelieving and contradicting people."[153]

The idea that the Jews were blind to the truth in their own scriptures became common among Christians for centuries after Augustine. Other words of Augustine from the same treatise, however, proved less durable, especially his declaration that Christians should demonstrate "great love" for the Jews and humility in regard to their situation:

> Dearly beloved, whether the Jews receive these divine testimonies with joy or with indignation, nevertheless, when we can, let us proclaim them with great love for the Jews. Let us not proudly glory against the broken branches; let us rather reflect by whose grace it is, and by much mercy, and on what root, we have been ingrafted. Then, not savoring of pride, but with a deep sense of humility, not insulting with presumption, but rejoicing with trembling, let us say: "Come you and let us walk in the light of the Lord," because His "name is great among the Gentiles."[154]

The "broken branches" and those which had been "ingrafted" referred to the apostle Paul's analogy of the Jews who rejected Christ ("the broken branches") and the Gentiles who accepted him (branches that had been grafted onto the olive tree of salvation).[155]

---

[153] Ibid.
[154] Ibid., 10.15.
[155] Romans 11:17–21.

FIT FOR SLAUGHTER

It was refreshing to see Augustine, after all his invective against the Jews, state that they should nonetheless be treated with the charity that the founder of Christianity had told his followers to display toward everyone. They should not be killed, but not be allowed to thrive. However, Augustine's great contemporary in the East, John Chrysostom (347–407), a prominent priest in Antioch who was to become patriarch of Constantinople and one of the most enduringly revered and respected of the Fathers of the Church, would have disagreed.

Chrysostom inveighed against the Jews in a series of eight sermons he preached to try to end the practice of Christians attending synagogue services and seeking cures for their ailments from Jews who offered remedies. His objective was to discourage the Christians of Antioch from not only frequenting the synagogues, but also from having friendly relationships with their Jewish neighbors. It is striking that Christians were attending Jewish synagogues in late fourth-century Antioch at all and shows that the antagonism between Christians and Jews that later became nearly universal was not dominant at that time and place.

Chrysostom, however, did his best to change that. He quoted Amos 5:21: "I hate, I despise your feasts, and I take no delight in your solemn assemblies." Then he added: "Does God hate their festivals and do you share in them? He did not say this or that festival, but all of them together.... Is not the place also an abomination? Before they committed the crime of crimes, before they killed their Master, before the cross, before the slaying of Christ, it was an abomination. Is it not now all the more an abomination?"[156]

---

[156] John Chrysostom, *Against the Jews*, trans. unknown, Homily 1, VII.1–2, https://www.tertullian.org/fathers/chrysostom_adversus_judaeos_01_homily1.htm.

Chrysostom not only affirms that the Jews killed Christ, but intimates that in doing so, they lost their basic humanity: "Christ was speaking to the Canaanite woman when He called the Jews children and the Gentiles dogs. But see how thereafter the order was changed about: they became dogs, and we became the children."[157] For this, he invokes the authority of the great apostle: "Paul said of the Jews: 'Beware of the dogs, beware of the evil workers, beware of the mutilation. For we are the circumcision.' Do you see how those who at first were children became dogs?"[158]

Yet when Paul wrote of "the dogs…the evil workers," in light of the controversies of his day, he was likely referring to the Christians who insisted that new converts to the faith had to be circumcised and keep the Jewish law rather than to the Jews who were outside his community altogether. But by the time of Chrysostom, such distinctions had been lost.

In words that would take on a chilling aspect in light of later events, Chrysostom continued: "Another prophet hinted at this when he said: 'Israel is as obstinate as a stubborn heifer.' And still another called the Jews 'an untamed calf.' Although such beasts are unfit for work, they are fit for killing. And this is what happened to the Jews: while they were making themselves unfit for work, they grew fit for slaughter."[159] He thus contradicted Augustine's recommendation that they not be slain, as they unwittingly bore witness to the truth of the Gospel wherever they wandered.

It is not surprising that after he said that they were "fit for slaughter," Chrysostom added that the Jews were unworthy of respect:

> Many, I know, respect the Jews and think that their present way of life is a venerable one. This is why I

---

[157] Ibid., II.1–2.
[158] Ibid., II.2.
[159] Ibid., II.5–6.

hasten to uproot and tear out this deadly opinion.
I said that the synagogue is no better than a theater
and I bring forward a prophet as my witness. Surely
the Jews are not more deserving of belief than their
prophets. "You had a harlot's brow; you became
shameless before all." Where a harlot has set herself up,
that place is a brothel. But the synagogue is not only
a brothel and a theater; it also is a den of robbers and
a lodging for wild beasts. Jeremiah said: "Your house
has become for me the den of a hyena." He does not
simply say "of wild beast," but "of a filthy wild beast,"
and again: "I have abandoned my house, I have cast
off my inheritance." But when God forsakes a people,
what hope of salvation is left? When God forsakes a
place, that place becomes the dwelling of demons.[160]

Then Chrysostom refers to Jesus's rebuke of "the Jews who had
believed in him" in the Gospel according to John: "But at any rate
the Jews say that they, too, adore God. No Jew adores God! Who say
so? The Son of God says so. For he said: 'If you were to know my
Father, you would also know me. But you neither know me nor do
you know my Father.' Could I produce a witness more trustworthy
than the Son of God? If, then, the Jews fail to know the Father, if they
crucified the Son, if they thrust off the help of the Spirit, who should
not make bold to declare plainly that the synagogue is a dwelling
of demons?"[161]

Christians should, therefore, end their practice of visiting synagogues. Chrysostom declares: "I hate the synagogue and abhor it."[162]
Why? "The temple was already a den of thieves when the Jewish

160   Ibid., III.1.
161   Ibid., III.2–3.
162   Ibid., V.2.

44

commonwealth and way of life still prevailed. Now you give it a name more worthy than it deserves if you call it a brothel, a stronghold of sin, a lodging-place for demons, a fortress of the devil, the destruction of the soul, the precipice and pit of all perdition, or whatever other name you give it."[163]

In another sermon, he went even further: "This is why I hate the Jews. Although they possess the Law, they put it to outrageous use. For it is by means of the Law that they try to entice and catch the more simpleminded sort of men. If they refused to believe in Christ because they did not believe in the prophets, the charge against them would not be so severe. As it is, they have deprived themselves of every excuse because they say that they do believe in the prophets but they have heaped outrage on him whom the prophets foretold."[164]

In the last of these sermons, Chrysostom delivered the coup de grâce: not only were the synagogues the dwelling places of demons, but the Jews themselves, he asserted, were engaged in demonic activity. To discourage Christians from going to the Jews to seek remedies for their ailments, Chrysostom preached: "What excuse will we have if for our fevers and hurts we run to the synagogues, if we summon into our own house these sorcerers, these dealers in witchcraft?... If you get some slight illness, will you reject him as your master and rush off to the demons and desert over to the synagogues? What pardon will you find after that? How can you call on Him for help again? Who else will be able to plead your cause even if he could speak with the freedom and confidence of a Moses? There is no one."[165]

---

[163] John Chrysostom, *Against the Jews*, trans. unknown, Homily 7, VII.6, https://www.tertullian.org/fathers/chrysostom_adversus_judaeos_07_homily7.htm.

[164] John Chrysostom, *Against the Jews*, trans. unknown, Homily 6, VI.11, https://www.tertullian.org/fathers/chrysostom_adversus_judaeos_06_homily6.htm.

[165] John Chrysostom, *Against the Jews*, trans. unknown, Homily 8, VI.6, 10, https://www.tertullian.org/fathers/chrysostom_adversus_judaeos_08_homily8.htm.

Patience in suffering was preferable to seeking cures from the foes of God himself: "When you see that God is punishing you, do not flee to his enemies, the Jews, so that you may not rouse his anger against you still further."[166] That idea has persisted to this day, as many majority-Muslim nations that have suffered natural disasters have rejected aid from Israel. They would rather suffer than get help from the Jews. Chrysostom adds that it was better to be sick and be rude to the Jews than to accept their help: "But if you put up with your fever for a little while, if you scorn those who want to chant over you an incantation or tie an amulet to your body, if you insult them roundly and drive them from your house, your conscience will immediately bring you relief like a drink of water."[167]

This was because the cures they offered were illusory: "Even if the Jews seem to relieve your fever with their incantations, they are not relieving it. They are bringing down on your conscience another more dangerous fever. Every day you will feel the sting of remorse; every day your conscience will flog you. And what will your conscience say? 'You sinned against God, you transgressed his Law, you violated your covenant with Christ. For an insignificant ailment you betrayed your faith.'"[168]

Notably, Chrysostom didn't say that the Jews' remedies didn't work. Instead, he based his idea entirely on the claim that it was wrong for the Christians to seek them out. He thus created an extremely peculiar scenario. The Jews were apparently welcoming the Christians who came to them seeking medicine and gave them remedies that were likely to have been at least as effective as anything else physicians of the fourth century offered to their patients and, in many

---

[166]   Ibid., VI.8.
[167]   Ibid., VII.1.
[168]   Ibid., VI.11.

cases, were clearly working since Chrysostom has to resort to telling Christians that they should prefer illness to being cured by Jews.

It is thus clear that the Jews of Antioch were performing a valuable service, and one from which the Christians benefited. Chrysostom did not say that the Jews were treating the Christians who came to them in ways that just made them sicker, and given his manifest hostility to the Jews, there can be little doubt that he would have said this if he could have. He did not accuse them of underhandedly administering poisons or even placebos to the Christians who came to them for cures. Instead, he charged that the success of the Jews' remedies was to be attributed to "witchcraft" and "demons" rather than to God, such that the Christians should prefer to remain ill.

This provides an insight into the nature of Christian antisemitism in the early centuries of the development of Christianity. The hostility was all going in one direction. Early Christians were not reacting to real, imagined, or exaggerated misdeeds of the Jews; rather, their suspicion and hostility were based on their understanding of Christian theology and conclusions that emanated from that understanding.

How very different the history of Europe, and the world, might have been if Chrysostom had seen the Christians of Antioch frequenting synagogues and seeking cures for their ailments from the Jews and preached in response a series of sermons demonstrating how, as Jesus says, "salvation is from the Jews."[169] He could have preached about the commonalities and the differences between Jewish and Christian understandings of the Old Testament without compromising his own faith in the slightest degree and emphasized that Christians should behave charitably toward the Jews, as they should toward anyone. He could thereby have established a paradigm of mutual respect instead of one of disdain, contempt, and even open hatred.

---

[169] John 4:22.

Of course, in establishing those attitudes as the norm in Christian attitudes toward Jews, Chrysostom, one of the most revered of all saints in Orthodox Christianity and a profoundly important figure for Roman Catholicism also, was by no means alone.

JEROME AND MOSES'S HORNS

Around 384, the Christian monk and renowned scholar Jerome (342–420) completed his Latin translation of the Bible, the *Vulgate*, which for centuries was the official Latin Bible of the Roman Catholic Church. In it, Jerome included a questionable translation of a passage from the Book of Exodus that fueled suspicions of the Jews for centuries. In the Revised Standard Version of the Bible, the passage reads: "the people of Israel saw the face of Moses, that the skin of Moses' face shone; and Moses would put the veil upon his face again, until he went in to speak with him."[170] Jerome's version, however, reads this way: "And they saw that the face of Moses when he came out was horned, but he covered his face again, if at any time he spoke to them."[171]

The Hebrew word *qaran* can indeed mean "horned," but it can also be rendered as "sending out rays of light," as is reflected in its English cognate, *corona*.[172] Jerome chose to render it as "horned." This may have been an innocent mistranslation, but Jerome did indeed hold a dim view of Jews, saying that they were "stained with

---

[170] Exodus 34:35.
[171] Rick Becker, "Glorious Exposure: Of Moses' Horns, St. Jerome, and the Last Judgment," *National Catholic Register*, April 11, 2019.
[172] Ibid.

the blood of Christ."[173] Whatever his intentions, Jerome's rendering of the Exodus passage was influential. Centuries later, when Michelangelo sculpted his famous statue of Moses, he gave him horns.

All this gave birth to the idea that not just Moses, but all Jews, were horned creatures, as indications of their demonic nature. This idea is still so widespread in the modern age that in 2008, an affiliate of Yeshiva University thought it necessary to publish an article entitled "Busting the Myth of Jews with Horns."[174]

THE SYNAGOGUE AT CALLINICUM

Augustine's profession of "great love for the Jews" rang hollow since he had emphasized that they should survive but not thrive. The same cannot be said of Chrysostom's statement that they were "fit for slaughter." A telling incident in 388 demonstrates that some Christians, including at least one senior cleric, thought virtually any misdeed was excusable if it was directed against those who—as the increasingly common charge insisted—had killed Christ. According to the eighteenth-century English historian Edward Gibbon, "the monks and populace of Callinicum, an obscure town on the frontier of Persia, excited by their own fanaticism, and by that of their bishop, had tumultuously burnt a conventicle of the Valentinians, and a

---

[173] Averyl Edwards, Annika Wurm, and Manuel Castillo, "Lost in Translation: Anti-Semitic Stereotypes Based on Mistranslations," University of North Carolina at Chapel Hill, n.d., https://jewishstudies.unc.edu/wp-content/uploads/sites/380/2017/05/AS2016.studentposter.Edwards.Final_.pdf.

[174] Esther Frederick, "Busting the Myth of Jews with Horns," The Marcos and Edina Katz YUTorah Online, May 27, 2008, https://www.yutorah.org/lectures/724208.

synagogue of the Jews."[175] The Valentinians were a heretical Gnostic Christian sect.

The bishop who had incited the mob "was condemned, by the magistrate of the province, either to rebuild the synagogue, or to repay the damage; and this moderate sentence was confirmed by the emperor." That emperor was Theodosius, who had made Christianity the official religion of the Roman Empire in 380 CE.[176] This "moderate sentence," however, although it was entirely just unless the empire were to descend into mob rule, enraged Ambrose, the bishop of Milan, who greatly influenced Augustine.

Ambrose wrote a letter to Theodosius, taking issue with the fact that the emperor had ordered that the mob "should be punished, and that the synagogue should be rebuilt by the Bishop himself."[177] He asked the emperor whether or not he had considered the possibility that the bishop, ordered to rebuild a synagogue, might renounce Christianity, or else defy the emperor to the point of martyrdom.

Ambrose also asked Theodosius to consider whether the synagogue should be rebuilt at all: "Shall then a building be raised for perfidious Jews out of the spoils of the Church, and shall that patrimony, which by Christ's mercy has been assigned to Christians, be transferred to the temples of the unbelieving? We read that temples were in former days erected from the spoils of the Cimbri and other enemies of Rome. Shall the Jews inscribe this title on the front of their synagogue: 'The temples of impiety built from the spoils of Christians?'"[178] He argued that there was "no adequate reason" that

175   Edward Gibbon, *The History of the Decline and Fall of the Roman Empire* (New York: Harper & Brothers, 1836), III.27.4, https://www.gutenberg.org/files/25717/25717-h/25717-h.htm.

176   Ibid.

177   Ambrose of Milan, Letter XL, To Theodosius, 6, in *The Letters of S. Ambrose, Bishop of Milan*, trans. anon. (Oxford: James Parker and Co., 1881), https://www.gutenberg.org/files/58783/58783-h/58783-h.htm.

178   Ibid., 10.

people "should be so severely punished for the burning of any building; much less seeing that it is a synagogue that has been burnt, a place of unbelief, a house of impiety, a receptacle of madness, which God Himself has condemned."[179]

The emperor, wrote Ambrose, should recall "how many churches the Jews burnt in the time of Julian's reign," when the apostate Christian emperor resolved to aid the Jews at the expense of the Christians. Ambrose claimed that the Jews had burned two churches at Damascus, "one of which is but just repaired, and that at the expense, not of the synagogue, but of the church, while the other is still a mass of shapeless ruins. Churches were likewise burnt at Gaza, Ascalon, Berytus, and nearly every town in that region, and yet no man asked for vengeance. At Alexandria too the most beautiful church of all was burnt down by the Gentiles and Jews. The church has not been avenged, shall then the synagogue be?"[180]

The obvious answer was, "Yes, both church and synagogue should be rebuilt," and the fact that "Gentiles and Jews" apparently participated in the destruction of churches should have prevented Ambrose from focusing his ire solely on the Jews. But he plowed on anyway, accusing the Jews of having lost nothing with the burning of the synagogue and asking: "of what could a fire deprive the treacherous Jews?"[181]

Ambrose asserted that claims of losses were "devices of the Jews who wish to accuse us falsely," and asked: "Nay, what are the calumnies into which they will not rush, who by false witnesses have slandered Christ Himself? Who are false even in matters relating to God? Whom will they not charge with the guilt of this sedition? whom will they not thirst after, even though they know them not? They

---

[179]   Ibid., 14. Language slightly modernized.
[180]   Ibid., 15.
[181]   Ibid., 18.

desire to see rank after rank of Christians in chains, to see the necks of the faithful placed under the yoke, the servants of God hidden in darkness, smitten with the axe, delivered to the fire, or sent to the mines, that their pains may be slow and lingering."[182]

Ultimately, Ambrose's appeal to Theodosius boiled down to this: "Will your Majesty give this triumph to the Jews over the Church of God? this victory over the people of Christ, this joy to the unbelievers, this felicity to the Synagogue, this grief to the Church?"[183] Identifying the Christians with the scriptural enemies of the Jews, he charged that the Jews would "place this solemnity among their feast-days; numbering it among those wherein they triumphed over the Ammonites, or Canaanites, or over Pharaoh king of Egypt, or which delivered them from the hands of Nebuchadnezzar king of Babylon. This festival they will add in memory of the triumph they have gained over Christ's people."[184]

Ambrose wrote all this privately to the emperor, but when Theodosius was unmoved, Ambrose began to address and admonish him from the pulpit. Finally, according to Gibbon, Theodosius gave Ambrose "a solemn and positive declaration, which secured the impunity of the bishop and monks of Callinicum."[185]

The destruction of the synagogue would not be punished, it would not be rebuilt, and its owners would not be compensated. A fateful precedent had been set. Ambrose's letter to Theodosius would also find numerous echoes throughout the ages as other Christians charged the Jews with being the enemies of Christ and the Christians and eager to celebrate their misfortune.

It was the Jews, however, who had actually suffered the misfortune. They would suffer this same misfortune again and again as

[182] Ibid., 19.
[183] Ibid., 20.
[184] Ibid.
[185] Ibid.

synagogues were destroyed in Rome, Antioch, and elsewhere in the empire. And so it would be again and again for centuries to come. One of the most striking aspects of Christian opposition to Jews and Judaism is that it is frequently marked by allegations that the Jews are scheming against the Christians and endeavoring to do harm to them; yet for the most part, the people who suffer actual harm are not the Christians, but the Jews.

GROWING HOSTILITY

After being on the receiving end of all this hostility, some Jews would fight back. The ecclesiastical historian Socrates Scholasticus (380–439) records that early in the fifth century, Cyril, the bishop of Alexandria, expelled the Jews from the city after they became embroiled in a controversy with the Christians, who favored regulations restricting popular dance shows that the Jews were staging in the city. The Jews of Alexandria, according to Socrates, burned a church and killed several Christians, whereupon Cyril, the bishop of Alexandria, "accompanied by an immense crowd of people, going to their synagogues—for so they call their house of prayer—took them away from them, and drove the Jews out of the city, permitting the multitude to plunder their goods. Thus the Jews who had inhabited the city from the time of Alexander the Macedonian were expelled from it, stripped of all they possessed, and dispersed some in one direction and some in another."[186]

The Christian emperors also promulgated laws that deprived Jews of various rights that Christians enjoyed. In 439, the Roman

---

[186] Socrates Scholasticus, Church History, VII.13, A.C. Zenos, trans. From *Nicene and Post-Nicene Fathers, Second Series*, Vol. 2, Philip Schaff and Henry Wace, eds. (Buffalo, NY: Christian Literature Publishing Co., 1890). Revised and edited for New Advent by Kevin Knight, http://www.newadvent.org/fathers/26017.htm.

Emperor Theodosius II, grandson of the emperor whom Ambrose exhorted to allow vigilantism and destruction of property when the victims were Jews and the target a synagogue, promulgated a series of laws that institutionalized a second-class status for the Jews. Jews were barred from obtaining "offices and dignities" and forbidden to exercise the "administration of city service" or to be a "defender of the city."[187] This was in order to prevent them from "the power to judge or decide as they wish against Christians, yes, frequently even over bishops of our holy religion themselves, and thus, as it were, insult our faith."[188]

The emperor further decreed: "Moreover, for the same reason, we forbid that any synagogue shall rise as a new building. However, the propping up of old synagogues which are now threatened with imminent ruin is permitted."[189] Those who defied the law and built synagogues would find the buildings they constructed converted into churches.

Lessening the need for new synagogues, he forbade Jews to convert Christians to Judaism, on pain of death: "To these things we add that he who misleads a slave or a freeman against his will or by punishable advice, from the service of the Christian religion to that of an abominable sect and ritual, is to be punished by loss of property and life."[190] That put an effective end to proselytism by the Jews, which had made Judaism a significant force in the empire and a serious rival to Christianity.

Nearly a century later, the Emperor Justinian went further, stipulating that no one who held "the Jewish superstition may offer

---

[187] "A Law of Theodosius II, January 31, 439: Novella III: Concerning Jews, Samaritans, Heretics, and Pagans," Internet Jewish History Sourcebook: Jews and the Later Roman Law 315–531 CE, https://sourcebooks.fordham.edu/jewish/jews-romanlaw.asp.
[188] Ibid.
[189] Ibid.
[190] Ibid.

testimony against orthodox Christians who are engaged in litigation, whether one or the other of the parties is an orthodox Christian."[191]

On occasion, the Jews returned the Christian hostility. At Caesarea in 556, Jews revolted against Justinian's rule, killing Christians, including the local governor, Stephanus, and burning churches.[192] Half a century later, the Jews welcomed the Persians who were trying to destroy the Roman Empire, leading the Roman Emperor Heraclius in 632 to order that all the Jews in the empire be converted to Christianity.[193] This edict was almost universally ignored, to the extent that nearly a century later, another Roman emperor, Leo III, also concerned about the prospect of Jews siding with the enemies of the empire, issued a decree that was almost identical in substance and likewise largely ignored.[194] In 874, Emperor Basil II also ordered the conversion of the Jews, although few actually converted.[195] Yet forced conversions to Christianity did continue, particularly during the reign of the Emperor Romanos I Lekapenos (919–944).[196]

It was clear that many of the Jews of the empire thought that any system was preferable to live under than that of the Christians. Unfortunately, they were to be proven wrong. Meanwhile, when they did push back against persecution from Christians, this was taken as an additional indication of the Jews' enmity toward Christ, his Church, and Christian believers.

---

[191] "A Law of Justinian, July 28, 531: Concerning Heretics and Manichaeans and Samaritans," Internet Jewish History Sourcebook: Jews and the Later Roman Law 315–531 CE, https://sourcebooks.fordham.edu/jewish/jews-romanlaw.asp.

[192] Elli Kohen, *History of the Byzantine Jews: A Microcosmos in the Thousand Year Empire* (Lanham, Maryland: University Press of America, 2007), 31.

[193] Simon Marcus and Yitzchak Kerem, "Greece," *Encyclopaedia Judaica*, second edition (Jerusalem: Keter Publishing House Ltd., 2007), vol. 8, 45.

[194] Ibid.

[195] Ibid., 46.

[196] Ibid., 47.

There were crosscurrents. In 598, Pope Gregory the Great, although he had been as critical of the Jews as Augustine, Chrysostom, and other Christian writers, decreed that the Jews "should have no infringement of their rights....We forbid to vilify the Jews. We allow them to live as Romans and to have full authority over their possessions."[197] Departing from the example of Ambrose of Milan, Gregory ordered that a bishop who had forcibly converted a synagogue into a church had to pay the Jews a fair price for the building (it could not be returned because it had now been consecrated to Christ) and that the Jews "should in no way appear to be oppressed, or to suffer an injustice."[198]

Nevertheless, the history of Christian antisemitism is long, and many of its essential and recurring characteristics were established in the writings of the early Church Fathers. The Jews, in the aggregate, bore the guilt for the killing of Christ, and as a people who were guilty of deicide, were inveterate enemies of God and his Church, who would stop at nothing to hinder its serene expansion and the salvation of the human race. Their practices, even when they appeared to be doing good, would only ensnare Christians in evil and ruin their souls. Also, as they did not display their evil in a way that would be obvious to everyone, they were clearly guilty of nefarious secret activities that were known only to the particularly observant and discerning.

---

[197]   David G. Dalin, *The Myth of Hitler's Pope* (Washington, DC: Regnery, 2005), 19.

[198]   Edward A. Synan, *The Popes and the Jews in the Middle Ages* (London: Macmillan, 1965), 46.

Chapter Three

A DESPISED PEOPLE

THE LOWLIEST OF PEOPLES

As a result of these fixed ideas, restrictions upon the Jews steadily increased in Christian Western Europe. In the middle of the eighth century, Pope Zachary reiterated an earlier edict that had forbidden Christians to marry Jews.[199] In the late 930s, Pope Leo VII told the archbishop of the German city of Mainz to exile from his diocese those Jews who would not become Christians.[200] This did not, however, mean that Jews could be attacked or despoiled with impunity; in the 1060s, Pope Alexander II praised bishops in Spain and southern France for protecting Jews from Christian attacks by Christians.[201] This did not, however, mean that they would be treated as equals.

---

[199] Ibid., 61.
[200] Ibid., 60.
[201] Ibid., 68–69.

Alexander's successor, Pope Gregory VII, ensured that Jews would remain in poverty and relegated to the lowest strata of society by forbidding them to hold positions that would involve them exercising authority over any Christians.[202]

When Pope Urban II called the First Crusade in 1095, crusaders made their way across Europe and attacked numerous Jewish communities, killing many Jews.[203] The crusaders wiped out entirely the Jewish communities of Speyer, Worms, and Mainz and decimated others in what was the largest-scale disaster the Jews had experienced since the Romans had expelled them from Judea. Many bishops in the areas through which the crusaders passed endeavored to stop this outrage but were unsuccessful. When the crusaders entered Jerusalem on July 14, 1099, they not only carried out a massacre of the Muslims in the city, but burned a synagogue that was crowded with Jews who had taken refuge there.

In the middle of the twelfth century, a Syrian chronicler named al-Azimi noted that the crusaders "turned to Jerusalem and conquered it from the hands of the Egyptians. Godfrey took it. They burned the Church of the Jews."[204] Another Syrian chronicler, Ibn al-Qalanisi, supplied more details: "The Franks stormed the town and gained possession of it. A number of the townsfolk fled to the sanctuary and a great host were killed. The Jews assembled in the synagogue, and the Franks burned it over their heads. The sanctuary was surrendered to them on guarantee of safety on 22 Sha'ban [14 July] of this year, and they destroyed the shrines and the tomb of Abraham."[205]

---

[202]   Ibid., 65.

[203]   Ibid., 70–74.

[204]   Carole Hillenbrand, *The Crusades: Islamic Perspectives* (Oxfordshire: Routledge, 2000), 64–65.

[205]   Ibid.

Early in the twelfth century, Pope Callixtus II reiterated that attacks on Jews were forbidden, but nevertheless, they continued.[206] In the mid-twelfth century, Bernard of Clairvaux, cofounder of the Knights Templar, said that "whoever touches a Jew so as to lay hands on his life, does something as sinful as if he laid hands on the Lord himself."[207] Yet he, too, was widely ignored. There was an entire cottage industry of attacks on Jews, such as the French theologian Peter of Blois's treatise "Against the Perfidious Jews."[208] The thirteenth-century English bishop Robert Grosseteste declared: "As murderers of the Lord, as still blaspheming Christ, and mocking his passion, [Jews] were to be in captivity to the princes of the earth."[209] He did, however, add a caveat reminiscent of Augustine, stating that they should not be killed, but wander the earth in misery: "As they have the brand of Cain, and are condemned to wander over the face of the earth, so were they to have the privilege of Cain, that no one was to kill them."[210]

Pope Innocent III in 1180 likewise excoriated the Jews as "the sons of the crucifiers, against whom to this day the blood cries to the Father's ears," but added a prohibition against forced baptism and declared that Christians were forbidden "wickedly to injure their persons, or with violence to take away their property, or to change the good customs which they have had until now in whatever region they inhabit."[211] Addressing Christian harassment of Jews directly, he commanded that "in the celebration of their own festivals, no one ought to disturb them in any way, with clubs or stones, nor ought any one

---

[206] Dalin, op. cit., 20.
[207] Synan, op. cit., 75.
[208] Ibid., 55.
[209] Ibid., 91.
[210] Ibid.
[211] Innocent III, "Constitution for the Jews (1199 AD)," Medieval Sourcebook, https://sourcebooks.fordham.edu/source/in3-constjews.asp.

try to require from them or to extort from them services they do not owe, except for those they have been accustomed from times past to perform."[212] He also prohibited the desecration of Jewish cemeteries. A century later, Pope Gregory X stated that "an accusation against Jews based solely on the testimony of Christians was invalid; Jewish witnesses must also appear."[213]

Yet the persecution was ongoing. In 1182, the Jews were expelled from France; a chronicler stated that King Philip "hated the Jews, and had heard many accusations against them, of blaspheming the name of Jesus Christ."[214] Yet the same monarch allowed them to return in 1198. Still, discrimination against them was justified, and so that they could not fool Christians into thinking they were one of their number and thus escape the humiliation of their status, the Fourth Lateran Council, which the Roman Catholic Church holds to be the twelfth ecumenical council, declared in 1215 that Jews' dress must be particular to them and clearly distinguishable from that of Christians.[215] Pope Gregory IX favored this decree to the extent that he wrote in 1233 to King Sancho VII of Navarre, admonishing him for allowing the Jews to appear in public without their badge indicating that they were Jews. He warned that the Jewish badge was necessary so that Jewish men would not mingle with Christian women "in a reprehensible way."[216]

Efforts were also made to impoverish the Jews, some of whom had grown wealthy in moneylending, a profession that was forbidden to Christians. While the Jews' dominance in this field was the direct result of their being barred from other professions and allowed to

[212] Ibid.
[213] Dalin, op. cit., 27–8.
[214] Malcolm Hay, *Europe and the Jews* (Chicago: Academy Chicago Publishers, 1992), 75.
[215] Synan, op. cit., 106.
[216] Shlomo Simonsohn, *The Apostolic See and the Jews: Documents, 492–1404* (Toronto: Pontifical Institute of Medieval Studies, 1988), 145.

operate in this one, they were then to be penalized from making the best of their situation. In 1194, England's King Richard I ("the Lion-hearted") commanded that "all the debts, pledges, mortgages, lands, houses, rents, and possessions of the Jews shall be registered...no contract shall be made with, nor payment, made to, the Jews, nor any alteration made in the charters, except before the said [church officials]."[217] King Richard forbade Jews from attending his investiture and had some who came to him bearing gifts flogged for their gesture of goodwill. A pogrom ensued in London, which Richard stopped not because he thought Jews should receive justice as much as anyone else, but because he needed financing from them in order to accomplish his military plans. The English theologian William de Montibus declared: "Jews are the sponges of kings, they are bloodsuckers of Christian purses, by whose robbery kings despoil and deprive poor men of their goods."[218]

Even the Magna Carta, the 1215 document in which King John granted certain rights to the barons of England and which became the foundation for constitutions that guaranteed rights to the citizenry, singled out the Jews. The Magna Carta's Clause 11 states: "And if anyone die owing a debt to the Jews, his wife shall have her dower and pay nothing of that debt."[219] The same clause adds that "debts owing to others than Jews shall be dealt with in the same manner," but in practice, this became the justification for Jews, not others, to be defrauded without penalty.[220]

In Pope Gregory IX's 1234 decretals, which formed the basis of the medieval Church's canon law, he decreed that Jews could not hold Christians as slaves and that Jews could retain their old synagogues

---

217 Amanda Borschel-Dan, "The Magna Carta's Very Jewish Underpinnings," *Times of Israel*, June 15, 2015.
218 Ibid.
219 Ibid.
220 Ibid.

but not build new ones. Various other restrictions were placed upon them. The decretals also stated that that the Jews by "their own fault submitted to perpetual servitude, when they crucified the Lord," and that "the perfidious Jews" must "under servile fear always show that they are ashamed of their guilt, and respect the honor of the Christian faith."[221] This did not mean that the Jews were reduced to slavery, but that they were not to be regarded as equals in Christian societies and could not hold positions of power or influence.

Having established their second-class status, Gregory took pains to emphasize that this did not mean that they could be mistreated in any way a Christian may have desired. Ambrose of Milan might have taken umbrage at this, but in 1235, Gregory decreed that the Jews were under his "veil of protection."[222] The following year, he demonstrated that these were not empty words: the pontiff wrote to King Louis IX of France, telling him that he had received "a tearful petition from the Jews residing in the kingdom of France, and worthy of pity."[223] He wanted the king to act to redress injustices that the Jews had suffered.

The Jews were complaining of having been mistreated by the crusaders of France, who had robbed and killed Jews as they made their way to the Holy Land. Gregory reminded Louis that "it is proper for kings to do judgment and justice" and that the Jews were under the protection of the pope.[224] Thus, he directed the king to ensure that restitution was made to the Jews for all their property that had been stolen and thereby show that "you hate iniquity and love justice."[225] He wrote to a number of French bishops, telling them also that this restitution had to be made. Nor was this the first time Gregory had

---

[221] *Decretalium D. Gregorii Papae IX. Compilatio, Liber Quintus*, 13, X, 5.6.
[222] Simonsohn, op. cit., 154.
[223] Ibid., 165.
[224] Ibid.
[225] Ibid.

acted in this way; he also had written to the French bishops in 1233, decrying the persecution of the Jews and ordering that those who were being held must be set free, as long as they forsook the biblical sin of usury.[226]

THE TALMUD ON TRIAL

In 1240, however, a Jew who had converted to Christianity and become a Franciscan friar, Nicholas Donin, came to Gregory with a series of quotations from the Talmud, the massive multivolume text of Rabbinic Judaism. Donin alerted Gregory to Talmudic passages that, he said, blasphemed Christ and his mother and taught that Jews could lawfully murder non-Jews, as well as steal from them and lie to them with impunity. (These charges we will examine in detail later.)

The Talmud was accordingly put on trial in Paris in the court of King Louis IX, whom Roman Catholics revere as a saint. Donin acted as prosecutor of the Talmud, with several rabbis attempting to defend it. The trial was actually an evangelistic exercise, with the Christians endeavoring to demonstrate that the Jews were misusing and misinterpreting their own scriptures and that they should acknowledge that the Christians were understanding them correctly and convert.[227]

The Talmud was found guilty and condemned to destruction. As many as ten thousand volumes were burned, which, in the days before the advent of the printing press, represented an incalculable and irreplaceable loss.

A close friend of Louis IX, Jean de Joinville, wrote in his biography of the king that Louis told him that "there was once a great

---

[226]   Ibid., 143.

[227]   Hyam Maccoby, ed. and trans., *Judaism on Trial: Jewish-Christian Disputations in the Middle Ages* (East Brunswick, New Jersey, Associated University Presses, 1982), 19–38.

disputation between clergy and Jews at the monastery of Cluny."[228] A poor knight who got around with the aid of a crutch was at the monastery, subsisting on the charity of the monks, and asked to speak first. Since he was a simple man, the assembled Christians were doubtful that this would make much of an impression but allowed him to do so. The knight then asked for the most learned of the Jews to be brought before him. When he was, the knight asked him: "Master, I ask you if you believe that the Virgin Mary, who bore God in her body and in her arms, was a virgin mother, and is the mother of God?"[229] The Jewish leader replied that he believed none of this. The knight responded that he was a fool and then cried out: "And truly, you shall pay for it!" Then he lifted up his crutch and hit the Jew in the head with it. He kept on beating him until he fell to the ground. The Jews quickly fled the monastery, "and so," says Joinville laconically, "ended the disputation."[230]

The abbot of the monastery, Joinville continues, "came to the knight and told him he had committed a deed of very great folly. But the knight replied that the abbot committed a deed of greater folly in gathering people together for such a disputation; for there were a great many good Christians there who, before the disputation came to an end, would have gone away misbelievers through not fully understanding the Jews." King Louis himself then sided with the knight: "And I tell all of you that no one, unless he be a very learned cleric, should dispute with them; but a layman, when he hears the Christian law mis-said should not defend the Christian law, unless it be he with his sword, and with that he should pierce the mis-sayer in

---

228 "St. Louis and the Jews of France, before 1270 CE," Internet Jewish History Sourcebook, https://sourcebooks.fordham.edu/jewish/1270-jews-stlouis.asp. Language slightly modernized for clarity.

229 Ibid.

230 Ibid.

the midriff, so far as the sword will enter."[231] All too many Christians heeded this advice, preferring to do violence with the Jews than to engage them in theological discussions.

During another disputation in Barcelona in July 1263, however, presenting the Jewish case was the renowned Jewish biblical scholar and philosopher Nachmanides, Moses ben Nachman. Not only was Nachmanides not subjected to physical violence; he was given complete freedom to state his views. King James I of Aragon heard him out and was deeply impressed, albeit unmoved by Nachmanides's arguments. The king told the scholar that he had never previously heard "an unjust cause so nobly defended."[232] Nachmanides was nonetheless banished from Spain and lived the rest of his life in Jerusalem.

In the late 1270s, Pope Nicholas III forced Jews to listen to sermons elaborating for them the truth of Christianity and exhorting them to convert; meanwhile, anyone who succumbed to this pressure and converted but then reverted to Judaism would be "turned over to the secular power," a fate that almost certainly would mean execution.[233]

The campaign against the Talmud would also continue; in 1320, Pope John XXII ordered the archbishop of Bourges in France to compel the Jews to turn over all their books, particularly the Talmud, to Christian authorities, who would examine them for blasphemy and burn those that were found to transgress against Christian sensibilities.[234] The Christian authorities, however, were not consistent in their hostility to the Talmud. In 1553, Pope Julius III ordered

---

[231]   Ibid.

[232]   Elinor Slater and Robert Slater, *Great Moments in Jewish History* (Middle Village, New York: Jonathan David Publishers, 1998), 168.

[233]   Synan, op.cit., 120.

[234]   Reginald L. Poole, "The Suppression of the Talmud by Pope John XXII," *The English Historical Review*, Volume VI, Issue XXII, April 1891, 372–373, https://academic.oup.com/ehr/article/VI/XXII/372/433175.

hundreds of copies of the Talmud to be publicly burned in Bologna, a city in the Papal States.[235] Early in the sixteenth century, on the other hand, Pope Leo X actually ordered a Christian printing house to print the Talmud, precisely so as to counter the false claims about its contents that continued to circulate.[236]

In 1413, Jews in Spain were summoned to the Catalonian city of Tortosa for another disputation under the auspices of Pope Benedict XIII, a claimant to the papal throne whose papal pretensions were recognized in Castile, Aragon, and Navarre, as well as in France, Sicily, and Scotland, but were ultimately rejected. There was no violence, but the whole affair was designed to compel the Jews to acknowledge that Jesus was the Jewish Messiah and convert to Christianity. While Nachmanides had been granted the freedom to make his case in Barcelona in 1263, by this time, the attitude of the Christians had hardened. The Jews were warned that if they rebutted the Christians' arguments, they risked being prosecuted for heresy.

The browbeating went on for nearly two years; finally, one of the rabbis, Astruc ha-Levi, dared to speak out about the injustice of it all:

> We are away from our homes. Our resources are diminished and are almost entirely gone. In our absence, great damage has occurred to our communities. We do not know the fate of our wives and children. We have inadequate maintenance here and even lack food. We have been put to extraordinary expenses. Why should people suffering from such woes be held accountable for their arguments, when contending with [Christian opponents] who are in the greatest prosperity and luxury?[237]

---

[235] David I. Kertzer, *The Kidnapping of Edgardo Mortara* (New York: Vintage, 1998), 13.
[236] Dalin, op. cit., 20–25, 31.
[237] Slater and Slater, op. cit.

He added that such disputations were pointless (to say nothing of rigged, since the Jews were not free to respond as they might): "A Christian living in the land of the Saracens may be defeated by the arguments of a pagan or a Saracen, but it does not follow that his faith has been refuted."[238] Ultimately, the Jews simply stopped responding altogether. The Christians were declared the winners, and the Jews told to be baptized, but all of them refused to do so. Angered, Benedict XIII prohibited study of the Talmud.

EXPULSIONS, GHETTOS, PERSECUTION

Meanwhile, in 1290, the Jews were expelled from England over claims that they had been trying to convert Christians to Judaism.[239] They were exiled from France again in 1306, recalled again in 1315, and exiled again in 1394, although that time the order to expel the Jews was widely ignored. In one German city, Erfurt, as many as three thousand Jews were massacred in 1349, and the survivors exiled. Their homes and possessions were burned. A century and a half later, in 1492, when *los Reyes Católicos*, the Catholic monarchs Ferdinand and Isabella, conquered the last Islamic kingdom in Spain, first expelled the Jews, and later the Muslims, from the country.

In 1498, Provence expelled its Jews as well. Jews began returning to France in the seventeenth century but were denied numerous rights and denied citizenship. Likewise, in 1555, Pope Paul IV issued a bull, *Cum nimis absurdum* (Since It Is Absurd), restricting the rights of the Jews in the Papal States and ordering that they be confined to one area of Bologna. "It is absurd and utterly unacceptable," wrote the pope, "that the Jews, who due to their own guilt were condemned

---

238   Ibid.
239   Dalin, op. cit., 121.

by God to eternal slavery, can, with the excuse of being protected by Christian love and thus tolerated living in our midst, show such ingratitude toward the Christians."[240]

The confinement of Jews to a ghetto was not enough. Fourteen years later, Pope Pius V ordered the Jews to be expelled from Bologna altogether. The pontiff told the nuns of the convent of Saint Peter the Martyr that they could use the land of the Jewish Cemetery of Bologna for their own purposes. All they needed to do in order to take possession of this gift was to "destroy all graves...of the Jews... and to take the inscriptions, the memorials, the marble gravestones, destroying them completely, demolishing them."[241] The pope directed the sisters to "exhume the cadavers, the bones and the fragments of the dead and to move them wherever they please."[242] Pope Sixtus V allowed the Jews of Bologna to return to the city in 1586, but in 1593, Pope Clement VIII exiled them again.

Occasionally, Jews were attacked over charges that they had murdered Christian children in order to drain them of their blood and mix it into Passover matzoh. These blood libels, which we will examine in more detail later, were generally based on no evidence at all or on confessions that were coerced under threat of torture or actual torture. Intriguingly, several medieval popes, including Innocent IV (who reigned from 1243 to 1254), Gregory X (1271–6), Martin V (1417–31), and Sixtus IV (1471–84), as well as the later popes Innocent X (1644–55) and Benedict XIV (1740–58) condemned the accusations as baseless. The fact that popes over two centuries had to do so, however, demonstrates how persistent such charges were. Paul III, who was pope for only a few weeks in 1503, condemned those

---

[240] Kertzer, op. cit., 13–14.
[241] Ibid., 14.
[242] Ibid.

who "pretend, in order to despoil them of their goods, that the Jews kill little children and drink their blood."[243]

In Orthodox Christianity, the teachings of the Fathers of the Church are accorded great respect. And so, the anti-Jewish writings of John Chrysostom and other influential thinkers carried immense weight for some Orthodox Christians. When much of the Orthodox world fell under Islamic occupation, Muslim rulers tended to encourage antagonism between the dhimmi communities to forestall the possibility of their banding together against their overlords.

There was, however, also a tradition of tolerance and respect in Orthodox Christianity. In 1568, Ecumenical Patriarch Metrophanes III of Constantinople (1565–72, 1579–80), wrote an encyclical letter to the Greek Orthodox in Crete. Responding to reports that Jews in Crete had endured persecution, the ecumenical patriarch wrote: "Injustice...regardless to whomever acted upon or performed against, is still injustice. The unjust person is never relieved of the responsibility of these acts under the pretext that the injustice is done against a heterodox and not to a believer. As our Lord Jesus Christ in the Gospels said, do not oppress or accuse anyone falsely; do not make any distinction or give room to the believers to injure those of another belief."[244]

SEIZING CHILDREN

There was often no problem, however, with many cases of Christians taking Jews' children, not to kill them, but to raise them as Christians. In 1814, the governor of the Italian city of Reggio issued an order

---

[243]   Synan, op. cit., 119; Dalin, op. cit., 23, 29, 32.

[244]   George C. Papademetriou, *Essays on Orthodox Christian-Jewish Relations* (Bristol, Indiana: Wyndam Hall Press, 1990), 88. A "heterodox" was someone who believed differently from Orthodox Christians.

stipulating that a seven-year-old Jewish girl, Saporina De'Angeli, be taken from her parents and raised as a Catholic because of reports that she had been surreptitiously baptized.[245] Thirty years later in the same city, police seized a nineteen-month-old Jewish baby, Pamela Maroni, from her parents because of reports that she, too, had been baptized. Like Sapronia De'Angeli, Pamela Maroni was raised as a Catholic.

In a notorious case in 1858, a Catholic woman who worked as a servant for one of the few Jewish families that still lived in Bologna claimed that she had baptized the family's six-year-old son. As it was illegal for a Catholic child to be raised by Jews, police arrived at the Mortara home and seized the boy from his family in order to ensure that he would be raised as a Catholic. Pope Pius IX brushed aside anguished requests from his family that the boy be returned. That boy, Edgardo Mortara, ultimately became a Catholic priest.[246]

Such cases were so common that in October 1851, Jewish leaders in Reggio and Modena petitioned the duke of Modena, Francesco V, for justice. They called his attention to "an extremely grave evil that in the recent past has afflicted us many times. We speak of the horrible danger that we face even today of, from one moment to the next, finding ourselves bereft of our offspring due to clandestine baptism. Experience teaches us that it is in the power of even the most abject and infamous person to reduce, in but a moment, a family to desperation, a whole Nation to mourning and fear."[247] Yet those who engaged in this practice maintained that they were doing the seized child a favor and saving his soul, and this argument was generally considered more persuasive than any appeal to the rights of parents.

This practice was not restricted to Italy. In Russia, a similar practice was enshrined in law. Beginning in the seventeenth century and

---

[245] Kertzer, op. cit., 33.
[246] Kertzer, op. cit., passim.
[247] Ibid., 34.

continuing until 1856, the Russian military forcibly drafted Jewish children and forbade them to practice Judaism, forcing them to give up their *tzitzit* (fringes or tassels worn on garments in accordance with the scriptural command: "You shall make yourself tassels on the four corners of your cloak with which you cover yourself") and *tefillin* (small boxes with straps containing scrolls inscribed with scripture passages).[248] Concerted efforts were made to convert them to Orthodox Christianity, with holdouts deprived of food, beaten, or even tortured. In 1827, a new law stipulated that "Jewish minors under 18 years of age shall be placed in preparatory training establishments for military training"; these training establishments were known as cantonist units.[249]

Once the conscripted Jewish boys finished the training at age eighteen, they went into the army, as Christians, for twenty-five years. As many as thirty to forty thousand Jews were converted in this way. Czar Nicholas I (1825–55) thought this practice was a necessary aspect of his efforts at "correcting" Jews in Russia so that they would become Christian, which was an essential element of being truly Russian.[250]

POGROMS

Large-scale pogroms against the Jews began in nineteenth-century Russia. In 1821, one of them was sparked in Constantinople, when Ottoman authorities had the Ecumenical Patriarch Gregory V imprisoned, tortured, and murdered. His lifeless body was hanged for three days in front of a door of the Patriarchate in order to terrorize

---

[248] Deuteronomy 22:12; Exodus 13:9.
[249] Yehuda Slutsky, "Cantonists," *Encyclopaedia Judaica*, op. cit., vol. 4, 437.
[250] Ibid., 439.

the Christians of the city into fearing to join the Greek war of independence. Then the Ottomans, who made consistent efforts to keep their subject peoples at odds with each other, compelled some of the Jews of Constantinople to cut down the ecumenical patriarch's body and cast it into the waters of the Golden Horn.[251]

The Christians of Constantinople recovered Gregory's body and, fearing further persecution from the Ottoman authorities, sent it to the Greek community in Odessa for burial. The word spread among the Odessa Christians that the Jews had been complicit in the ecumenical patriarch's death, whereupon they rampaged through the Jewish area of the city, murdering seventeen Jews and injuring over fifty.[252]

From 1881 to 1884, 1903 to 1906, and 1917 to 1921, there were major pogroms in Russia, in which thousands of Jews were murdered, sparking large-scale emigration of Jews from Russia to the United States. Many of these pogroms had a specifically Christian character. Jews were attacked in Warsaw, then a part of the Russian Empire, on Christmas Day 1881; on Easter Sunday that year, two Jews were murdered and 120 injured in Balta, and numerous Jewish women were raped.[253]

AN ACCURSED PEOPLE

The Jews of Europe could not look to the Protestant Reformation that began in the sixteenth century for any relief. The pioneering

---

[251] Thomas Gordon, *History of the Greek Revolution* (Edinburgh and London: T. Cadell, 1833), I, 187.

[252] "Pogroms," American Jewish Joint Distribution Committee, https://web.archive.org/web/20070121190823/http://www.moria.farlep.net/vjodessa/en/pogroms.html.

[253] Yehuda Reshef and Michael Berenbaum, "Pogroms," *Encyclopaedia Judaica*, op. cit., vol. 16, 279–80.

reformer Martin Luther in 1543 wrote a lengthy treatise entitled "On the Jews and Their Lies," in which he reiterated the theological hostility of Augustine, Chrysostom, and other early Church Fathers in a cruder, more violent form. "I had made up my mind to write no more either about the Jews or against them," Luther began, but explained that when he heard that "those miserable and accursed people" were luring Christians to convert to Judaism, he decided to write his "little book," in order to oppose the Jews' "poisonous activities."[254]

Luther marveled that there could be any such conversions: "I would not have believed that a Christian could be duped by the Jews into taking their exile and wretchedness upon himself."[255] But this was Satan's handiwork: "However, the devil is the god of the world, and wherever God's word is absent he has an easy task, not only with the weak but also with the strong."[256]

Luther was writing to warn Christians about the Jews, not to convert the Jews, which he believed to be a hopeless task. Unlike those Christians who disputed with the Jews over the Talmud and engaged them in debates, as unequal as they were, Luther asserted that since the Jews had "failed to learn any lesson from the terrible distress that has been theirs for over fourteen hundred years in exile," they wouldn't learn anything from "our talking and explaining."[257]

The Jews should have learned from their long-suffering exile, Luther asserted, "for such ruthless wrath of God is sufficient evidence that they assuredly have erred and gone astray."[258] The divine wrath against them had been so relentless, Luther asserted, that it was "proof

---

[254] Martin Luther, *On the Jews and Their Lies*, Martin H. Bertram, trans., *Luther's Works, Vol. 47: The Christian in Society IV*, Franklin Sherman, ed. (Minneapolis: Fortress Press, 1971), part 1, https://web.archive.org/web/20050113123449/http://jdstone.org/cr/files/martin_luther/onthejewsandtheirlies01.html.
[255] Ibid.
[256] Ibid.
[257] Ibid.
[258] Ibid.

that the Jews, surely rejected by God, are no longer his people, and neither is he any longer their God."[259]

God now has to put up with their arrogance: "God has to endure that in their synagogues, their prayers, songs, doctrines, and their whole life, they come and stand before him and plague him grievously (if I may speak of God in such a human fashion). Thus he must listen to their boasts and their praises to him for setting them apart from the Gentiles, for letting them be descended from the holy patriarchs, and for selecting them to be his holy and peculiar people, etc. And there is no limit and no end to this boasting about their descent and their physical birth from the fathers."[260] Here Luther sounds more like a jealous sibling sniping at one who is perceived as more favored than a pious and sober analyst of scripture.

The great reformer accordingly recommended that various measures be taken to ensure that this arrogant people would be humbled. "With prayer and the fear of God," Luther declared, "we must practice a sharp mercy to see whether we might save at least a few from the glowing flames."[261] The "sharp mercy" he had in mind was meant to spare the Jews from hellfire by subjecting their synagogues to earthly fire. Luther's first recommendation was "to set fire to their synagogues or schools and to bury and cover with dirt whatever will not burn, so that no man will ever again see a stone or cinder of them."[262]

Luther declared that this criminal act should be done "in honor of our Lord and of Christendom, so that God might see that we are Christians, and do not condone or knowingly tolerate such public lying, cursing, and blaspheming of his Son and of his Christians."[263] He further advised that "their houses also be razed and destroyed. For

---

[259] Ibid.
[260] Ibid.
[261] Ibid., part XI.
[262] Ibid.
[263] Ibid.

they pursue in them the same aims as in their synagogues."[264] Where, then, would the Jews live? "Instead they might be lodged under a roof or in a barn, like the gypsies. This will bring home to them the fact that they are not masters in our country, as they boast, but that they are living in exile and in captivity, as they incessantly wail and lament about us before God."[265]

Luther also called for the confiscation of "all their prayer books and Talmudic writings, in which such idolatry, lies, cursing, and blasphemy are taught."[266] Rabbis should be "forbidden to teach henceforth on pain of loss of life and limb."[267]

The Jews were to be deliberately exposed to danger when traveling: "I advise that safe-conduct on the highways be abolished completely for the Jews. For they have no business in the countryside, since they are not lords, officials, tradesmen, or the like. Let them stay at home."[268] They were to be impoverished: "I advise that usury be prohibited to them, and that all cash and treasure of silver and gold be taken from them and put aside for safekeeping."[269] They should be forced to do manual labor: "I recommend putting a flail, an ax, a hoe, a spade, a distaff, or a spindle into the hands of young, strong Jews and Jewesses and letting them earn their bread in the sweat of their brow, as was imposed on the children of Adam."[270] Finally, he declared that "if we are afraid that they might harm us or our wives, children, servants, cattle, etc., if they had to serve and work for us," that they be expelled from Germany altogether.[271]

---

[264]   Ibid.
[265]   Ibid.
[266]   Ibid.
[267]   Ibid.
[268]   Ibid.
[269]   Ibid.
[270]   Ibid.
[271]   Ibid.

Luther made all these recommendations, he said, because treating the Jews kindly would only embolden them: "God's anger with them is so intense that gentle mercy will only tend to make them worse and worse, while sharp mercy will reform them but little. Therefore, in any case, away with them!"[272]

In comparison with Luther, Augustine and Chrysostom, and even Ambrose of Milan, looked positively philosemitic. Luther's rhetoric, and even more his recommendations, were so incendiary that it is easy to see a connection between them and the Jew-hatred in Germany that ultimately led to the National Socialist regime of Adolf Hitler and its genocide of the Jews. There can be little doubt that Luther's hostility contributed to an atmosphere in which Jews were regarded with hatred, suspicion, and fear, and some Christians could even think themselves justified and righteous in brutalizing and even killing them.

CHRIST-KILLERS? NO

Perhaps in reaction to Luther's incandescent hatred of the Jews, the counterreformation Catholic Church took an entirely different tack. Remarkably, in 1566, the catechism of the Council of Trent struck a massive blow against Catholic antisemitism by denying its central claim: that Jews collectively bore the guilt for Christ's death. Christ, it explained, died even for the Jews themselves: he "not only suffered for sinners, but even for those who were the very authors and ministers of all the torments He endured."[273] As he died to redeem mankind from sin, the guilt for his death was something that all sinners shared:

---

[272] Ibid.
[273] The Catechism of Trent, Article IV: "Suffered Under Pontius Pilate, Was Crucified, Dead, and Buried," http://www.cin.org/users/james/ebooks/master/trent/tcreed04.htm.

"In this guilt are involved all those who fall frequently into sin; for, as our sins consigned Christ the Lord to the death of the cross."[274]

In fact, Christians bore even greater guilt than the Jews, because they had the benefit of knowing the fullness of the divine plan: "This guilt seems more enormous in us than in the Jews, since according to the testimony of the same apostle: *If they had known it, they would never have crucified the Lord of glory*; while we, on the contrary, professing to know Him, yet denying Him by our actions, seem in some sort to lay violent hands on Him." Nor could the guilt for his death be laid at the feet of the Jews even if Christ had been an ordinary man whose death had no greater significance than the death of any other man, for "men of all ranks and conditions were gathered together against the Lord, and against His Christ. Gentiles and Jews were the advisers, the authors, the ministers of His Passion: Judas betrayed Him, Peter denied Him, all the rest deserted Him."[275]

Yet this striking statement had little effect on popular attitudes. The two attitudes—hostility to the Jews for killing Christ and charity toward them in recognition that the "guilt seems more enormous in us than in the Jews"—would continue. By the late nineteenth century, Catholic antisemitism was alive and well in the Vatican's two major publications, the daily newspaper *L'Osservatore Romano* and the biweekly *La Civiltà Cattolica*. In 1880, *La Civiltà Cattolica* urged governments to place restrictions on the rights of the Jews, calling for "exceptional laws for a race that is so exceptionally and profoundly perverse."[276] Eighteen years later, *L'Osservatore Romano* appeared nostalgic for the days when European countries were expelling the Jews

---

[274] Ibid.
[275] Ibid.
[276] Jules Gomes, "The Vatican's Mouthpieces Haven't Ended Their 150-Year-Old Jew-Hatred," Jihad Watch, May 22, 2024.

en masse, warning that they "cannot and must not live among others as any other people in the world...do."[277]

The ambiguity of the Roman Catholic Church's stance toward the Jews was summed up in the mid-twentieth century figure of Eugenio Pacelli, Pope Pius XII (1939–58), whom some revere for saving thousands of Jews from the National Socialists, and whom others revile for not doing enough and even, they contend, silently approving of the Germans' genocidal activities.

Pacelli and the National Socialist regime even negotiated an agreement, officially called the "Concordat between the Holy See and the German Reich." In his capacity as cardinal secretary of state, Pacelli signed this agreement in July 1933. While it lessened the National Socialists' hostility to the Roman Catholic Church, as Catholic leaders had hoped it would do, it also restrained the Church from speaking out against Hitler's race theories and hatred of the Jews.

Despite the Church's Concordat with the National Socialist German Reich, in 1937, Pius XII's predecessor, Pope Pius XI, took the unusual step of issuing an encyclical letter in German rather than the customary Latin. Entitled *Mit Brennender Sorge* (With Burning Sorrow), the encyclical was a strong condemnation of National Socialist antisemitism, declaring: "Whoever exalts race, or the people, or the State, or a particular form of State, or the depositories of power, or any other fundamental value of the human community—however necessary and honorable be their function in worldly things—whoever raises these notions above their standard value and divinizes them to an idolatrous level, distorts and perverts an order of the world planned and created by God; he is far from the true faith in God and from the concept of life which that faith upholds."[278]

---

[277]   Ibid.
[278]   Pius XI, *Mit Brennender Sorge*, March 14, 1937.

The National Socialists were furious, forbade distribution of the encyclical in Germany, and even claimed that Pius XI was half-Jewish.[279] Yet although it bore his name, Pius XI was not actually the author of *Mit Brennender Sorge*; it was the work of Cardinal Eugenio Pacelli, the paradoxical future Pope Pius XII.

Mit Brennender Sorge, for all its ringing words against the idolatry of race and blood, had no effect on National Socialist antisemitism, which we will discuss in greater detail later on. Yet there wouldn't have been as many National Socialists in Germany had it not been for centuries of Christian antisemitism that ensured that Hitler's scapegoating and demonizing of the Jews would find a receptive audience. There were no doubt numerous professing Christians who took part in various ways in the Holocaust, and the Christians who objected to the treatment of the Jews in National Socialist Germany were few.

The horrors of the Holocaust moved the Roman Catholic Church to repudiate the fundamental basis for Christian antisemitism once again. The Second Vatican Council, which the Roman Catholic Church holds to be the twenty-first ecumenical council, reiterated the Catechism of the Council of Trent's rejection of the idea that the Jews bore collective guilt for the crucifixion of Christ:

> True, the Jewish authorities and those who followed their lead pressed for the death of Christ; still, what happened in His passion cannot be charged against all the Jews, without distinction, then alive, nor against the Jews of today. Although the Church is the new people of God, the Jews should not be presented as rejected or accursed by God, as if this followed from the Holy Scriptures.

---

[279]   Dalin, op. cit., 39.

Furthermore, in her rejection of every persecution against any man, the Church, mindful of the patrimony she shares with the Jews and moved not by political reasons but by the Gospel's spiritual love, decries hatred, persecutions, displays of anti-Semitism, directed against Jews at any time and by anyone.[280]

This Vatican II statement heralded a new era in relations between the Catholic Church and the Jews. In 2000, Pope John Paul II issued an appeal to the Jews for reconciliation: "We hope that the Jewish people will acknowledge that the Church utterly condemns anti-Semitism and every form of racism as being altogether opposed to the principles of Christianity. We must work together to build a future in which there will be no more anti-Judaism among Christians or anti-Christian sentiment among Jews."[281] His successor, Pope Benedict XVI, in 2005, sent greetings to the Church's "brothers and sisters of the Jewish people, to whom we are joined by a great spiritual heritage, rooted in God's irrevocable promises."[282]

Taking note of the new surge in antisemitism, in 2024, the US Conference of Catholic Bishops required a note to be included with all material containing the text of Good Friday services. Drawn from the statements of the Second Vatican Council, the note read:

> The passion narratives are proclaimed in full so that all see vividly the love of Christ for each person. In light of this, the crimes during the Passion of Christ cannot be attributed, in either preaching or catechesis, indiscriminately to all Jews of that time, nor to Jews

---

[280] Second Vatican Council, "Declaration on the Relation of the Church to Non-Christian Religions (Nostra Aetate)," October 28, 1965.

[281] Pope John Paul II, "Visit to the Chief Rabbis of Israel, March 23, 2000," *L'Osservatore Romano*, March 29, 2000.

[282] Dalin, op. cit., 15.

today. The Jewish people should not be referred to as though rejected or cursed, as if this view followed from Scripture. The Church ever keeps in mind that Jesus, his mother Mary, and the apostles all were Jewish. As the Church has always held, Christ freely suffered his passion and death because of the sins of all, that all might be saved.[283]

The statement adds that "we cannot lay responsibility for the trial on the Jews in Jerusalem as a whole. Still less can we extend responsibility to other Jews of different times and places."[284] This is simple common sense. No one in any other context would hold members of any group today responsible for what some other members of the same group did two millennia ago or assume that every member of a group had a particular character because of a long-ago incident. Yet it is a staple of Christian antisemitism that the Jews' alleged responsibility for the crucifixion of Christ, and their rejection of Christ, imprinted an indelible character upon every Jew who ever lived thereafter. Christian doctrines of individual responsibility, of no one bearing the guilt of another's sin, and of the universality of sin and evil within the soul of every human being, rather than being uniquely concentrated among people of one group in particular, are forgotten.

There was a similar movement in the Orthodox Church. In 2007, twelve priests issued a statement that noted: "Sadly, there are some Orthodox Christians who propagate disgusting anti-Semitism under the banner of Orthodoxy, which is incompatible with Christianity."[285] They called for liturgical changes to avoid giving the impression that the Jews were collectively responsible for the death of

---

283   Michelle La Rosa and JD Flynn, "The USCCB's Good Friday Pastoral Note," The Pillar, March 12, 2024.

284   Ibid.

285   Etgar Lefkovits, "Priests: Remove Anti-Semitic Liturgy," *Jerusalem Post*, April 20, 2007.

Christ. The changes were not forthcoming, as liturgical changes are extremely difficult to bring about in Orthodox Christianity; however, there was clearly a growing tendency to avoid the age-old blaming of modern-day Jews for the arrest and crucifixion of Christ.

In 2014, Ecumenical Patriarch Bartholomew of Constantinople visited Yad Vashem, Israel's memorial to the victims of the Holocaust, and stated: "We condemn any acts of terrorism, anti-Semitism and xenophobia. We must publicly profess that the crime against the believers of any faith is an abomination of the face of God."[286] In a November 2021 speech to the American Jewish Committee, the ecumenical patriarch noted the closeness of the Jewish and Christian traditions:

> The book of Genesis reminds us of these words of creation: "Let us make humankind in our image, according to our likeness." (Genesis 1:26) As you know so well, both of our religious traditions have explored in depth the meaning of this expression. Commenting upon this passage, the Great Midrash— also known as the Midrash Ha-Gadol—offers a beautiful interpretation, that God consulted His own heart, namely, consulted Himself while creating humankind. Thus, the imago Dei becomes the seal of God's love for the entire world. The patristic tradition certainly built upon this hermeneutic: our dignity as human beings is based on this divine imprint in each person as the most precious gift.[287]

---

[286] "Speech of Ecumenical Patriarch Bartholomew I of Constantinople at Yad Vashem," Yad Vashem, May 27, 2014, https://www.yadvashem.org/blog/speech-of-ecumenical-patriarch-bartholomew-i-of-constantinople-at-yad-vashem.html.

[287] "Remarks of His All-Holiness Ecumenical Patriarch Bartholomew at the AJC Human Dignity Award," Greek Orthodox Archdiocese of America, November 1, 2021, https://www.goarch.org/-/2021-11-01-remarks-ecumenical-patriarch-bartholomew-ajc-human-dignity-award.

NOT OVER

Amid this conciliatory atmosphere, it was easy to think that Christian antisemitism was a thing of the past, an ugly relic of history, now consigned to its dustbin. This was, however, not the case. No multiplication of statements from the Vatican or any other authority could overcome what some Christians saw as the collective guilt of the Jews for rejecting their Messiah. All the anti-Jewish statements of Chrysostom and the rest live on in some circles, particularly among Orthodox Christians who revere the Fathers and can sometimes be tempted to forget that they were fallible men of their time.

As opposition to Israel steadily entered the mainstream in the West, and antisemitism once again became fashionable after October 7, the ugliest features of Christian antisemitism began to reappear.

On February 2, 2024, Pope Francis wrote to Karma Ben Johanan, a professor of comparative religion at Hebrew University of Jerusalem, lamenting the fact that "this war has also produced divisive attitudes in public opinion worldwide and divisive positions, sometimes taking the form of anti-Semitism and anti-Judaism."[288] The pope stated that he could repeat what his predecessors had said, "the relationship that binds us to you is particular and singular," and that "the path that the Church has walked with you, the ancient people of the covenant, rejects every form of anti-Judaism and anti-Semitism, unequivocally condemning manifestations of hatred towards Jews and Judaism as a sin against God."[289] He asserted that Roman Catholics were "very concerned about the terrible increase in attacks against Jews around the world. We had hoped that 'never again' would be a refrain heard

---

[288] Pope Francis, "Full Text: A Letter from Pope Francis to His 'Jewish Brothers and Sisters in Israel,'" *America*, February 3, 2024.
[289] Ibid.

by the new generations, yet now we see that the path ahead requires ever-closer collaboration to eradicate these phenomena."[290]

At least one Roman Catholic, however, was very concerned about other issues entirely and took strong issue with the pope's letter. The Roman Catholic traditionalist polemicist E. Michael Jones, who has written books entitled *The Jewish Revolutionary Spirit*, *The Jews and Moral Subversion* and *The Holocaust Narrative*, challenged Francis's basic premises, working from earlier Christian exegeses of the New Testament (punctuation as in the original):

> Pope Francis refers to Israel as the Holy Land. Pope Francis condemns anti-Semitism without defining the term. Pope Francis condemns anti-Judaism with no recognition that it is indistinguishable from the Gospel message. Was Jesus Christ an anti-Semite when he told the Jews in John 8 "Your father is Satan"? No. Was he anti-Jewish? Yes, because the Jews are the people who killed Christ and are enemies of the entire human race (I Thess 2:14-5). They are the people who prevent Paul from spreading the Gospel.. All of the fundamental texts of the Catholic faith, from the Gospels, to the Epistles, to the Acts of the Apostles, to the writings of the Church fathers are anti-Jewish. Sooner or later the Church will clarify this issue. In the meantime, read The Jewish Revolutionary Spirit for the full story.[291]

Jones blithely ignored his Church's statements about how all Jews could not be held responsible for the actions of some of them.

---

[290] Ibid.
[291] E. Michael Jones, X, February 3, 2024, https://twitter.com/EMichaelJones1/status/1753845338773832039.

Nevertheless, as a believing Roman Catholic, he was sure that one day the Church would come around to his way of thinking. It had to; after all, Jesus himself had promised: "When the Spirit of truth comes, he will guide you into all the truth."[292] Jones was certain that his own judgment, rather than that of the only marginally orthodox (at best) leftist Pope Francis, would prove to be that truth, for it was founded upon "the fundamental texts of the Catholic faith, from the Gospels, to the Epistles, to the Acts of the Apostles, to the writings of the Church fathers," all of which, he said, were anti-Jewish.

The application of the texts in question not just to Jews of a particular time and place, but to all of them collectively as Jews, was something that Jones didn't even see as needing to be explained. When he saw Israel begin its defensive war against Hamas, he saw it through the frame of reference of what he took to be the warnings of the Lord, the scripture, and the Fathers of the Church against the eternal enemies of the Church and the Christians. These were the Jews, behaving as they had always behaved. Christians must oppose them, as they always had. That was all there was to it.

For a Christian, there were many other ways to regard these issues. While Christian antisemites tended to assume, or to insist with elaborate arguments, that the very existence of the Jews after Christ was inherently anti-Christian and directed toward the destruction of Christians, Christianity, and Christian civilization, in reality, most Jews lived their lives without thinking about Christ or Christianity at all. The ancient charges of deicide, as mainstream as they were, were incompatible with the fundamental tenet of Christian theology that it was the sin of all human beings that put Christ on the cross, not one particular group. The statement "his blood be upon us and upon our children" was not an everlasting indictment of the Jews, but a statement of the mechanism of redemption.

---

[292] John 16:13.

The idea that Jews must be held in contempt or hated, much less mistreated, contradicted the fundamental Christian obligation of charity. The anti-Jewish statements of the Fathers of the Church failed on that score and could thus reasonably be seen as not normative for Christians and as evidence that sanctity did not confer infallibility.

It was possible, therefore, to be Christian and not hate Jews. Although many Christians lost sight of this amid the fog of propaganda after October 7, it remained true.

Chapter Four

APES AND PIGS

DID THE NAZIS BRING ANTISEMI-TISM TO THE ISLAMIC WORLD?

The Anti-Defamation League and other Jewish organizations dedicated to fighting antisemitism have warned in recent years of a rise in Jew-hatred, and they were quite right: after October 7, that hatred broke out into the open. Yet these organizations have concentrated overwhelmingly on antisemitism that has emanated from right-wingers, many of whom identify themselves as Christians. Yet within the same period, there has also been a rise in Islamic and leftist Jew-hatred—in fact, an even greater one, which organizations that defend Jews have almost entirely ignored. In fact, in the case of Islamic antisemitism, there are widespread denials that it even exists or is an integral aspect of the Islamic faith.

At a November 2023 panel at George Washington University, "Antisemitism in the Middle East: Unpacking the Root Causes and Implications for Regional Stability," Evin Ismail, a senior lecturer in political science at the Swedish Defense University, announced confidently that "I view Islamism as a politicization of Islam. And Islam is understood as a spiritual faith. To make this distinction clear, many scholars have stated that the Quran is not antisemitic. However, Islamists have developed an Islamist antisemitism where they claim that Muslims are in a permanent war with Jews."[293]

Ismail claimed not only that the Qur'an was not antisemitic, but that the introduction of antisemitism into Islam transformed the hitherto presumably peaceful religion into its politicized and bastardized form, "Islamism": "My main argument is antisemitism is an integral part of Islamism, antisemitism as in the ideology that politicizes Islam and not the religion itself, was born out of antisemitism and still depends on it for its survival. Here the Muslim Brotherhood plays a key role as the first Islamist movement."[294] The Muslim Brotherhood was founded in 1928, so in Ismail's view, we should see no antisemitism in the Islamic world before that date.

The German historian Matthias Küntzel, who was also on this panel, agreed, although he appeared to place the introduction of antisemitism into the Islamic world nine years later: "The Hamas massacre of Oct. 7, this ecstatic killing, proved that Nazi-like antisemitism flourished still today. And it proves that we have to find out how this Nazi-like hatred of Jews reached the Arab world and Hamas. Islamic antisemitism, it was only from the year 1937 onwards that Berlin began massively to intervene in the Middle East conflict. It wanted to prevent the establishment of even a tiny Jewish state."[295]

[293] "Program on Extremism Panel Analyzes Roots of Antisemitism in the Middle East," GWToday, December 4, 2023.
[294] Ibid.
[295] Ibid.

According to George Washington University's GWToday, Küntzel claimed that initially, "the Nazis had difficulties spreading their propaganda in the Middle East because Muslims were not ready to accept the racist antisemitism. Nazi propaganda then sought to embed antisemitism into the consciousness of the Arab world through the use of tailored antisemitic interpretations of Islam and the Quran."[296]

Tal-Or Cohen Montemayor of CyberWell then noted that "traditional media was hijacked by the Nazis in the Middle East to popularize this idea of antisemitism or antisemitism that's rooted in Islam, through radio and traditional media."[297]

This was just one panel, but it was representative of a tendency. The Jerusalem Center for Public Affairs features on its website a 2005 Küntzel article in which he declares: "Anti-Semitism based on the notion of a Jewish world conspiracy is not rooted in Islamic tradition but, rather, in European ideological models. The decisive transfer of this ideology to the Muslim world took place between 1937 and 1945 under the impact of Nazi propaganda."[298]

Günther Jikeli, a professor at Indiana University and associate director of the Institute for the Study of Contemporary Antisemitism, wrote in 2018: "It has been shown that Nazis successfully exported racist and genocidal antisemitism to the Muslim world and found partners in some Muslim leaders, such as Amin al-Husseini, the mufti of Jerusalem who helped disseminate modern antisemitic attitudes in the Muslim world."[299] In Jikeli's article, this sentence carries a footnote that cites a book by Matthias Küntzel.

---

[296] Ibid.
[297] Ibid.
[298] Matthias Küntzel, "National Socialism and Anti-Semitism in the Arab World," Jewish Political Studies Review 17:1–2, Spring 2005, https://www.jcpa.org/phas/phas-kuntzel-s05.htm.
[299] Günther Jikeli, "Discrimination against Muslims and Antisemitic Views among Young Muslims in Europe," in *Antisemitism Today and Tomorrow: Global Perspectives on the Many Faces of Contemporary Antisemitism*, Mikael Shainkman, ed. (Boston: Academic Studies Press, 2018), 112.

Jikeli lays some of the blame at the feet of Christians as well: "A much earlier export of antisemitic tropes took place in the nineteenth century, when Christian missionaries spread the blood libel in the Arab world."[300] Unlike Evin Ismail and others, Jikeli does acknowledge that antisemitism is not entirely a gift of National Socialism and Christianity to the Islamic world: "Some have highlighted the discrimination against Jews in premodern Islamic societies and negative views of Jews in Islamic scripture. Parts of the Koran and the Hadith convey derogatory views of Jews or suggest an enmity between Muslims and Jews and are used to justify anti-Jewish hostility."[301] He does not, however, find this compelling, as it "does not explain why today's antisemitism in Muslim countries includes modern and global-genocidal forms of antisemitism that were not present in traditional Muslim societies."[302]

Largely unexplained and unexamined is why National Socialist anti-Jewish literature and other modern forms of antisemitism found such an eagerly receptive audience in the Islamic world. The scholars who have formulated and propagated these fashionable theories don't seem to consider the possibility that many Muslims were perfectly capable of seeing world events through the prism of Qur'anic passages that excoriated the Jews; in fact, the core Islamic idea that the Qur'an is the perfect book that is valid for all times and in all places essentially requires them to do this. Consequently, the idea that Muslims were largely indifferent to the Qur'an's anti-Jewish material and were not imbibing modern charges against the Jews until the National Socialists or Christians brought these "tropes" to them is based on a shallow and inadequate understanding of the role of the

---

[300] Ibid., 112–3.
[301] Ibid., 112.
[302] Ibid.

Qur'an in Islamic theology and how it is understood to apply in the life of individual Muslims.

Many of these scholars are also attempting to prevent the image of Islam from being sullied by association with National Socialist Jew-hatred. Those Muslims who were receptive to Amin al-Husseini's appeals were falling for "tailored antisemitic interpretations of Islam and the Quran." The Qur'an, as Evin Ismail said, was "not antisemitic." Only when Islam was twisted into "Islamism" did it become so.

These claims, as comforting as they are with their promise of a tolerant, benign Islam that rejects antisemitism, or at very least is incompatible with modern-day anti-Jewish conspiracy theories, are as false as they are misleading.

THE QUR'AN'S VIEW OF THE JEWS

Antisemitism is deeply embedded within the Qur'an and Islamic tradition. The Qur'an's treatment of Jews is consistent and unambiguous: those who do not accept that Muhammad is a prophet and become Muslims are untrustworthy schemers who hate the Muslims and try to frustrate their plans whenever and wherever they can. That the Qur'an's picture of the Jews does not include the blood libel or the claim that they secretly control the world does not exonerate the Qur'an or Islam in their traditional formulations and interpretations from charges of a deep and abiding Jew-hatred.

Islam's most common prayer, the Fatihah (Opening), is also the first chapter of the Qur'an. In it, the believer asks Allah: "Guide us to the straight path, the path of those whom you have favored, not of those who have earned your anger, or of those who have gone astray."[303] In an Islamic tradition, Muhammad states that "the Jews are those who Allah is angry with."[304] Those who have gone astray, he adds, are the Christians.

One way in which the Jews have incurred Allah's anger is by twisting the message that he sent them through the prophets. In the Qur'an, the biblical prophets and Jesus Christ are all Muslims who taught Islam. The Qur'an says of itself that it simply confirms what they taught before. When the teachings of Judaism and Christianity have not corresponded to those of Islam, Muslims throughout the history of Islam have charged that this is because the Jews and Christians have tampered with their scriptures in order to efface their Islamic content, creating the religions of Judaism and Christianity in the process.

The Qur'an appears generously to promise salvation to the Jews and other non-Muslims: "Indeed, those who believe, and those who are Jews, and Christians, and Sabeans, whoever believes in Allah and the last day and does right, surely their reward is with their Lord, and no fear will come upon them, neither will they grieve."[305]

This apparent generosity is, however, illusory. Islamic tradition makes it clear that the Jews and other non-Muslims only enter paradise because they have accepted that Muhammad was a prophet and become Muslims. The renowned medieval Islamic scholar Ibn Kathir explains: "After Allah described the condition—and punishment—of those who defy His commands, fall into His prohibitions and transgress set limits by committing prohibited acts, He stated that the earlier nations who were righteous and obedient received the rewards for their good deeds. This shall be the case, until the Day of Judgment."[306]

303 Qur'an 1:6–7.
304 Jami at-Tirmidhi, vol. 5, book 44, no. 3954, Sunnah.com, https://sunnah.com/urn/639380.
305 Qur'an 2:62.
306 Ibn Kathir, op. cit., I, 247.

Being "righteous and obedient," however, meant becoming Muslim: "Therefore, whoever follows the unlettered Messenger and Prophet shall acquire eternal happiness and shall neither fear from what will happen in the future nor become sad for what has been lost in the past."[307] The "unlettered Prophet" is Muhammad. Ibn Kathir adds later that "Allah does not accept any deed or work from anyone, unless it conforms to the Law of Muhammad that is, after Allah sent Muhammad. Before that, every person who followed the guidance of his own Prophet was on the correct path, following the correct guidance and was saved."[308]

In the Qur'an, accordingly, the biblical prophets, as Muslims, curse the Jews for their rejection of the true religion: "Those among the children of Israel who went astray were cursed by the tongue of David, and of Jesus, son of Mary. That was because they rebelled and used to transgress."[309] They knew that Muhammad was speaking the truth, but obstinately concealed the fact: "Is it ever so that when they make a covenant, a party of them sets it aside? The truth is, most of them do not believe. And when a messenger from Allah comes to them, confirming what is with them, a faction of those who have received the book cast the book of Allah behind their backs, as if they did not know."[310]

Allah gave the Jews their law, says the Qur'an, because of their evildoing; presumably, if they had behaved better, not as many restrictions would have been placed upon them: "Because of the wrongdoing of the Jews, we forbade them good things which had been lawful for them, and because they kept many people from Allah's way, And for their taking usury when they were forbidden to take it, and of their devouring people's wealth by means of false pretenses, we have

---

307   Ibid.
308   Ibid., I. 249.
309   Qur'an 5:78.
310   Qur'an 2:100–1.

prepared for those among them who disbelieve a painful doom."[311]
Another Qur'anic passage elaborates on this: "To those who are Jews,
we forbade every animal with claws. And of the oxen and the sheep,
we forbade to them the fat of them, except what is upon the backs or
the entrails, or what is mixed with the bone. We awarded them that
for their rebellion. And indeed, we truly are truthful."[312]

Their rebellion apparently had to do with their unwillingness to
receive and obey Allah's message: Allah tells his prophet not to "let
those who compete with one another in the race to disbelief grieve
you."[313] This group was "the Jews," who were "listeners for the sake
of falsehood, listeners on behalf of other people who do not come to
you, changing words from their context and saying: If this is given to
you, receive it, but if this is not given to you, then beware."[314]

The Jews would "distort the book with their tongues, so that you
might think that what they say is from the book, when it is not from
the book. And they say, It is from Allah, when it is not from Allah, and
they knowingly speak a lie about Allah."[315] And again, "some of those
who are Jews change words from their context and say, We hear and
disobey, hear as one who does not hear, and Listen to us, distorting
with their tongues and slandering religion. If they had said, We hear
and we obey, hear and look at us, it would have been better for them,
and more upright. But Allah has cursed them for their disbelief, so
they do not believe, except for a few."[316] Allah asks his prophet: "Have
you any hope that they will be true to you when a party of them used

---

[311] Qur'an 4:60–1.
[312] Qur'an 6:146.
[313] Qur'an 5:41.
[314] Ibid.
[315] Qur'an 3:78.
[316] Qur'an 5:46; cf. 4:46.

to listen to the word of Allah, and then used to change it knowingly, after they had understood it?"[317]

Not only did the Jews change "words from their context" and dare to "lie about Allah"; they even denied that there had been any divine revelation, whereupon the Qur'an challenges them with the revelation Moses received: "And they do not measure the power of Allah in its true measure when they say, Allah has revealed nothing to a human being. Say, Who revealed the book that Moses brought, a light and guidance for mankind, which you have put on parchments which you show, but you hide much of it, and you were taught what you did not know, nor your fathers? Say, Allah. Then leave them to their play of vain discourse."[318]

While the Jews preferred to conceal much of what Allah had revealed to them through Moses, they prided themselves on being the chosen people, an idea that the Qur'an ridicules, including the Christians' idea that they are God's children in the mockery: "The Jews and Christians say, We are sons of Allah and his loved ones. Say: Why then does he punish you for your sins? No, you are just mortals of his creating. He forgives those whom he wills, and punishes those whom he wills. To Allah belongs the dominion of the heavens and the earth and all that is between them, and to him is the journeying."[319]

For refusing to believe and obey Moses, "humiliation and poverty struck them and they were visited with wrath from Allah. That was because they disbelieved in Allah's signs and killed the prophets wrongfully. That was for their disobedience and transgression."[320] Mistreating and even killing the prophets Allah sent to them was a recurring feature of their history: "And indeed we gave the book to Moses and we caused a succession of messengers to follow after him,

---

[317] Qur'an 2:75.
[318] Qur'an 6:90–1.
[319] Qur'an 5:18.
[320] Qur'an 2:61.

and we gave Jesus, son of Mary, clear proofs, and we strengthened him with the holy spirit. Is it always the case that when a messenger comes to you with what you yourselves do not desire, you grow arrogant, and some of them you disbelieve and some you kill?"[321]

The Qur'an contends that the Jews even claim that the power of Allah himself was limited: "The Jews say, Allah's hand is chained. Their hands are chained and they are cursed for saying this. No, but both his hands are spread out wide in bounty. He bestows it as he wills."[322] Allah asks in dismay of both the Jews and Christians: "Why don't the rabbis and priests forbid them to speak evil and devour illicit gain? Indeed their handiwork is evil."[323]

This evil handiwork included defrauding the Muslims: "Among the people of the book," a term that Islamic tradition applies primarily to Jews and Christians, "there is he who, if you trust him with a great amount of treasure, will return it to you. And also among them is he who, if you trust him with a piece of gold, will not return it to you unless you keep standing over him."[324]

These were specifically the Jews. The passage makes this clear as it piles on further charges: "That is because they say, We have no duty to the Gentiles. They knowingly speak a lie about Allah."[325]

In general, the Jews are heartless. Allah gave them various signs, but they still did not heed: "Then, even after that, your hearts were hardened and became as rocks, or worse than rocks, for hardness. For indeed there are rocks from which rivers gush, and indeed there are rocks that split in two so that water flows from them. And indeed

---

[321] Qur'an 2:87.
[322] Qur'an 5:64.
[323] Qur'an 5:63.
[324] Qur'an 3:75.
[325] Ibid.

there are rocks that fall down in the fear of Allah. Allah is not unaware of what you do."[326]

These dishonest and evil people were unworthy for Muslims to befriend: "O you who believe, do not take the Jews and the Christians for friends. They are friends of one another. He among you who takes them for friends is of them. Indeed, Allah does not guide wrongdoing people."[327] The Jews and Christians only wanted to lead Muslims away from Islam: "Many of the people of the book long to make you unbelievers after your belief, through envy on their own account, after the truth has become clear to them."[328]

While portraying the Jews as scheming and dishonest enemies of Allah and the Muslims, the Qur'an denies the central charge of Christian antisemitism, stating that Jews didn't actually kill Christ, even though they claim to do so and even thought they had done so: "And because of their saying, We killed the Messiah, Jesus son of Mary, the messenger of Allah, they did not kill him nor crucify him, but it seemed so to them, and indeed, those who disagree about this are in doubt about it, they have no knowledge of it except pursuit of a supposition, they did not kill him for certain."[329]

Other passages also reflect a faulty understanding of Judaism on the part of those who composed and compiled the Qur'an. One of the most curious statements in the entire Qur'an claims that they believe in Ezra as the son of God, in a manner that is apparently equivalent to the Christian belief in Jesus: "And the Jews say, Ezra is the son of Allah, and the Christians say, The Messiah is the son of Allah. That is their saying with their mouths. They imitate the

---

[326] Qur'an 2:74.
[327] Qur'an 5:51.
[328] Qur'an 2:109.
[329] Qur'an 4:157.

statements of those who disbelieved before. May Allah curse them. How perverse they are."[330]

The Qur'an goes on to charge that the Jews also join the Christians in revering their earthly religious authorities as additional gods: "They have taken as lords besides Allah their rabbis and their monks and the Messiah, the son of Mary, when they were called to worship only one God. There is no God except him. May he be glorified from all that they ascribe as partners."[331] They want to do nothing less than blow out the light of divine revelation and plunge the world into spiritual darkness: "They want to put out the light of Allah with their mouths, but Allah refuses except that he will perfect his light, however much the unbelievers hate it."[332]

Meanwhile, the Jews have no reservations about committing various sins: "They did not restrain one another from the wickedness they did. Indeed what they used to do was evil."[333] For all their misdeeds, the Jews who do not become Muslims are headed straight for hell: "Because of the wrongdoing of the Jews, we forbade them good things which had been lawful for them, and because they kept many people from Allah's way, and for their taking usury when they were forbidden to take it, and of their devouring people's wealth by means of false pretenses, we have prepared for those among them who disbelieve a painful doom."[334]

Islamic tradition amplifies the Qur'an's antisemitism even beyond the virulent Jew-hatred of the Islamic holy text. The Qur'an says: "Therefore woe to those who write the book with their hands and then say, This is from Allah, that they may sell it for a small price. Woe to them for what their hands have written, and woe to them

---

[330]   Qur'an 9:30.
[331]   Qur'an 9:31.
[332]   Qur'an 9:32.
[333]   Qur'an 5:79.
[334]   Qur'an 4:160–1.

for that they earn by it."[335] The Qur'anic text does not mention who exactly is guilty of this crime, but in the traditional and mainstream commentaries on the book, there is no doubt. The *Tafsir al-Jalalayn* says that the Jews "removed the description of the Prophet, may Allah bless him and grant him peace, which was in the Torah and the verse of stoning and other things which they wrote differently from how they were originally revealed!"[336]

In another reference to an unspecified group, the Qur'an says: "Indeed Allah heard the saying of those who said, Allah is poor and we are rich. We will record their saying along with their killing of the prophets wrongfully and we will say, Taste the punishment of burning."[337] Among other Qur'an commentators, the renowned Islamic scholar Ibn Kathir identifies these miscreants also as the Jews.[338]

The Jews, along with the polytheists, are the worst enemies of the Muslims: "You will find the Jews and the idolaters the most vehement of mankind in hostility to those who believe."[339] Muslims are to fight against them and subjugate them under the hegemony of Islamic law: Allah gave Muhammad a revelation commanding Muslims to fight even against Jews and Christians until they accepted Islamic hegemony, symbolized by payment of a poll tax (*jizya*) and discriminatory regulations that would ensure that they would be constantly reminded of their subordinate position: "Fight against those who do not believe in Allah or the last day, and do not forbid what Allah and his messenger have forbidden, and do not follow the religion of truth,

---

335   Qur'an 2:79.
336   Jalalu'd-Din al-Mahalli and Jalalu'd-Din as-Suyuti, *Tafsir al-Jalalayn*, Aisha Bewley, trans. (London: Dar Al Taqwa Ltd., 2007), 28.
337   Qur'an 3:181.
338   Ibn Kathir, *Tafsir Ibn Kathir* (abridged) (Riyadh: Darussalam, 2000), II, 334.
339   Qur'an 5:82.

even if they are among the people of the book, until they pay the jizya with willing submission and feel themselves subdued."[340]

APES AND PIGS

The Jews' disobedience had led Allah to take away their human nature itself: "And you know about those among you who broke the Sabbath, how we said to them, Be apes, despised and hated. And we made it an example to their own generation and to succeeding ones, and a warning to those who fear Allah."[341]

Another passage has Allah transforming recalcitrant "people of the book": "He whom Allah has cursed, on whom his wrath has fallen, and of whose sort, Allah has turned some into apes and pigs."[342] In another reference to this group of Jews who broke the Sabbath, the Qur'an adds: "So when they took pride in what they had been forbidden, we said to them, Be apes, despised and hated."[343]

These are not obscure passages to which no one pays attention. Just weeks before the October 7 attacks, the federally funded Muslim Association of Canada was the recipient of unwelcome media scrutiny for inviting a sheikh, Nashaat Ahmed, to speak at a conference. According to Canada's *National Post*, Ahmed had been "accused of openly praying for the Jewish people to be destroyed" and referred to Jews "as evil beasts, the worst of the earth's living creatures, and the descendants of apes and pigs."[344]

---

[340] Qur'an 9:29.
[341] Qur'an 2:65–6.
[342] Qur'an 5:59–60.
[343] Qur'an 7:166.
[344] Terry Glavin, "Antisemitic Egyptian Sheikh Was to Be Hosted by Ottawa-Funded Muslim Group," *National Post*, September 1, 2023.

In March 2023, Britain's highest-ranking diplomat in Jerusalem, Consul-General Diane Corner, held an official meeting with Mahmoud al-Habbash, a leading Sharia judge in the Palestinian Authority and Mahmoud Abbas's spiritual adviser. Corner appeared indifferent to the fact that the previous September, al-Habbash had exhorted Muslims not to permit al-Aqsa mosque to be "abandoned as prey in the hands of the grazing herds of humanoids, of people or creatures that Allah created in the form of humans, and He said of them: 'Shall I inform you of [what is] worse than that as penalty from Allah? [It is that of] those whom Allah has cursed and with whom He became angry and made of them apes and pigs.'"[345]

Likewise, the general supervisor of the Palestinian Authority's Ministry of Religious Affairs in the Palestinian city of Tubas, Sheikh Muhammad Abd al-Ilah, said this in February 2021 in reference to Donald Trump's "deal of the century" Middle East peace plan: "We are here and will remain here behind the wise leadership, which rejects the deal of the century, which is expressed by the sale of Palestine at no cost to the descendants of the apes and pigs."[346]

Such rhetoric is dispiritingly common. A Muslim preacher in Malmö, Sweden, Basem Mahmoud, declared in October 2020: "In all times, it is the same deceptive villains who stand in the way of the faithful. Everyone knows that the West is ruled by Jews. The Jews are their rulers. The Jews are the offspring of pigs and apes. They are hostile to Muslims, but they will be helpless against Islam."[347] When he was accused of hate speech, Mahmoud replied, quite reasonably, that he was only quoting the Qur'an and that he could not "change

---

[345] "Abbas' Advisor on Islam: Jews are 'humanoids... creatures that Allah created in the form of humans... apes and pigs," Palestinian Media Watch, September 30, 2022.

[346] "Jews are 'the descendants of the apes and pigs' - PA Min. of Religious Affairs official," Palestinian Media Watch, February 16, 2021.

[347] "VIDEO: Imam om judarna: 'Grisars och apors avkomma,'" *Samnytt*, June 16, 2022.

his religion for the sake of the Jews."[348] Yet Swedish authorities, like their counterparts all over the Western world, had unanimously determined that the Qur'an was entirely benign and presented no cause for concern for its potential to incite any kind of violence or unrest.

Dr. Fadi Yousef Kablawi, imam of the North Miami Islamic Center in Florida, in March 2021, criticized Muslims who engaged in negotiations with non-Muslims, specifically those who participated in peace talks with Israel: "Who do you go to? The brothers of the apes and pigs. Huh? The offspring of pigs and apes—that's who you seek your honor from?" He was appalled that Muslims would accord Jews such respect: "Criminals—[those] people are criminals. There is no corruption in the world that the [Jews] are not behind. [You should] know it for a fact."[349]

"MAY'S ALLAH'S CURSE BE ON THE JEWS"

The voluminous hadith collections record what Islamic tradition contends are Muhammad's words and deeds, and when these meet the traditional criteria for authenticity (which primarily involve having an unbroken chain of narrators who are considered reliable), Muslims regard them as second only to the Qur'an in authority. These canonical traditions contain a great deal of anti-Jewish material. Muhammad is depicted as intensifying the Qur'an passages in which Jews are dehumanized and transformed into apes and pigs: "A group of Bani Isra'il," that is, the tribe of Israel, "was lost. I do not know what happened to it, but I think (that it underwent a process of metamorphosis) and assumed the shape of rats. Don't you see when

[348] Ibid.
[349] "Miami Imam Dr. Fadi Yousef Kablawi: There Can Be No Peace, Normalization with the Brothers of Pigs and Apes; Jews Refuse to Convert to Islam; The Pope, Catholics Are Idol Worshipers," MEMRI, March 12, 2021.

the milk of the camel is placed before them, these do not drink and when the milk of goat is placed before them, these do drink."[350]

The hadith also amplifies the Qur'an's curses of the Jews. Muslims could bring on the final victory of Islam in the last days by killing this accursed people: "The last hour would not come unless the Muslims will fight against the Jews and the Muslims would kill them until the Jews would hide themselves behind a stone or a tree and a stone or a tree would say: Muslim, or the servant of Allah, there is a Jew behind me; come and kill him; but the tree Gharqad would not say, for it is the tree of the Jews."[351]

Ninth-century traditions that form the core of what Islam presents to this day as the details of Muhammad's life are no kinder to the Jews. When Muhammad moves with his followers from Mecca to Medina and becomes for the first time a political and military leader as well as a religious one, he encounters three Jewish tribes: the Banu Qaynuqa, Banu Nadir, and Banu Qurayza. Initially, he makes a covenant with them, but after winning a decisive victory over the pagan Quraysh (not to be confused with the Qurayza Jews) at Badr, the first great battle in Islamic history, Muhammad went to the Qaynuqa and demanded that they accept his new religion: "O Jews, beware lest God bring upon you the vengeance that He brought upon Quraysh and become Muslims. You know that I am a prophet who has been sent—you will find that in your scriptures and God's covenant with you."[352]

The Qaynuqa Jews refuse, whereupon Muhammad's first extant biography, that of the ninth-century Muslim writer Ibn Hisham, notes that they "were the first of the Jews to break their agreement with the

[350] Imam Muslim, *Sahih Muslim*, translated by Abdul Hamid Siddiqi, Kitab Bhavan, revised edition 2000, 2997.

[351] Ibid., 2922.

[352] Ibn Ishaq, *The Life of Muhammad: A Translation of Ibn Ishaq's Sirat Rasul Allah*, A. Guillaume, trans. (Oxford: Oxford University Press, 1955), 363.

apostle and to go to war, between Badr and Uhud, and the apostle besieged them until they surrendered unconditionally."[353] Yet it was either that or give up their identity as Jews and become Muslims.

Another biographer of Muhammad says that this was the occasion when this passage of the Qur'an was revealed: "And if you fear treachery from any people, then throw it back to them fairly. Indeed, Allah does not love the treacherous" (8:58). Muhammad is depicted as receiving this revelation and then remarking, "I fear the Banu Qaynuqa."[354]

The ninth-century historian al-Waqidi gives the impression that this had at least something to do with the sexual outrage of a pious Muslim woman by the Jews. He recounts that a Muslim woman "came to the market of the Banu Qaynuqa," where she "sat down at a goldsmith's with a trinket of hers."[355] But then, "a Jew of the Banu Qaynuqa came and sat behind her, and without her knowledge fixed her outer garment to her back with a pin. When the woman stood up her pudenda showed and they laughed at her."[356] The offender was then killed, whereupon the Banu Qaynuqa "gathered and surrounded and killed the Muslim" who had killed the Jew.[357] Then, says al-Waqidi, the Jews "abandoned the agreement with the Prophet and opposed him, fortifying themselves in their fortress."[358]

The picture of the perverted Jew avid to defile Gentile women would become a staple of anti-Jewish literature among both Muslims and Christians. Muhammad was so outraged by this incident that he strode into the Qaynuqa's marketplace and proclaimed: "O

---

[353]   Ibid.

[354]   Tabari, op. cit., 86.

[355]   Muhammad ibn Umar al-Waqidi, *The Life of Muhammad: Al-Waqidi's Kitab al-Maghazi*, Rizwi Faizer, Amal Ismail and AbdulKader Tayob, trans., Rizwi Faizer, ed. (London: Routledge, 2011), 88.

[356]   Ibid.

[357]   Ibid.

[358]   Ibid.

Jews, beware lest God bring upon you the vengeance that He brought upon Quraysh and become Muslims. You know that I am a prophet who has been sent—you will find that in your scriptures and God's covenant with you."[359] Thus, the Jews were not only perverts who outraged the honor of decent women, but rebels against God himself, daring to ignore, or even to tamper with, the divine revelations he had sent them.

Muhammad decided that the Qaynuqa Jews must leave Medina. He besieged them and exiled them from the city.

After exiling the Banu Qaynuqa, Muhammad addressed another aspect of the problem of Jews outraging the modesty of Muslim women by determining to have a Jewish poet, Ka'b bin al-Ashraf, who "composed amatory verses of an insulting nature about the Muslim women," killed.[360] Muhammad asked for a volunteer to kill Ka'b, gave permission to the volunteer to deceive Ka'b in order to gain his trust and get close to him. Muhammad screamed, "Allahu akbar!" when he got the news that Ka'b had been murdered.[361]

Not hesitating to punish the Jews collectively for the misdeeds of a few, Muhammad thereupon commanded his followers to "kill any Jew that falls into your power."[362] This was not limited to combatants; first among the victims was a Jewish merchant, Ibn Sunayna. This man had had "social and business relations" with the Muslims and was not recorded as having committed any offenses.[363]

Seeing all this, one of the other tribes of Medina, the Banu Nadir, resolved to kill Muhammad; once again, however, the only record of this comes from Islamic tradition. Muhammad exiled them from the

[359] Ibn Ishaq, op. cit., 363.
[360] Ibid., 367.
[361] Ibn Sa'd, *Kitab al-Tabaqat al-Kabir*, S. Moinul Haq, trans. (New Delhi: Kitab Bhavan, n.d.), I, 37.
[362] Ibid., 36; Ibn Ishaq, op. cit., 369.
[363] Ibn Ishaq, op. cit.

city as well. Shortly after that, when the pagan Quraysh of Mecca laid siege to Medina, the Jews of the third remaining Medinan Jewish tribe, the Banu Qurayzah, were inside the besieged city with the Muslims. Muhammad, however, determined that they had betrayed them and were secretly aiding the Quraysh. Muhammad called out to them in Qur'anic language that numerous jihadis emulate even today: "You brothers of monkeys, has God disgraced you and brought His vengeance upon you?"[364]

The Jews surrendered, and Muhammad appointed one of his warriors to determine their fate. He decreed that all the men be beheaded, and the women and children enslaved. One of the Jews is depicted as agreeing with this sentence: "God's command is right. A book and a decree, and massacre have been written against the Sons of Israel."[365] He was nonetheless beheaded with the rest; according to Ibn Hisham, there were "600 or 700 in all, though some put the figure as high as 800 or 900."[366]

Then came the turn of the Jews Muhammad had previously exiled. They had settled in the oasis of Khaybar, north of Medina. The prophet of Islam and his men attacked by surprise, as the Jews were heading out one morning to tend their farms. It is to this massacre that present-day supporters of the Palestinian Arabs are referring when they chant, "Khaybar, Khaybar, O Jews, the army of Muhammad will return." Muhammad himself was in the thick of the fighting and, according to his ninth-century biographer Ibn Sa'd, "killed ninety-three men of the Jews."[367]

The Muslims tortured and ultimately killed one of the Jewish leaders, Kinana ibn al-Rabi, in an attempt to get him to reveal where the Jews' treasure was hidden. Once the Jews of Khaybar were

---

[364] Ibid., 461.
[365] Ibid., 464.
[366] Ibid.
[367] Ibn Sa'd, op. cit., II, 132–33.

thoroughly defeated, Muhammad decreed that they be exiled as well, with as much of their property as they could manage to take with them, as long as they left their gold and silver behind.[368] Some of them begged him to be allowed to stay, and he relented, as long as they agreed to one key caveat: "If we wish to expel you we will expel you."[369] Muhammad also commanded that the Jewish women be enslaved.[370]

Muhammad further ordered that one of these newly enslaved women, Zaynab bint al-Harith, cook him dinner. According to Islamic tradition, she poisoned his food, but Muhammad was able to discern that it was poisoned before he had eaten too much of it. Zaynab explained: "You know what you have done to my people."[371] Islamic tradition disagrees about whether Muhammad had her put to death or showed her mercy and allowed her to live. In any case, the effects of this poisoning lingered; on his deathbed, Muhammad is depicted as saying that the pain he was feeling stemmed from what he had eaten at Khaybar.

Thus, the Jews are charged with killing Muhammad, as well as with killing Jesus.

Muhammad took a Jewish woman, Safiya bint Huyayy, the widow of Kinana ibn al-Rabi and the daughter of another man the Muslims had just killed, from among the spoils of war. According to Ibn Hisham, Safiya was brought to the Islamic prophet "along with another woman."[372] As they were led "past the Jews who were slain," the woman with Safiya "shrieked and slapped her face and poured dust on her head."[373] A disgusted Muhammad ordered: "Take this

---

[368] Ibid., II, 137.
[369] Ibn Ishaq, op. cit, 515.
[370] Ibn Sa'd, op. cit., II, 137.
[371] Ibn Ishaq, op. cit.
[372] Ibn Ishaq, op. cit., 514.
[373] Ibid., 515.

she-devil away from me."[374] Al-Waqidi states that Muhammad chided the man who had led these women past their dead relatives: "Has graciousness left you that you take a young girl past the dead?"[375] The man replied: "O Messenger of God, I did not think that you would hate that. I wanted her to see the destruction of her people."[376]

Muhammad was so taken with Safiya that upon her conversion to Islam, he made her his latest wife instead of keeping her as a sex slave. His other wives, however, were not so welcoming. Safiya herself is depicted as recounting: "I suffered his wives who looked down on me saying, 'O daughter of a Jew.' But I used to see the Messenger of God, and he was gracious and generous to me. One day when he visited me I was crying. He said, 'What is the matter with you?' I said, 'Your wives look down on me and say, "O daughter of a Jew ."'"[377] Muhammad was incensed. Safiya says that he told her how to respond: "I saw that the Messenger of God was angry. He said, 'When they speak to you or dismiss you, say, "My father is Aaron and my uncle, Moses."'"[378]

This sounded agreeably broad-minded, but Muhammad is said also to have ordered that Jews and Christians in Muslim lands "must pay the poll tax—for every adult, male or female, free or slave, one full dinar"—and he explained how to determine that amount precisely—"or its equivalent in clothes." The consequences of refusal to pay were severe: "He who pays that to God's apostle has the guarantee of God and His apostle, and he who withholds it is the enemy of God and His apostle."[379]

---

[374] Ibid.
[375] Al-Waqidi, op. cit., 331.
[376] Ibid.
[377] Al-Waqidi, op. cit., 332.
[378] Ibid.
[379] Ibn Ishaq, op. cit., 643.

On his deathbed, one tradition has Muhammad exclaiming to his youngest and favorite wife: "O Aisha! I still feel the pain caused by the food I ate at Khaybar, and at this time, I feel as if my aorta is being cut from that poison."[380] This would mean that it was the Jewish woman who prepared his meal at Khaybar who ultimately killed him. He also stated his desire to remove Jews and Christians from Arabia: "If I live—if Allah wills—I will expel the Jews and the Christians from the Arabian Peninsula."[381] Although gravely ill, he managed one more swipe at his greatest enemies: "May Allah's curse be on the Jews for they built the places of worship at the graves of their Prophets."[382]

The Qur'an promises that those who disobey him will suffer in this world: "As for those who disbelieve, I will punish them with a heavy punishment in this world and the hereafter, and they will have no helpers."[383] Believers in Allah are charged with administering his punishment: "Fight them, and Allah will punish them by your hands, and he will lay them low and give you victory over them, and he will heal the hearts of people who are believers. And he will remove the anger of their hearts."[384]

This amounts to an open-ended threat of violence against Jews everywhere.

---

[380] Sahih Bukhari, vol. 5, book 64, no. 4428.

[381] Jami at-Tirmidhi, book 21, no. 1606.

[382] Muhammed ibn Ismail al-Bukhari, *Sahih al-Bukhari: The Translation of the Meanings*, Muhammad M. Khan, trans., Darussalam, 1997, vol. 8, book 86, no. 437.

[383] Qur'an 3:56.

[384] Qur'an 9:14–5.

Chapter Five

HUMILIATION AND DISGRACE

AFTER MUHAMMAD

The Qur'an and the life of Muhammad as depicted in Islamic tradition were consistent in their portrayal of Jews as accursed enemies of Allah, burning with rage and jealousy against the Muslims and determined to thwart them in every way possible. This was remarkably similar to the antisemitic Christian idea that in rejecting Christ, the Jewish people as a whole had become antichrist, determined to impede the serene progress of the Church in every way possible. And just as all too many Christians acted upon this assumption throughout history, so also did all too many Muslims.

Abu Bakr, one of Muhammad's staunchest followers, succeeded him as the first caliph, or successor, the first to be the Islamic community's political, military, and spiritual leader after the death of the prophet of Islam. He also shared something else with Muhammad: he was poisoned by the Jews. According to the tenth-century Muslim historian al-Tabari, "The cause of his death was that the Jews fed him poison in a grain of rice; it is also said in porridge."[385]

Umar ibn al-Khattab, who succeeded Abu Bakr as caliph, acted to ensure that the subject peoples knew their place; the provisions he put in place in order to ensure that the Jews and Christians would "feel themselves subdued," as the Qur'an directed, became enduring elements of Islamic law. This was known as the dhimmah, the contract of protection.

Accordingly, a Muslim jurist of the thirteenth century, Ghazi ibn al-Wasiti, recalled that Umar "commanded that both Jews and Christians should be forbidden to ride upon saddles; that no one belonging to the 'Protected People' should be allowed to enter a public bath on Friday, except after Prayer-time. He ordered, further, that a guard should be set to watch both Jews and Christians whenever they slaughtered an animal, so that the guard should mention the name of Allah and of his Prophet [at such a slaughter]."[386]

In his fourteenth-century commentary on the Qur'an, Ibn Kathir explains for the Jews and Christians to "feel themselves subdued" means that they had to be "disgraced, humiliated and belittled. Therefore, Muslims are not allowed to honor the people of Dhimmah or elevate them above Muslims, for they are miserable, disgraced and humiliated."[387] Ibn Kathir quotes a saying attributed to Muhammad: "Do not initiate the Salam [the greeting of peace] to the Jews and Christians, and if you meet any of them in a road, force them to its narrowest alley."[388] Ibn Kathir then adds: "This is why the Leader of

---

[385]   Muhammad al-Tabari, *The History of al-Tabari*, vol. 11, *The Challenge to the Empires*, Khalid Yahya Blankinship, trans. (State University of New York Press, 1993), 1–2.
[386]   Ibid., 182–83.
[387]   Ibn Kathir, op. cit., IV, 406.
[388]   Ibid.

the faithful Umar bin Al-Khattab, may Allah be pleased with him, demanded his well-known conditions be met by the Christians, these conditions that ensured their continued humiliation, degradation and disgrace."[389]

The same conditions applied to the Jews as well. These included a prohibition on building new synagogues or repairing old ones, as well as numerous regulations that were designed to remind the subject people of their place, with conversion of Islam held out as an opportunity to escape all this misery and live a decent life. The Christian dhimmis pledged:

> We will not...prevent any of our fellows from embracing Islam, if they choose to do so. We will respect Muslims, move from the places we sit in if they choose to sit in them. We will not imitate their clothing, caps, turbans, sandals, hairstyles, speech, nicknames and title names, or ride on saddles, hang swords on the shoulders, collect weapons of any kind or carry these weapons.... We will not encrypt our stamps in Arabic, or sell liquor. We will have the front of our hair cut, wear our customary clothes wherever we are, wear belts around our waist, refrain from erecting crosses on the outside of our churches and demonstrating them and our books in public in Muslim fairways and markets. We will not sound the bells in our churches, except discreetly, or raise our voices while reciting our holy books inside our churches in the presence of Muslims....[390]

---

389   Ibid.
390   Ibn Kathir, vol. 4, p. 407.

For the Jews, the same rules were in effect, and raising their voices during synagogue worship could likewise break the covenant. The penalty was simple and clear: if the contract of protection was broken, the protection was revoked, and the errant dhimmi's life was forfeit.

DISTINCTIVE CLOTHING

The Qur'an says of the Jews: "They will be stricken with disgrace wherever they are found, except for a rope from Allah and a rope from men. They have brought on anger from their Lord, and wretchedness is laid upon them. That is because they used to disbelieve the signs of Allah, and killed the prophets wrongfully. That is because they were rebellious and used to transgress."[391]

Applying this dictum, the caliph al-Mansur in 772 ensured that Jews would be readily distinguishable from the Muslims by ordering that the dhimmis in Jerusalem receive a distinctive symbol stamped onto their hands.[392] As we have seen, some Christian rulers would later adopt this provision as well. In the Islamic world, the mark was meant to humiliate as well as to distinguish. Early in the eleventh century, the Fatimid caliph al-Hakim in Cairo ordered Jews to wear heavy blocks of wood in the shape of a calf around their necks.[393] In fourteenth-century Damascus, the capital of the Abbasid caliphate, the Islamic jurist Ibn Qayyim al-Jawziyya emphasized that "those who are of the opinion that to pray in a church or synagogue is loathsome also say that they are places of great infidelity and polytheism. Indeed, their loathsomeness is greater than that of bathhouses, cemeteries or dunghills since they are places of Divine Wrath.... Moreover, are they

---

[391] Qur'an 3:112.
[392] Moshe Gil, *A History of Palestine 634–1099* (Cambridge University Press, 1992), 473.
[393] Gil, op. cit., 376.

not the houses of the enemies of Allah, and Allah is not to be adored in the houses of his enemies?"[394]

Ibn Qayyim also said that "verily, Allah has annulled the sounding of the Christian bell and the Jewish [ram's] horn and has replaced them with the call of monotheism and devotion."[395] This was an indication that the sound of the bell or the ram's horn could bring swift punishment, for he continued: "'Humiliation and derision are to be the lot of those that disobey my word.' The *dhimmis* are the most disobedient of His command and contrary to His word; consequently, it befits them to be humiliated by distinguishing them from the comportment of the Muslims whom Allah has exalted through their obedience to Him and His Prophet above those that have disobeyed Him."[396]

He reiterated the importance of forcing the Jews to wear distinctive clothing:

> That a distinctive sign [*ghiyar*] must be imposed upon them is clear from the Prophet's statement, "He of the people who resembles them [the *dhimmis*] shall be deemed of their number." ...Moreover the distinctive dress serves other purposes. He [the Muslim] will thereby know that he is not to go to meet him, he is not to seat him among Muslim company, he is not to kiss his hand, he is not to stand up for him, he is not to address him with the terms brother or master, he is not to wish him success or honor as is customary toward a Muslim, he is not to give him Muslim

[394] Bat Ye'or, *The Dhimmi: Jews and Christians Under Islam*, David Maisel, Paul Fenton, and David Littman, trans. (Madison, New Jersey: Fairleigh Dickinson University Press, 1985), 196–97.
[395] Ibid.
[396] Ibid.

charity, he is not to call him as a witness, either for accusation or defence.[397]

Al-Marrakushi, a historian writing in the thirteenth century, observed that Abu Yusuf, the Almohad caliph in Spain, in 1198, forced the Jews in his domains to wear distinctive clothing. He "ordered the Jewish inhabitants of the Maghreb to make themselves conspicuous among the rest of the population by assuming a special attire consisting of dark blue garments, the sleeves of which were so wide as to reach to their feet and—instead of a turban—to hang over their ears a cap whose form was so ill-conceived as to be easily mistaken for a pack-saddle. This apparel became the costume of all the Jews of the Maghreb and remained obligatory until the end of the prince's reign and the beginning of that of his son Abu Abd Allah" in 1224.[398] For his part, Abu Abd Allah ordered the Jews, according to al-Marrakushi, "to wear yellow garments and turbans, the very costume they still wear in the present year 621," that is, 1224.[399]

MULTICULTURAL AL-ANDALUS

Many who learn of these restrictions assume that they were largely a dead letter, left unenforced by rulers who were more enlightened than the letter of the law would allow. Unfortunately, however, while there were times and places in which they were not fully enforced, the laxity generally resulted in Muslim protests and the reapplication of the laws upon the subject peoples, often with violence.

One of the persistent myths and fantasies of our age is that medieval Muslim Spain was a paradise of coexistence and mutual respect

---

[397] Ibid.
[398] Ibid., 189.
[399] Ibid.

between Muslims, Jews, and Christians. In reality, life was only remotely bearable for the subject peoples if they always remembered their subservient position. When a Jew in eleventh-century Granada was appointed to a position of responsibility, the Jews of the area were given a grisly reminder of that fact. Samuel ibn Naghrillah and his son Joseph were both given positions of prestige and power in the city, but some Muslims were outraged that Islamic law was being breached by allowing dhimmis to have power over Muslims.

A Muslim jurist, Abu Ishaq, wrote in fury to the Berber King Badis, demanding that this injustice be redressed. Of Badis himself, Abu Ishaq wrote: "He has chosen an infidel as his secretary when he could, had he wished, have chosen a Believer."[400] This had led the Jews to forget that they had second-class status: "Through him, the Jews have become great and proud and arrogant—they, who were among the most abject."[401] Recalling the Qur'an passages dehumanizing the Jews, he wrote: "And how many a worthy Muslim humbly obeys the vilest ape among these miscreants."[402]

Abu Ishaq exhorted Badis to restore the proper order of an Islamic society: "Put them back where they belong and reduce them to the lowest of the low, roaming among us, with their little bags, with contempt, degradation and scorn as their lot, scrabbling in the dunghills for colored rags to shroud their dead for burial."[403] What was happening was simply wrong: "These low-born people would not be seated in society or paraded along with the intimates of the ruler."[404] This was a matter of the divine will: "God has vouchsafed in His revelations a warning against the society of the wicked. Do not

---

[400] Darío Fernández-Morera, *The Myth of the Andalusian Paradise* (Wilmington, Delaware: ISI Books, 2016), 182–3.
[401] Ibid.
[402] Ibid.
[403] Ibid.
[404] Ibid.

choose a servant from among them but leave them to the curse of the accurst!"[405]

Other rulers were aware that this was how the Jews ought to be treated: "Turn your eyes to other countries and you will find the Jews are outcast dogs. Why should you alone be different and bring them near when in all the land they are kept afar?"[406] Badis had allowed the Jews to enrich themselves: "They collect all the revenues, they munch and they crunch. They dress in the finest clothes while you wear the meanest."[407] Nor were the Jews worthy of the respect Badis had accorded them: "They are the trustees of your secrets, yet how can traitors be trusted?"[408]

Abu Ishaq urged Badis to set things right by killing the leader of the Jews, a man to whom he referred in Qur'anic language: "Their chief ape has marbled his house and led the finest spring water to it. Our affairs are now in his hands and we stand at his door. He laughs at God and our religion.... Hasten to slaughter him as an offering, sacrifice him, for he is a precious thing...."[409] He wanted Badis to kill other Jews as well: "Do not consider it a breach of faith to kill them, the breach of faith would be to let them carry on. They have violated our covenant with them.... God watches His own people and the people of God will prevail."[410]

Abu Ishaq's anger was contagious, and his exhortations did not go unheeded. On December 30, 1066, enraged Muslims rampaged through Granada and killed four thousand Jews in Granada, while plundering numerous Jewish homes. Joseph ibn Naghrila

---

[405] Ibid.
[406] Ibid.
[407] Ibid.
[408] Ibid.
[409] Ibid.
[410] Ibid.

was crucified, in accord with the Qur'an's command to crucify or otherwise put to death those who "wage war against Allah and his messenger."[411]

The pogrom in Granada took place because the Jews failed to maintain their prescribed position of subservience. The laws regarding the subjugation of the dhimmis were in general strictly enforced.

In the middle of the twelfth century, the Almohads advanced in North Africa and massacred Jews in large numbers. According to Ibn Baydhaq, a Muslim historian, when the Almohad caliph Abd al-Mumin captured Tlemcen in North Africa in the early 1140s, he "killed all those who were in it, including the Jews, except those who embraced Islam."[412] Proceeding to Sijilmasa in 1146, Abd al-Mumin killed the Jews there also: "one hundred and fifty persons were killed for clinging to their [Jewish] faith."[413] When the conquest was complete, "the Jews in all [Maghreb] localities [conquered]...groaned under the heavy yoke of the Almohads; many had been killed, many others converted; none were able to appear in public as Jews.[414]

Ibn Naqqash, a fourteenth-century Muslim historian, states that in 1301, the vizier of Gharb in North Africa visited Cairo and discovered, to his dismay, that the local Jews and Christians were "attired in the most elegant clothes" and "rode on mules, mares, and expensive horses."[415] They were even "considered worthy of being employed in the most important offices, thus gaining authority over the Muslims."[416] He compared their impunity unfavorably to the situation back home in Gharb, where both Jews and Christians were "main-

---

[411] Richard Gottheil and Meyer Kayserling, "Granada," *Jewish Encyclopedia* (1906), http://jewishencyclopedia.com/articles/6855-granada; Qur'an 5:33.

[412] Andrew Bostom, *The Legacy of Islamic Antisemitism* (Amherst, New York: Prometheus Books, 2007), 102.

[413] Ibid.

[414] Ibid.

[415] Bat Ye'or, op. cit., 193.

[416] Ibid.

tained with constraints of humiliation and degradation. Thus they were not permitted to ride on horseback, nor to be employed in the public administration."[417]

The emir Rukn agreed that the vizier was right and "assembled the Christians and Jews on Thursday, 20 Rajab, and informed them that they would no longer be employed either in the public administration or in the service of the emirs. They were to change their turbans: blue ones for the Christians, who were moreover to wear a special belt [*zunnar*] around their waists; and yellow turbans for the Jews."[418] The situation of the dhimmis changed virtually overnight: "By the twenty-second of Rajab all the Jews were wearing yellow turbans and the Christians blue ones; and if they rode on horseback, they were obliged to ride with one of their legs bent under them. Next, the *dhimmis* were dismissed from the public administration and the functions that they occupied in the service of the emirs. They were then prohibited to ride horses or mules. Consequently, many of them were converted to Islam."[419]

Ibn Naqqash adds that the emir extended these regulations to all the lands he ruled: "The Sultan gave orders to all the provinces recently added to his states and in which there were houses owned by Jews and Christians, in order that all those that were higher than the surrounding Muslim abodes should be demolished to their height. Furthermore all the *dhimmis* who owned a shop near that of a Muslim, should lower their *mastaba* [ground floor] so that those of the Muslims would be higher. Moreover, he recommended vigilance in the observance of the distinctive badges [*ghiyar*] in accordance with ancient custom."[420]

---

[417] Ibid.
[418] Ibid.
[419] Ibid.
[420] Ibid.

HUMILIATION

Humiliation was the constant objective. Toward the end of the fifteenth century, a Berber Islamic scholar, Muhammad al-Maghili, who had destroyed the synagogue in Tlemcen and expelled the Jews from the city, detailed the rules for collecting the jizya from the dhimmis:

> On the day of payment they shall be assembled in a public place like the *suq*. They should be standing there waiting in the lowest and dirtiest place. The acting officials representing the Law shall be placed above them and shall adopt a threatening attitude so that it seems to them, as well as to the others, that our object is to degrade them by pretending to take their possessions. They will realize that we are doing them a favor [again] in accepting from them the *jizya* and letting them [thus] go free. Then they shall be dragged one by one [to the official responsible] for the exacting of payment. When paying, the *dhimmi* will receive a blow and will be thrust aside so that he will think that he has escaped the sword through this [insult]. This is the way that the friends of the Lord, of the first and last generations will act toward their infidel enemies, for might belongs to Allah, to His Prophet, and to the Believers.[421]

Along with the humiliation came the stigma of being designated in the Qur'an as among the worst enemies of the Muslims, which made it easy for Jews to be blamed for any misfortune that befell the Islamic community.

---

[421] Ibid., 201; John Hunwick, *Jews of a Saharan Oasis: The Elimination of the Tamantit Community* (North Princeton, New Jersey, Markus Wiener Publishers, n.d.).

In the Ottoman Empire in 1660, much of the ancient capital of Constantinople, conquered from the Christians in 1453, was destroyed by a fire. The Jews were blamed and summarily banished from the city. This had likely been inevitable after some calamity or other, for in the city's royal mosque was an inscription that referred to Muhammad banishing the Jews from Medina. The same mosque's endowment deed referred, gratuitously, to "the Jews who are the enemy of Islam."[422]

Those enemies had to be reminded constantly of their status. Nearly a century and a half later, an Egyptian historian, Abd al-Rahman al-Jabarti, explained that the Egyptians hated Napoleon and his men when the French occupied Egypt because they had dared to allow "the lowliest Copts, Syrian and Orthodox Christians, and Jews" to ride horses and even to carry weapons.[423] In the middle of the nineteenth century, however, the Ottoman Empire abolished the dhimma under pressure from Britain and France. Technically, the Jews and Christians now had equal rights with the Muslims, although this was rarely the case in practice.

In Morocco, however, Sharia rules remained in force. In 1880, a visitor to the country recounted that "a deputation of Israelites, with a grave and reverend rabbi at their head," had contemplated requesting permission from the local Muslim official "for them to wear their shoes in the town. 'We are old, Bashador,' they said, 'and our limbs are weak; and our women, too, are delicately nurtured, and this law presses heavily upon us.'"[424] However, they decided against even presenting this request, "the granting of which would

---

[422] Caroline Finkel, *Osman's Dream: The History of the Ottoman Empire* (New York: Basic Books, 2007), 279–80.

[423] Ibid., 202.

[424] Bat Ye'or, op. cit., 321.

exasperate the populace, and might lead to consequences too terrible to contemplate."[425]

In 1888, however, the Anglo-Jewish Association did appeal to Moroccan authorities for the abolition of the dhimmi laws. They noted that Jews had to "live in the ghetto.... On leaving the ghetto they are compelled to remove their footwear and remove their headcovering.... Jews are not permitted to build their houses above a certain height.... Jews 'are not allowed to drink from the public fountains in the Moorish quarter nor to take water therefrom' as the Jews are considered unclean."[426] This appeal fell on deaf ears.

ZIONISM

Jews who tried to escape the persecution they had experienced from both Christians and Muslims by returning to their ancient homeland found a Muslim leader there who was determined to prevent them from staying there, or ideally from coming at all. One Arab leader, Amin al-Husseini, believed that the new arrivals were coming to land that belonged to the Muslims and that they had no right to be there, since the Qur'an directs Muslims to "drive them out from where they drove you out."[427]

In traditional Islamic theology, this led to the idea that Muslims had a command from Allah to recover any land they had once ruled but had been lost to them. As al-Husseini saw it, Palestine was now being trodden down by the children of apes and pigs, the "most vehement of mankind in hostility to those who believe." This must not be

---

[425] Ibid.

[426] Tudor Parfitt, "*Dhimma* Versus Protection in Nineteenth Century Morocco," in *Israel and Ishmael: Studies in Muslim-Jewish Relations*, Tudor Parfitt, ed. (London: Palgrave Macmillan, 2000), 157–59.

[427] Qur'an 2:191.

allowed to stand. Allah had, along with this command to drive them out, given to al-Husseini a key weapon he could use to accomplish this: "Make ready for them all that you can of force and of warhorses, so that by them you may strike terror in the enemy of Allah and your enemy."[428]

Terror would be the centerpiece of al-Husseini's program. In 1919, he began fomenting jihad attacks and riots. In one of these in Jerusalem in 1920, six Jews were murdered and two hundred more were injured. The British high commissioner, who was, ironically, a Jew named Herbert Samuel, rewarded al-Husseini for this by appointing him mufti of Jerusalem. Thus encouraged, al-Husseini instigated more riots; not long after he was made mufti, Muslims killed forty-three Jews in Petah Tikva and Jaffa.[429]

The mufti claimed that the Jews were conspiring to gain control of the entire region: "Palestine does not satisfy the Jews, because their goal is to rule over the rest of the Arab nations, over Lebanon, Syria, and Iraq, and even over the lands of Khyber in Saudi Arabia, under the pretext that this city was the homeland of the Jewish tribes in the seventh century."[430] However, he saw the Jews as pursuing an even larger conflict against the Muslims. In a 1937 article, "Islam and the Jews," he wrote:

> The battle between Jews and Islam began when Mohammed fled from Mecca to Medina…In those days the Jewish methods were exactly the same as they are today. Then as now, slander was their weapon. They said Mohammed was a swindler…They tried to undermine his honor…They began to pose senseless and unanswerable questions to Mohammed…and

---

[428] Qur'an 8:60.
[429] Parfitt, op. cit.
[430] Ibid.

then they tried to annihilate the Muslims. Just as the Jews were able to betray Mohammed, so they will betray the Muslims today...the verses of the Koran and the Hadith assert that the Jews were Islam's most bitter enemy and moreover try to destroy it.[431]

As World War II raged in Europe, al-Husseini made his way to Berlin, where he found men of like mind in the National Socialist high command and even had a cordial meeting with Adolf Hitler. From Berlin, al-Husseini made radio broadcasts in Arabic exhorting Muslims to support the National Socialists, demonstrating that Qur'anic antisemitism was not at all far from National Socialist antisemitism, albeit considerably older.

The mufti explained the congruence of National Socialist and Islamic goals: "It is the duty of Muhammadans in general and Arabs in particular to...drive all Jews from Arab and Muhammadan countries.... Germany is also struggling against the common foe who oppressed Arabs and Muhammadans in their different countries. It has very clearly recognized the Jews for what they are and resolved to find a definitive solution [*endgültige Lösung*] for the Jewish danger that will eliminate the scourge that Jews represent in the world."[432]

In line with this, he told his listeners in Syria, Lebanon, Mandatory Palestine, Iraq, and Egypt to "sabotage the oil pipe lines, blow up bridges and roads along British lines of communication, kill British troops," and more, including "mislead them by false information," and to do it all "in the name of the Koran and for the honor of

---

[431] Jeffrey Herf, "Haj Amin al-Husseini, the Nazis and the Holocaust: The Origins, Nature and Aftereffects of Collaboration," Jerusalem Center for Public Affairs, January 5, 2016, http://jcpa.org/article/haj-amin-al-husseini-the-nazis-and-the-holocaust-the-origins-nature-and-aftereffects-of-collaboration/.

[432] Gilbert Achcar, *The Arabs and the Holocaust: The Arab-Israeli War of Narratives* (Henry Holt and Company, 2010), 157.

Islam."[433] This reflected the actual teachings of the Qur'an, which directs Muslims to "kill them wherever you find them" and even to mislead unbelievers when one is threatened by them, in order to guard against the threat they pose.[434]

Al-Husseini also told Muslims that they could gain a place in paradise by killing Jews. This was based on the Qur'an's guarantee of paradise to those who "kill and are killed" for Allah, as well as a canonical Islamic tradition in which Muhammad states that that the last hour would not come until the Muslims killed Jews.[435] Thus, Muslims could hasten the advent of the last hour and the final victory of the Muslims by killing Jews.

As might be expected of the mufti of Jerusalem, al-Husseini frequently cited the Qur'an. In one broadcast, he said of the Jews: "They cannot mix with any other nation but live as parasites among the nations, suck out their blood, embezzle their property, corrupt their morals.... The divine anger and curse that the Holy Koran mentions with reference to the Jews is because of this unique character of the Jews."[436] In yet another, he thundered: "Kill the Jews wherever you find them. This pleases God, history and religion."[437]

The mufti found time to recruit Muslims for a Muslim SS company in Bosnia, which murdered nine-tenths of the Jews there.[438] In May 1941, he went on the air with a call to Muslims in Iraq to wage jihad against British troops there. Iraqi Muslims, however, took this as a cue to begin killing Jews. In a pogrom known as the Farhud, or

[433] David G. Dalin and John F. Rothmann, *Icon of Evil: Hitler's Mufti and the Rise of Radical Islam* (New Brunswick, New Jersey: Transaction Publishers, 2009), 53.
[434] Qur'an 2:191; 4:89; 9:5; 3:28.
[435] Sahih Muslim 2922.
[436] Dalin and Rothmann, op. cit., 54.
[437] Ibid.
[438] Dalin, "Hitler's Mufti," op. cit.

"violent dispossession," 128 Jews were killed, and over a thousand Jewish homes and businesses were destroyed.[439]

Toward the end of the war, French troops arrested al-Husseini, but the British objected to French plans to put him on trial. Not for the first time, the bearers of the Mandate to create a Jewish National Home were quick to appease the Arabs. He managed to escape prosecution. In October 1945, the head of Mandatory Palestine's Criminal Investigation Division, Arthur Giles, who called himself "Bey," a Turkish honorific, thought the mufti could be put to better use. He expressed the opinion that al-Husseini could serve as a unifying figure for the Arabs, as well as to "cool off the Zionists.... Of course, we can't do it, but it might not be such a damn bad idea at that."[440]

At the same time, the Arab Higher Committee, a group of Arab leaders in Mandatory Palestine that al-Husseini had established in 1936, and officials from several Muslim countries were working to get al-Husseini out of France. The French learned of plans to spirit the mufti out of the country but did nothing to impede them, as they knew that there would be riots in Morocco and Algeria if they did anything to prevent his escape. In May 1946, al-Husseini flew to Syria and traveled from there to Egypt, which granted him asylum. He was one of the few who had any involvement with National Socialist efforts to exterminate the Jews who escaped all prosecution.

Once in Egypt, al-Husseini began working to prevent the imminent creation of the state of Israel. Hajj Amin al-Husseini emphasized that this was not just a war but a jihad, saying: "I declare a holy war, my Muslim brothers! Murder the Jews! Murder them all!"[441] He had

---

[439] "Hajj Amin al-Husayni: Arab Nationalist and Muslim Leader," United States Holocaust Memorial Museum, https://www.ushmm.org/wlc/en/article.php?ModuleId=10007666.

[440] Richard Breitman and Norman J. W. Goda, *Hitler's Shadow: Nazi War Criminals, U.S. Intelligence, and the Cold War* (Washington, DC: National Archives, 2012), 21–2.

[441] Saul S. Friedman, *A History of the Middle East* (Jefferson, North Carolina: McFarland, 2006), 249.

plenty of support for this call; Muslim Brotherhood founder Hassan al-Banna said: "All Arabs shall arise and annihilate the Jews. We shall fill the sea with their corpses."[442]

Abdul Rahman Azzam, the secretary-general of the Arab League, said: "I personally wish that the Jews do not drive us to this war," but he wasn't issuing a call for peace; he was just boasting about how terrible the coming war would be, so awesome in its brutality that he didn't want to see it.[443] Azzam continued: "This will be a war of extermination and momentous massacre which will be spoken of like the Tartar massacre or the Crusader wars."[444]

These calls were heard. The Arab Liberation Army, under al-Husseini's leadership, also murdered three hundred Jews at Kfar Etzion, south of Jerusalem. Jihadis also killed twenty Jewish girls by blowing up a house. Forty-one Jews were killed in Haifa in December 1947. The following month, Jews were burned alive at the Ein Zeitun settlement. Also in January 1948, thirty-five Jews were killed, and the corpses sexually mutilated.

The next month, Muslims planted a bomb in the offices of the *Jerusalem Post*, killing one person and wounding twenty others. In March 1948, forty-six people were killed and 130 injured in a bombing at a market that Jews frequented, and fourteen more people were killed in another bombing at the Jewish Agency building. One hundred and five Jews were murdered in another attack in April 1948. The following month, Muslims destroyed thirty-five synagogues. In June 1948, other jihadis disemboweled several Jewish women.[445]

On April 4, 1948, posters appeared in Jerusalem saying: "The Government is with us, Allenby is with us, kill the Jews; there is no

---

442   Ibid.
443   David Barnett and Efraim Karsh, "Azzam's Genocidal Threat," *Middle East Quarterly* (Fall 2011), 85–88.
444   Ibid.
445   Ibid.

punishment for killing Jews."[446] Edmund Allenby was an English officer whom the Muslims admired, and who admired them; he had died twelve years before this, so his mention on these posters was a claim of his blessing for the killing of Jews. A mob chanted, "Palestine is our land, kill the Jews," and, "We will drink the blood of the Jews," and roamed through Jerusalem, ultimately killing five Jews and injuring 216 others.[447]

And so on. Modern Israel has had to fight for its life ever since the moment of its birth. And while policymakers and negotiators have steadfastly ignored the fact, those who have opposed the existence of the Jewish state and devoted themselves to destroying it consistently couch their opposition in terms of Islam. Losing territory that was once ruled under Islamic law is considered an insult to Islam. Islam is supposed to be in a perpetual springtime of ever-increasing growth; hence the popularity of the color green on the flags of so many majority-Muslim countries. Making the insult sting all the more was the fact that the lost territory was a Jewish state.

The Qur'an says that "humiliation and poverty struck them and they were visited with wrath from Allah. That was because they disbelieved in Allah's signs and killed the prophets wrongfully."[448] Thus, humiliation and poverty was the natural and deserved lot of the Jews. For them instead to be governing a state, and even worse, on Muslim land, was an intolerable affront to Islam. That state would have to be destroyed, however long it took.

---

[446]   Bruce Hoffman, *Anonymous Soldiers: The Struggle for Israel, 1917–1947* (New York: Knopf Doubleday Publishing Group, 2015), 10.
[447]   Ibid., 10–11.
[448]   Qur'an 2:61.

A RELIGIOUS WAR

After October 7, numerous Muslim clerics around the world made it abundantly clear that they considered the war between Israel and Hamas to be a religious war and that their hatred of Israel was based on Islamic theological principles as much, or more, than upon alleged Israeli atrocities. Dr. Fadi Kablawi explained at the Masjid As Sunnah An Nabawiyyah in North Miami that "the war in Gaza is a war on Islam. You better believe that or stop being naïve and a fool."[449] Sounding a bit like E. Michael Jones, Dr. Sayed Moustafa al-Qazwini said at the Islamic Education Center of Orange County, California, that the Jews were "the enemies of mankind, the enemies of humanity."[450]

Contradicting analysts who remained confident that the establishment of a Palestinian state would solve everything, a Michigan imam named Usama Abdulghani said at a pro-Hamas rally that "those lions" were "defending not just Palestine, but they are fighting on behalf of the entire nation of Muhammad the Messenger."[451]

Two weeks after the massacre, the imam Mahmoud Abdel-Hady of the Maryum Islamic Center in Ellicott City, Maryland, said "When we are together with the Book of Allah and the Sunna of the Messenger of Allah, Jerusalem will be ours. There is no doubt about

---

449   "Florida Imam Dr. Fadi Kablawi: The War in Gaza Is Not a War against Hamas, It Is a War against Islam; The West Is Collapsing, It Shot Itself in the Head and Will Never Rise; Oh Allah, Show Us the Black Days You Inflict upon the Jews!," MEMRI, November 10, 2023.

450   "California Imam Dr. Sayed Moustafa al-Qazwini: The Jews Killed Their Prophets, Have a Sense of Entitlement, Are Liars; The Enemies of Gaza Are the Enemies of Mankind, Humanity," MEMRI, November 17, 2023.

451   "At Dearborn, Michigan Pro-Hamas Rally Praising the October 7 Attack, Held in Front of Henry Ford Centennial Library, Imam Abdulghani Says: October 7 Was a Day of God, a Miracle; The Honorable 'Lions' of Palestine Are Not Only Defending Palestine but Are Fighting on Behalf of Muhammad the Messenger; The Friends of the Zionist Occupiers and Colonialists Must Know That Their Time Is Over," MEMRI, October 14, 2023.

that. This is a promise from Allah and it is going to happen. Now, eventually, this is where we are going, where the world is going."[452]

The following day, Umar Mitchell, an imam at the Colorado Muslims Community Center in Aurora, Colorado, gave a lesson to children that was heavily dependent on the Qur'an's statements about the Jews. The Jews, he said, "were given covenants, promises, and agreements that they were supposed to follow. What did they do every single time? They don't obey. They break their covenant. They lie and break their contract."[453] He added that "the Israelites were sent many, many messengers and prophets. They killed some of them. They even tried to kill Jesus."[454] Mitchell continued:

> If that wasn't all bad enough, Allah had given them one day that they don't do any business. What day was that? For the Jews, what is their day they don't do anything—just devote it to worship? What day is it? Saturday. So the people were prevented from doing business. So there's a group of fishermen... Who knows this story? You guys don't know the story about the fishermen who were not supposed to fish on Saturday? In the Baqara Chapter of the Quran, they are told not to fish, so they say: "You know what, we'll cast our nets on Friday, we'll leave the nets out there all Saturday, we'll do our worship—everything is good—then come Sunday, we're going to eat."... What did Allah do to them as a punishment? Yes?

452   "Maryland Imam Mahmoud Abdel-Hady: The Muslims and the Oppressed Will Eventually Be in Control of Things, Considering the Birth Rate of Muslims; October 7 Was a 'Great Victory,' Like the Viet Cong's Tet Offensive," MEMRI, October 21, 2023.

453   "Colorado Imam Teaches Children at Mosque: Jews Cannot Be Trusted; Allah Turned Jewish Fishermen into Monkeys; The Jews Killed Their Prophets, Tried to Kill Jesus," MEMRI, October 22, 2023.

454   Ibid.

Yes. He made them into monkeys. Literal physical monkeys. Monkeys. Does this sound like a people you want to do business with?[455]

In Australia, the imam Abu Ousayd of the Al Madina Dawah Centre in Sydney invoked the genocidal hadith: "Towards the end of times, when the Muslims will be fighting the Jews, the trees will speak, the stones will speak and they will say 'oh Muslim, oh believer, there is a Yahud (Jew) behind me, come and kill him.'"[456] Islamic scholar Karim AbuZaid also referred to it, at the Colorado Muslims Community Center: "Remember, one day Allah will give Muslims drones too—rocks. A rock, one day, will call upon the Muslim: 'Come, behind me there is [a Jew].' A drone, that is a drone. The rock will call a Muslim: 'Come, he is behind me.'"[457]

Imam Alhajie Jallow said at the Madinah Community Center in Madison, Wisconsin: "O Jews, you unjust, criminal, corrupt oppressors: stop! You will all most definitely be killed. The Jews, the aggressors, the evil... You describe them, what they do. By Allah, all of them will be killed by Muslims. They will all be executed by Muslims. They will all be killed, this is a divine promise that will inevitably be fulfilled. This is a promise from Allah and it is going to happen. They will all be killed. They will all be killed. And on that day, the believers will rejoice in Allah's victory."[458]

---

[455] Ibid.

[456] David Southwell, "Radical Cleric at Sydney Islamic Centre Broadcasts Sermon on Teachings about 'Killing Jews' and Supports Fellow Preacher who Called for a Jihad," *Daily Mail Australia*, November 7, 2023.

[457] "Colorado Islamic Scholar Karim AbuZaid: Muslims Should Not Shy Away from Talking about Martyrdom, There Is a Prize for Being Killed for the Sake of Allah – It's Like the Airline Upgrading You from Economy to First Class," MEMRI, November 10, 2023.

[458] "Madison, Wisconsin Friday Sermon by Imam Alhajie Jallow Following October 7 Attack: Our Brothers in Gaza Are Heroes; Only Jihad Can Bring Glory and Victory to the Muslims; the Jews Will Be Killed, Executed by the Muslims," MEMRI, October 13, 2023.

At the Islamic Center of Warren, Michigan, Imam Abdou Alwaly Zindani preached: "One Jewish man in New York was talking to a Palestinian businessman. First, the [Palestinian] said: 'Don't worry, Jewish man. One day will come, and we will slaughter you like a sheep and the stone and the tree will work undercover with us. They will tell us: 'Hey Muslim, come. Somebody is hiding here, get up and kill him.'"[459]

Another imam in Australia, Ahmad Zoud of Masjid As-Sunnah Lakemba in Sydney, engaged in a bit of projection as he declared: "These are the Jews. However, not all of the Jews are like that; just most of them. The most important characteristic of the Jews is that they are bloodthirsty. They love to shed blood. From an early age, they raise their children on terrorism, violence, and killing. Jews remain Jews. They are not changed by the passing of time. Oh Muslims, servants of Allah, betrayal and treachery are among the characteristics of the Jews. Betrayal is one of their traits, and treachery is a characteristic deeply rooted in them."[460]

In a more contemporary vein, Dr. Khalid Siddiqi told a congregation at Yaseen Belmont Masjid in California that the Jews controlled American politics: "The most hating people for the Muslims are Jews."[461] This was a classic case of projection. Particularly after October 7, Muslims were frequently hateful and violent toward Jews, not the other way around. Siddiqi continued: "The Freemason movement is a Jewish movement, which [seeks] the reconstruction of the

---

[459] "Michigan Friday Sermon by Imam Abdou Zindani: One Day the Muslims Will Slaughter the Jews Like Sheep; Oh Allah, Make Us Soldiers for You, Make Us Die the Way You Want Us to Die," MEMRI, January 5, 2024.

[460] "Australian Imam Ahmad Zoud in Sydney Friday Sermon: The Jews Are Bloodthirsty and Treacherous Criminals, Terrorists, and Monsters—Not All the Jews Are Like This, Just Most of Them," MEMRI, December 22, 2023.

[461] "San Francisco Bay Area Islamic Scholar Dr. Khalid Siddiqi: The Jews Make Up Only 1% of the Universe, Yet Probably Cause 99% of the Problems in the World," MEMRI, November 4, 2023.

Temple of Solomon…. These are very smart people. You know we have the Republican Party and we have the Democratic Party, and what is their design? In the entire universe, their population is one percent, and probably they are the cause of 99% of the problems of the world. So, 50% of the Jews are in the Republican Party and 50% in the Democratic Party. They never lose. Even after losing the elections, they are still winners. They are designed that way."[462]

Other imams demonstrated an awareness of antisemitic claims regarding Jewish beliefs. Sheikh Maher Hamoud, the secretary-general of the Union of Resistance Ulama, said on December 27, 2023, on Palestinian Islamic Jihad's Palestine Today TV that the aftermath of October 7 had "emphasized the ancient character that we read about, that we learnt about through the Talmud, the Torah, and the moral values of the Israelites in the Quran, and throughout the history of humanity. The most important of the characteristics that were highlighted now is that they believe that anyone who is not a Jew is a beast that had been created in order to serve the Chosen People, and that they are allowed to treat others unjustly, take their money, and kill them."[463]

At Masjid Al-Iman in Fort Lauderdale, Florida, an imam spread falsehoods about the Talmud (which we will examine in detail later):

> We will mention what the Jews believe, because you wonder: How come? Why are they such a breed of human beings? It is simply because they are indoctrinated that way. That is their creed…. I will give you the proof from two passages from the Talmud, which is one of the books that the Zionists refer to….

---

[462] Ibid.

[463] "Lebanese Sunni Islamic Scholar Sheikh Maher Hamoud: 'The Jews Believe That Non-Jews Are Beasts Created to Serve Them; Some Jews Add the Blood of Gentile Children to Their Matzos,'" MEMRI, December 27, 2023.

"Allah created the foreigner, the non-Jew..."—listen to this—"in human form so that they would be suitable to serve the Jews." This message goes to those who bow—from amongst this Islamic nation—to the Zionists, to the Jews. This is how they look at you. This is how they see you, as an animal that is in the form of a human being, [created] just to serve them.... We are talking about babies in the incubators in the [Gaza] hospitals—shooting everybody. That's why, because in their creed, we're all animals, and we are worthless. It is an honor for them, and they will be raised in the ranks if they do that.... Now you wonder why they go, they fly from Brooklyn... from under the tunnels there is an airline that goes underground.... I'm joking. They go from under the tunnels straight to Palestine. To do what? To steal the land. Why? Because for them it is permissible to steal from someone who is not a Jew.[464]

The imam's little joke about tunnels was bitterly ironic in light of the massive and complex network of Hamas tunnels that the IDF discovered running underneath Gaza in the wake of the October 7 massacre. There had been a concerted effort to divert attention away from the Hamas tunnels, including a massive outcry over unauthorized digging at the Chabad headquarters in Brooklyn, with all manner of wild claims circulating. Jew-haters everywhere tried to shift the focus away from the reality of the Hamas tunnels to completely unfounded allegations of nefarious activities that the Jews were supposedly perpetrating in their imaginary tunnels underneath Brooklyn.

---

464   "Fort Lauderdale, Florida Friday Sermon: Why Are the Jews Such a Breed of Humans? Their Talmudic Creed Makes It an Honor for Them to Shoot Gazan Babies in Their Incubators; They View Non-Jews as Worthless Animals," MEMRI, April 19, 2024.

Through that controversy and others, Islamic antisemitism received, as always, far less notice. The Roman Catholic Church repudiated Christian antisemitism in the 1960s. No Islamic authority has done anything similar. Clearly, Islamic antisemitism is very much alive.

Chapter Six

NATIONAL AND INTERNATIONAL SOCIALIST JEW-HATRED

THE FRENCH REVOLUTION'S PARADIGM

The storming of the Bastille on July 14, 1789, heralded the coming of a new order to France, one that rejected the ancient monarchical autocracy and would respect the rights of man. Groups that held positions of power and privilege would be brought down, and the oppressed would be exalted.

The French Revolution was the first socialist utopia, the first time that people with the ethos and outlook of the contemporary Left tried to establish an earthly paradise. It would not be the last.

The revolutionaries' glowing vision of this new order, a veritable secular messianic age, quickly dissolved in a pool of blood. The French revolutionaries discovered that they could only enforce equality among human beings of vastly differing temperaments, abilities, priorities, and cultural perspectives by force; those who resisted fell victim to the Reign of Terror.

Amid all the chaos, confusion, anarchy, and bloodlust, several groups that had hitherto been denied rights suddenly found the restrictions upon them removed. Among these were the Jews. Count Stanislas of Clermont-Tonnerre argued in favor of the rights of the Jews in the National Assembly, but he did so in a paradoxical way, declaring that "all must be denied to Jews as a nation; all must be given to Jews as individuals."[465] He maintained that "the existence of a nation within a nation is unacceptable to our country."[466]

Historian Milo Lévy-Bruhl explains that the count's position was that the Jews should be allowed to become Frenchmen, as long as they gave up being Jews, at least in part: "The Jews had to abandon completely their own laws for the laws of France. Their religious freedom would be guaranteed within the limits of national law. In exchange, they would be granted the full rights of a French citizen."[467]

Those who insisted that the Jews must not be granted French citizenship argued that the Jews would never give up their distinctive beliefs, practices, and customs:

> They will not renounce their own laws! Even if they declare their intent to do so, their morals will not allow them to be true Frenchmen!

[465]   Milo Lévy-Bruhl, "The Jews and the French Revolution," K-Larevue.com, May 27, 2021, https://k-larevue.com/en/jews-and-the-french-revolution/.
[466]   "France," Center for Jewish History, https://www.cjh.org/lapidus/France.html.
[467]   Lévy-Bruhl, op. cit.

They should be protected from violence, of course, as any foreigner should be. But that doesn't mean we'd have to consider them citizens. One can be a man without being a citizen.

Their laws and morals have kept them away from the rest of the population for too long. Even if they agree to submit to our laws, and agree in good faith, an adaptation period is required. How else to regenerate their morals—to abandon usury, for example?[468]

After a great deal of disagreement and debate, in September 1791, a Jacobin named Adrien Jean-François Duport proposed a Law Regarding the Jews and stated:

I believe that freedom of worship does not permit any distinction in the political rights of citizens on account of their creed. The question of the political existence of the Jews has been postponed. Still, the Muslims and the men of all sects are admitted to enjoy political rights in France. I demand that the motion for postponement be withdrawn, and a decree passed that the Jews in France enjoy the privileges of full citizens.[469]

The law was passed. Even then, however, Jews encountered a great deal of suspicion and continued to suffer discrimination of various kinds. Many French citizens, even as the revolution endeavored to level out all distinctions and inequities among human beings, believed that the Jews were not and could not be French. Their beliefs, customs, and culture were simply too different from those of the French. Lingering French antisemitism culminated in 1894 in the Dreyfus

---

[468] Ibid.

[469] "On This Day: French Jews Given Full Rights under Law," *Jerusalem Post*, September 27, 2021.

Affair, in which a Jewish military officer, Captain Alfred Dreyfus, was falsely accused of treason. The controversy over this accusation roiled France for twelve years and made it clear that the French Revolution may have granted Jews French citizenship, but that didn't mean that they were universally accepted as such.

The French Revolution also created a new difficulty for the Jews and established a paradigm for the latter-day authoritarian regimes that endeavored to abolish ancient inequities and establish a new regime of justice and equality: the Jews were welcomed as long as they stopped being Jews. If they gave up their distinctive beliefs and practices and melted into the larger society, many, although by no means all, of the majority population would find that acceptable.

If, however, they maintained themselves as a distinct group, they were an affront to the very idea of the utopian leveler regime itself. How could equity between all groups be established if one group refused to conform and stubbornly held itself out from the whole? The liberal state offered Jews citizenship, freedom, and protection, but at the price of their identity.

Contemporary historian David Aberbach explains that while the French had granted equal rights to the Jews, "most Europeans were reluctant to accept Jews as equals. The prospect of emancipation was often a trigger for popular anti-Jewish riots." What's more, "emancipation was granted not as a natural human right, on principles of pluralism and tolerance, but with general expectation that Jews would vanish through total assimilation, even baptism—a modern version of the old Christian hope of Jewish acceptance of the Christian faith." The expectation that the Jews would disappear was contained in the adage that "all must be denied to Jews as a nation; all must be given to Jews as individuals." The idea that Jews were only gaining rights as individuals and not as part of a larger community militated against the continued existence of that community as such.

Thus, the Jews again faced the dilemma that they had dealt with in numerous contexts throughout history. The pagans, Christians, and Muslims who had excoriated, discriminated against, and persecuted the Jews all held out the possibility of relief; all the Jews had to do was end their existence as a separate people and become indistinguishable from the larger community. This was a price that many Jews were happy to pay and did pay; others, however, refused to do so. And so, the persecutions continued.

With the advent of modern authoritarianism, this tendency became even more pronounced.

INTERNATIONAL SOCIALISM

Fifty-four years after the French revolutionaries initiated a Reign of Terror against those who refused to accept their paradise of liberty, equality, and fraternity, two German intellectuals published their own vision of a utopian future, likewise to be attained by authoritarianism and the use of brute force against those who refused to cooperate voluntarily.

The Communist Manifesto of Karl Marx and Friedrich Engels declared: "A spectre is haunting Europe—the spectre of Communism. All the Powers of old Europe have entered into a holy alliance to exorcise this spectre: Pope and Czar, Metternich and Guizot, French Radicals and German police-spies."[470] The old powers, confronted with this spectre, warned that Communism "abolishes eternal truths, it abolishes all religion, and all morality, instead of constituting them

---

[470] Karl Marx and Friedrich Engels, *The Communist Manifesto*, 1848, https://www.fulltextarchive.com/book/The-Communist-Manifesto/.

on a new basis; it therefore acts in contradiction to all past historical experience."[471]

To this, Marx and Engels responded: "What does this accusation reduce itself to? The history of all past society has consisted in the development of class antagonisms, antagonisms that assumed different forms at different epochs. But whatever form they may have taken, one fact is common to all past ages, viz., the exploitation of one part of society by the other. No wonder, then, that the social consciousness of past ages, despite all the multiplicity and variety it displays, moves within certain common forms, or general ideas, which cannot completely vanish except with the total disappearance of class antagonisms."[472]

This was not in any sense a denial: Communism did indeed wish to destroy all religion, as part of its larger program to end "the exploitation of one part of society by the other."[473] Judaism would be destroyed along with the other religions in the quest to establish an international state that would enforce economic justice with guns and gulags.

Karl Marx made his hostility to Judaism clear five years before he cowrote *The Communist Manifesto*. In 1843, the Hegelian philosopher Bruno Bauer published a book entitled *The Jewish Question*, in which he considered whether it was possible for a Jew to be a citizen of a modern state of the kind that the Left envisioned: "The question is whether the Jew as such," Bauer wrote, "that is, the Jew who realizes that he is forced by his true nature to live in eternal separation from others—is able to receive general human rights and grant them to

---

[471] Ibid.
[472] Ibid.
[473] Ibid.

others."[474] This was the same question that had so vexed the French revolutionaries half a century before.

Of those general human rights, Bauer asks if Jews have "really earned" them.[475] He contended that a Jew's very Jewishness prevented this: "As long as he remains a Jew, the limited nature of his Jewishness triumphs over the human nature that would link him, with other men, and separates him from non-Jews. By this separation he proclaims the special nature that makes him a Jew to be his true and highest nature, to which all human nature must yield."[476] Thus, in order to join the state that respected the universal rights of man, the Jew had to cease being a Jew.

Marx disagreed with Bauer, but only because he had an even larger vision of the destruction of Judaism and the erasure of a particularly Jewish identity. Marx was interested not just in the destruction of Judaism, but of the disappearance also of the Jewish influence in the larger society. "For us," said Marx, "the question of Jewish capacity for emancipation becomes the question of which element in society must be overcome in order to abolish Judaism. For the Jews' capacity for emancipation depends on the Jews' relation to the emancipation of our whole enslaved world."[477]

At this point, Marx began to resort to age-old stereotypes and caricatures of the Jews. He asked: "What is the object of the Jew's worship in this world?"[478] Then he answered his own question: "Usury. What is his worldly god? Money."[479] Accordingly, "emancipation from usury and money, that is, from practical, real Judaism, would

---

[474]   Karl Marx, *A World Without Jews*, Dagobert D. Runes, trans. (New York: Philosophical Library, 1959), 22. The title of this book was apparently given to it by the translator and does not correspond to the title of Marx's work, which was "On the Jewish Question."
[475]   Ibid.
[476]   Ibid., 22–3.
[477]   Ibid., 36–7.
[478]   Ibid., 37.
[479]   Ibid.

constitute the emancipation of our time."[480] For "the organization of society so as to abolish the preconditions of usury, and hence its possibility, would render the Jews impossible."[481]

This was the utopian vision Marx offered in *The Communist Manifesto*: "Finally, when all capital, all production, all exchange have been brought together in the hands of the nation, private property will disappear of its own accord, money will become superfluous, and production will so expand and man so change that society will be able to slough off whatever of its old economic habits may remain."[482] Thus, in Marx's perfect society, Jews and non-Jews will have been "emancipated" from "practical, real Judaism," which he identified with "usury and money," the hallmarks of the old order Communists were determined to destroy.

Ultimately, then, Marx's vision was far more radical than Bauer's. Bauer called for the Jews' rejection of Judaism in order to join the secular state that respected the universal rights of man; Marx wanted to abolish Judaism and eradicate its influence in society, and since he identified Judaism with the core elements of the exploitative system, he was determined to destroy, the destruction of Judaism was a core element of the Marxist program. As Marx himself put it: "The social emancipation of Jewry is the emancipation of society from Jewry."[483]

Marxism, as its founding theorist formulated it, thus went even farther than the French revolutionaries, as well as the Christians, Muslims, and others who had decried and persecuted Jews in the past. Not only did Marx insist that the Jews could only participate in his new society if they ceased being Jews, but he also identified their ceasing being Jews, and the eradication of Judaism itself, with the core goals of his entire program. If a classless, moneyless society in which

480   Ibid.
481   Ibid.
482   Marx and Engels, *The Communist Manifesto*, op. cit., 18.
483   Marx, *A World Without Jews*, op. cit., 45.

the proletariat was no longer exploited was to be established, and the Jews were the chief exploiters, then the Jews would have to go. In his foundational work of Communist theory, *Das Kapital* (Capital), Marx uses Shakespeare's Jewish moneylender, Shylock, as his model capitalist.

It is remarkable, in light of all this, that so many Jews became Marxists, particularly in Russia, where there were a great many Jews among the Bolsheviks who established the Soviet Union. It is even more remarkable that in the twentieth century, the idea that Marxism was fundamentally and essentially Jewish, and was, in fact, a central element of a Jewish plot to gain global hegemony, became a staple of attacks upon Jews.

One of the foremost theorists responsible for the widespread identification of Marxism with Jews and Judaism was a German named Adolf Hitler.

NATIONAL SOCIALISM

In July 1925, Adolf Hitler, the Leader (*Führer*) of the National Socialist German Workers Party, published his lengthy manifesto, *Mein Kampf* (My Struggle), which he had written while in prison for his role in the Beer Hall Putsch, an attempted coup in Munich in 1923. Recounting his own political and intellectual development, he recalls that as a youth, down and out in Vienna, he one day has a most unpleasant encounter.

> Once as I was strolling through the Inner City, I suddenly encountered an apparition in a black caftan and black hair locks. Is this a Jew? was my first thought.
>
> For, to be sure, they had not looked like that in Linz. I observed this man furtively and cautiously, but the

longer I stared at this foreign face, scrutinizing feature for feature, the more my first question assumed
a new form:

Is this a German?[484]

Hitler's ultimate answer to this question would devastate the Jews
of Europe and convulse the entire world.

Another great formative moment for his thought came when, he
says, "inspired by the experience of daily life, I now began to track
down the sources of the Marxist doctrine."[485]

This study didn't take him as long as he had expected, for Hitler
determined that the sources of Marxist doctrine turned out to be the
people he had come to despise: "If I reached my goal more quickly
than at first I had perhaps ventured to believe, it was thanks to my
newly acquired, though at that time not very profound, knowledge
of the Jewish question."[486] He claimed that "this was the time of the
greatest spiritual upheaval I have ever had to go through."[487] Ultimately, this study was to change the course of his life and that of millions of others: when he had completed it, Hitler says, "I had ceased
to be a weak-kneed cosmopolitan and become an anti-Semite."[488]

For Hitler, Marxism was entirely a Jewish production, and a
malignant one: "The Jewish doctrine of Marxism," he asserted,
"rejects the aristocratic principle of Nature and replaces the eternal
privilege of power and strength by the mass of numbers and their
dead weight."[489] Hitler was a Social Darwinian, exalting those with
superior abilities and despising Marxism for its stated determination

---

[484] Adolf Hitler, *Mein Kampf*, Ralph Manheim, trans. (Boston: Houghton Mifflin, 1943), 56.
[485] Ibid., 63.
[486] Ibid., 64.
[487] Ibid.
[488] Ibid.
[489] Ibid., 65.

to exalt the downtrodden. Those with superior abilities were, in his view, the Germans, the master race. Hitler was not interested in equality or the universal rights of man; his National Socialism exalted the Germans above all others.

Yet while he rejected internationalist Marxism, he did not reject socialism as a whole. His National Socialist vision involved all individual Germans subordinating their will to that of the nation and people (*volk*) as a whole, as the leader, Hitler, would determine it. The German government would, in turn, provide for the needs of all Germans, for "the entire economy suffers bitterly from the individual's insecurity in earning his daily bread."[490]

This was simply another form of collectivism, in which the dictatorship of the master race and its exaltation replaced the dictatorship of the proletariat. Jews could have no part in it any more than they could have a part in the workers' paradise. This was, Hitler explained, because Marxism, which he identified as Jewish, "denies the value of personality in man, contests the significance of nationality and race, and thereby withdraws from humanity the premise of its existence and its culture."[491]

Without the exaltation of nationality and race, National Socialism was nothing. Both the idolatry of race and blood and the idolatry of the worker leveled out all other distinctions between people; everyone in the perfect state was a German or a worker. Neither utopia had any room for a distinct people who maintained its own distinct identity and culture.

Hitler thus believed, as did Marx, that the Jews were the foremost enemies of the perfect society he envisioned and that the emancipation of Germany depended upon the eradication of the Jews, just as Marx stated that the emancipation of the workers depended upon

---

[490] Ibid., 26.
[491] Ibid.

their eradication as well. For if Marxism prevailed, it would lead to the dissolution of all human culture: "As a foundation of the universe, this doctrine would bring about the end of any order intellectually conceivable to man. And as, in this greatest of all recognizable organisms, the result of an application of such a law could only be chaos, on earth it could only be destruction for the inhabitants of this planet."[492]

The victory of the Jews, with their Marxism, would mean nothing less than the death of the human race: "If, with the help of his Marxist creed, the Jew is victorious over the other peoples of the world, his crown will be the funeral wreath of humanity and this planet will, as it did thousands of years ago, move through the ether devoid of men."[493]

An avenging god, however, had sent Hitler himself as the antidote: "Eternal Nature inexorably avenges the infringement of her commands. Hence today I believe that I am acting in accordance with the will of the Almighty Creator: *by defending myself against the Jew, I am fighting for the work of the Lord.*"[494]

TWO MORE VIRULENT STRAINS OF JEW-HATRED

As with older forms of Jew-hatred, National Socialism and Marxism both despised the Jews for remaining stubbornly different. Both demanded the eradication of Jews and Judaism. Yet both also introduced new and even more sinister aspects to their contempt for the Jews than had been seen in previous belief systems that inculcated hatred for Jews.

---

[492] Ibid.
[493] Ibid.
[494] Ibid. Emphasis in the original.

It had been possible for Jews to become polytheists, offer sacrifice to the Roman gods, and thereby become integrated members of Roman society. It likewise remained possible for Jews to become Christians or Muslims, although in both cases, there were occasions in which the new converts were subjected to lingering suspicion. With Marxism and National Socialism, however, the situation was decidedly different.

Marx identified Judaism with usury and thus identified the fundamental opponent of the entire Marxist enterprise as the Jew. To be a Jew was to be automatically a class enemy, an enemy of the people. In equating Judaism with capitalism itself, Marx made Jews the primary and paradigmatic enemy of the Communist state. Jews could still cease to be Jews and become Communists, and many did, but as in Christian Spain and elsewhere, suspicions lingered regarding the new converts. Because their Jewishness made them the very foe that Communism was dedicated to destroying, they could never entirely alleviate that suspicion.

National Socialism went even further and made the situation for Jews significantly worse. There was no way for a Jew to become a German as Adolf Hitler understood what being a German involved. To convert to Christianity was not enough; to have served in the German army and even been awarded medals for heroism in World War I was not enough. "Aryan" and "Jew" were fixed and immutable racial categories; in National Socialist Germany, Jewish blood was generally treated as a kind of infection that rendered the carrier Jewish. There was no way a carrier could rid himself of it and render himself acceptable to the guardians of the state's purity and health.

BITTERLY OPPOSED, BUT WITH A COMMON ENEMY

As rival utopian authoritarian scenarios, National Socialism and Marxism were vociferously opposed to one another. Yet they had a common foe. Marx equated Jews with capitalism, and so Judaism and Jews had to be erased in order to establish the paradisal just society in which everyone worked to the extent of his abilities and received compensation in proportion to his needs. Hitler equated Jews both with non-Germanness and with the Marxist imperative to place the master race on the same level as inferior races.

Hitler wrote of Marxism in *Mein Kampf:* "By the categorical rejection of the personality and hence of the nation and its racial content, it destroys the elementary foundations of all human culture, which is dependent on just these factors. This is the true inner kernel of the Marxist philosophy in so far as this figment of a criminal brain can be designated as a 'philosophy.' With the shattering of the personality and the race, the essential obstacle is removed to the domination of the inferior being—and this is the Jews."[495]

Marx, meanwhile, saw the Jews as likewise a threat, but for essentially the opposite reason. For him, "the real nature of the Jew is amply fulfilled in bourgeois society."[496] Therefore, "as soon as society can abolish the empirical nature of the Jew, that is, usury and its preconditions, being a Jew will become impossible."[497] Marx wanted to make being a Jew impossible because being a Jew was essentially to be a capitalist, while Hitler wanted to make being a Jew impossible because being a Jew meant being a Marxist.

Thus, while Hitler declared the undying enmity of National Socialism for Marxism, and Communists and National Socialists

---

[495] Hitler, *Mein Kampf,* op. cit., 320.
[496] Marx, *A World Without Jews*, op. cit., 44.
[497] Ibid., 45.

brawled in the streets of Weimar Germany, both of these systems for establishing an authoritarian utopia were largely based on the idea that the Jews were the cause of all the troubles they were dedicated to remedying.

NOT JEWS, BUT CAPITALISTS

Along with making the Jews the focus of hatred for opposite reasons, there was another fundamental difference between Marxist and National Socialist hatred of the Jews. While National Socialism and the paranoia and hatred of Adolf Hitler are inseparable, not all of Marx's thought automatically became Marxist dogma. Marx's great Russian acolyte, Vladimir Ilyich Ulyanov, a.k.a. Lenin, rejected Marx's equation of usury, and capitalism in general, with the Jews.

During the revolutions in Russia of February and October 1917 and the subsequent Russian civil war, both sides scapegoated and attacked the Jews. The Red Army, like the other armies that were vying for power in Russia, had no compunction about attacking civilians and looting towns, particularly as it was retreating and the soldiers were full of frustration and rage. Jews were a favored target.

In the town of Dimitriev in Kursk in March 1918, Orthodox Christians emerged from church and surrounded the office of the local Communist Party commissar, chanting: "Beat the Yids and the commissars. Save Russia!"[498] Like Hitler when he wrote *Mein Kampf* a few years later, these people equated Marxism with Jews and considered an attack on the one to be an attack on the other. The word that translated here as "Yid" is *zhid*, an extremely derogatory

---

[498] Vladimir P. Buldakov, "Freedom, Shortages, Violence: The Origins of the 'Revolutionary Anti-Jewish Pogrom' in Russia, 1917–1918," in *Anti-Jewish Violence: Rethinking the Pogrom in East European History*, Jonathan Dekel-Chen, David Gaunt, Natan M. Meir, and Israel Bartal, eds. (Bloomington: Indiana University Press, 2010), 84.

and offensive term in Russian. In his memoirs, Soviet leader Nikita Khrushchev refers to *zhid* as "a very offensive term, an insult to the Jewish nation."[499]

Yet the Red Army, which the people of Kursk and many other places assumed to be a Jewish entity, was hardly friendlier to Jews. That same month, as the Red Army retreated before the advancing Germans in the town of Glukhov in Chernigov province in Ukraine, it led mobs in particularly brutal attacks on Jews. Historian Vladimir P. Buldakov notes that "for two-and-a-half days, the town was at the mercy of an enraged mob. Almost every schoolboy was killed and not even twelve-year-olds were spared. Men were taken from their homes, beaten with the butts of rifles, stabbed, or shot. Peasants from neighboring villages removed the loot in wagons. The pogrom was carried out under the slogan 'Surrender all weapons! We are going to slaughter all the bourgeoisie and the Yids!'"[500] Four hundred Jews were murdered.

So as one mob chanted, "Beat the Yids and the commissars," the other countered with, "We are going to slaughter all the bourgeoisie and the Yids!" Both assumed that they were acting in the service of a righteous cause and that the Jews were on the other side, yet their accusations against the Jews were mutually exclusive.

Meanwhile, although the brutality of the Red Army in Glukhov may have been in line with the words of Karl Marx, this behavior was actually against Red Army policy. Army leaders were determined to combat antisemitism, and so was Lenin himself. The head of the Red Army, Leon Trotsky, was Jewish.

In March 1919, without referring to Marx's 1843 document on the "Jewish question," the leader of Soviet Russia denied that

---

[499] Nikita Khrushchev, *Khrushchev Remembers*, Strobe Talbott, trans. (Boston: Little, Brown, 1970), 152.

[500] Buldakov, op. cit.

document's central premise. Lenin declared that pogroms were a practice of the old regime; the implication was that they should not be part of the new. "When the accursed tsarist monarchy was living its last days," he said, "it tried to incite ignorant workers and peasants against the Jews. The tsarist police, in alliance with the landowners and the capitalists, organized pogroms against the Jews."[501] This was just an attempt to distract the exploited workers with a scapegoat: "The landowners and capitalists tried to divert the hatred of the workers and peasants who were tortured by want against the Jews."[502]

Lenin asserted that "in other countries, too, we often see the capitalists fomenting hatred against the Jews in order to blind the workers, to divert their attention from the real enemy of the working people, capital."[503] He considered Jew-hatred to be a symptom of the problems the Communists were dedicated to overcoming: "Hatred towards the Jews persists only in those countries where slavery to the landowners and capitalists has created abysmal ignorance among the workers and peasants."[504] Thus, "only the most ignorant and down-trodden people can believe the lies and slander that are spread about the Jews."[505]

Jew-hatred, Lenin continued, was a hangover from the times of superstition: "This is a survival of ancient feudal times, when the priests burned heretics at the stake, when the peasants lived in slavery, and when the people were crushed and inarticulate. This ancient, feudal ignorance is passing away; the eyes of the people are being opened."[506]

---

[501] V. I. Lenin, "Anti-Jewish Pogroms," March 1919, https://www.marxists.org/archive/lenin/works/1919/mar/x10.htm.
[502] Ibid.
[503] Ibid.
[504] Ibid.
[505] Ibid.
[506] Ibid.

Marxism-Leninism was not synonymous with Marxism. Lenin contradicted Marx directly, asserting that "it is not the Jews who are the enemies of the working people. The enemies of the workers are the capitalists of all countries."[507] While for Marx, the Jews were the capitalists of all countries, for Lenin, they were just another group whom the capitalists were oppressing.

The Bolshevik leader's denunciation of antisemitism and the codification of that denunciation in the laws of the nascent Soviet Union were one reason why many Jews joined the Communists and began to identify with the international Left. Some of the Bolshevik leaders were Jews, including Leon Trotsky, although there were more Jews among the Bolsheviks' rivals in the Communist movement, the Mensheviks. These men, however, were not remotely observant Jews or interested in preserving Jewish beliefs, culture, and traditions. As Marxists, they were atheists who regarded Judaism, like other religions, as a superstition that had impeded the progress of mankind.

Jewish activist and historian Simon Dubnov fled the Soviet Union in 1922, only to be murdered by the National Socialists in 1941. Of Trotsky, whose given name was Lev Davidovich Bronstein, Dubnov said: "They appear under Russian pseudonyms because they are ashamed of their Jewish origins. It would be better to say that their Jewish names are pseudonyms; they are not rooted in our people."[508]

STALIN AGAINST ANTISEMITISM

What's more, Jews who joined the Bolshevik revolution thinking that antisemitism would finally be a thing of the past were to be disappointed. Lenin's denunciation of antisemitism was not uniformly

---

[507] Ibid.
[508] Seth J. Frantzman, "Was the Russian Revolution Jewish?," *Jerusalem Post*, February 7, 2018.

heeded. The Red Army carried out another pogrom in 1920, this time while it was retreating from the Poles. Generally, however, it was much kinder to the Jews than the anti-Communist White Army tended to be. Jews were granted rights that the Russian Empire had never accorded them; they began to take up positions of responsibility and professions in which they had never been seen before. Zvi Gitelman, a contemporary scholar of the situation of Jews in the Soviet Union, observes that "never before in Russian history—and never subsequently—has a government made such an effort to uproot and stamp out antisemitism."[509]

Joseph Stalin was at this time likewise firm in his stated opposition to antisemitism, writing to the Jewish News Agency in the United States in January 1931 that "national and racial chauvinism is a vestige of the misanthropic customs characteristic of the period of cannibalism. Anti-semitism, as an extreme form of racial chauvinism, is the most dangerous vestige of cannibalism."[510] Like Lenin, he condemned Jew-hatred as a diversion of focus from the real enemy: "Anti-semitism is of advantage to the exploiters as a lightning conductor that deflects the blows aimed by the working people at capitalism. Anti-semitism is dangerous for the working people as being a false path that leads them off the right road and lands them in the jungle."[511]

However, the Soviet Union had a decidedly inconsistent attitude toward the Jews. Emblematic of this was the establishment in 1928 of the Jewish Autonomous Oblast, a place where the Jews of the Soviet Union could theoretically live together in peace, albeit while conforming to the dictates of the Communist state. It was also

---

[509] Zvi Gitelman, "Soviet Antisemitism and Its Perception by Soviet Jews," in *Antisemitism in the Contemporary World*, Michael Curtis, ed. (Boulder, Colorado: Westview Press, 1986), 189.

[510] Joseph Stalin, "Reply to an Inquiry of the Jewish News Agency in the United States," January 12, 1931, https://www.marxists.org/reference/archive/stalin/works/1931/01/12.htm.

[511] Ibid.

an alternative to Zionism, designed to make the Jews of the Soviet Union less anxious to leave the workers' paradise altogether.

Yet the Jewish Autonomous Oblast was not an attractive destination for Jews, or for much of anyone else. It was impossibly remote, in the Soviet Far East, north of China, where Stalin wanted to increase the population as a deterrent to Chinese expansionist ambitions. From Chernigov, within the historic Pale of Settlement where most of the Jews in Russia had lived, to Birobidzhan in the Jewish Autonomous Oblast, it was over five thousand miles. Few Jews made the arduous journey to their inhospitable new homeland; at the height of Jewish settlement in the Oblast, Jews made up only about a quarter of the population. Today, fewer than a thousand Jews remain there. From the beginning, it was more symbol than substance, a monument to the Communist state's efforts to demonstrate how all-inclusive and welcoming it was.

STALIN FOR ANTISEMITISM

Meanwhile, Soviet efforts against antisemitism had largely ended by the mid-1930s, and ultimately, the Marxist-Leninist state would prove to be inhospitable for Jews to an extent that would have warmed Karl Marx's ice-cold heart. Alexander Nikolayevich Yakovlev, a longtime Soviet official who served as a member of the Politburo in the late 1980s, states that despite Stalin's rejection of antisemitism in his 1931 letter to the Jewish News Agency, the Soviet dictator was obsessed with the Jews and renewed persecutions after he had attained full power.

Stalin moved to destroy Jewish institutions in the Soviet Union just as Germany's National Socialist leader was concluding that the Bolshevik Revolution had given the Jews of Russia a total victory within the country. In his unpublished 1928 second book, Hitler wrote that in the Soviet Union, "Jewry, pressing toward the upper strata and therefore toward supreme leadership, has exterminated the former alien upper class with the help of the Slav race instinct. Thus it is a quite understandable process if Jewry has taken over the leadership of all areas of Russian life with the Bolshevik revolution."[512]

Hitler wasn't alone in making this assumption. Historian Paul Johnson notes that "in the outside world," few people knew about "the survival of anti-Semitism, in new forms, in Soviet Russia, the destruction of Jewish institutions and the growing physical threat to Jews under Stalinism. It was simply assumed that, since the Jews were among the principal instigators of Bolshevism, they must be among its principal beneficiaries. The all-important distinction between the great mass of Jews, who were observant, assimilationist or Zionist, and the specific group of Non-Jewish Jews who had actually helped to create the revolution, was not understood at all."[513]

Stalin didn't even hesitate to enter into a non-aggression pact with National Socialist Germany. The Soviet leader, so decidedly against Jew-hatred eight years before that he likened it to cannibalism, turned cannibal himself. He began laying the groundwork for the accord with Germany and signaling his goodwill to the National Socialists by demonstrating that his distaste for the Jews was comparable to the Führer's.

On May 3, 1939, the Soviet leader sent troops from the People's Commissariat for Internal Affairs (NKVD), that is, the secret police, to surround the Commissariat for Foreign Affairs. Stalin ordered one of his loyal courtiers, Vyacheslav Molotov, whose wife was Jewish, to "purge the ministry of Jews. Clean out the 'synagogue.'"[514] Molotov later remarked: "Thank God for these words! Jews formed

---

[512] Adolf Hitler, *Hitler's Second Book: German Foreign Policy*, Arthur Kemp, trans. (Ostara Publications, 2014), 157.

[513] Paul Johnson, *A History of the Jews* (New York: Harper & Row Publishers, 1987), 455.

[514] Antony Beevor, *The Second World War* (New York: Little, Brown and Company, 2012), 17.

an absolute majority in the leadership and among the ambassadors. It wasn't good."[515] Molotov took over as foreign minister as a Jew, Maxim Litvinov, was replaced. Numerous Jewish officials of the foreign ministry were arrested and interrogated in hopes of uncovering a Jewish plot against the state.[516]

On August 23, 1939, as the pact was concluded, Stalin promised the National Socialist German foreign minister, Joachim von Ribbentrop, that he would put an end to Jewish "domination" in the Soviet Union.[517] In removing Litvinov and the Jewish officials of the Soviet foreign ministry, Stalin had already begun to do this.

The Soviet Union's pact with the National Socialists entitled it to occupy eastern Poland; once this was done, Stalin had the Jews there deported to the Jewish Autonomous Oblast. When National Socialist Germany turned on the international socialists and invaded the Soviet Union, they were able to apprehend Jews who might otherwise have escaped them. About a million of the three million Jews in the Soviet Union perished in the Holocaust (which we will examine later).

STALIN AGAINST ANTISEMITISM AGAIN

Stalin, now eager to distinguish himself from the man he had courted so assiduously in 1939, eased up on some of his antisemitic policies and even oversaw the creation of a Jewish Anti-Fascist Committee in the Soviet Union.[518] He even briefly supported Zionism, assuming that a Jewish state would be socialist and give the Soviets leverage

[515] Arnold Beep, "The Pact between Devils: The Myth of Stalin as the Great Anti-fascist," *Freedom News*, May 9, 2023.
[516] Ibid.
[517] Richard Pipes, *Alexander Yakovlev: The Man Whose Ideas Delivered Russia from Communism* (Ithaca, New York: Cornell University Press, 2015).
[518] Johnson, *History of the Jews*, op. cit., 525.

against Britain in the Middle East. The Soviet Union accordingly voted at the United Nations in favor of the creation of the State of Israel.

When the Muslim Arab nations neighboring Israel immediately declared war on the new state, the Soviet Union facilitated concrete help to enable the Jewish state to survive. Historian Hugh Fitzgerald observes that "in 1948, Czechoslovakia was the one country willing to sell arms to Israel, including, most importantly, a half-dozen airplanes which became the Israeli Air Force. That tiny air force played an important role in preventing an Egyptian force from marching through the Sinai straight to Tel Aviv. After that first delivery of planes, the Czechs then provided more planes, ultimately delivering to Israel twenty-five Avia S-199 fighters, and 61 Supermarine Spitfire fighter aircraft."[519] By that time, Czechoslovakia had fallen within the Soviet orbit; the Czechs armed the Israelis on Stalin's orders.

STALIN FOR ANTISEMITISM AGAIN

Stalin's support for Zionism did not mean favorable treatment for the Jews in the Soviet Union. After the end of World War II, Stalin resumed deporting Jews from Eastern Europe to the Jewish Autonomous Oblast. He also turned against the Jews whose support he had worked to secure during the war. In 1944, the Jewish Anti-Fascist Committee had written to Stalin, requesting the creation of an autonomous Jewish Soviet republic in the Crimea, which Stalin had rendered largely depopulated in May of that year by deporting nearly two hundred thousand Crimean Tatars to Uzbekistan, on the grounds that some of them had collaborated with the National

---

[519] Hugh Fitzgerald, "Czech Defense Minister Calls for Leaving the UN," *Jihad Watch*, November 2, 2023.

Socialist Germans. Several years later, Stalin seized upon this letter as evidence that the pro-American Zionists were attempting to establish a foothold for the United States inside the Soviet Union.[520] On January 13, 1948, the chairman of the Jewish Anti-Fascist Committee, Solomon Mikhoels, was murdered on Stalin's orders.[521] The other members of the committee were arrested and finally executed in 1952 after four years of torture.[522]

The Soviet Union's support for Israel, meanwhile, did not last long. As the world fell into the binary division of the Cold War, it was clear by the fall of 1948 that Israel would be on the American side of the divide, and so the Soviets turned increasingly to aiding the Islamic jihad against the Jewish state. By 1951, the Soviet press was denouncing Zionism as a "reactionary national movement" that involved "Fascist methods of government and discrimination against the Arab population in Israel."[523]

Demonstrating the malleability of socialist theory, which proclaimed of itself that it was based on scientific analysis, Soviet propaganda began to assert that Zionism was a reactionary movement from its very beginning. The fact that Stalin had initially favored it was swept under the rug as the Soviet press charged that Zionist visionary Theodor Herzl had in 1903 offered the assistance of Zionists to the czar's interior minister, Vyacheslav von Plehve, to help Russian authorities tamp down revolutionary sentiments among young Jews. This was stretching credulity considerably beyond the breaking point: it is extraordinarily unlikely that Herzl would have offered von Plehve help of any kind, as the interior minister had been responsible for

---

[520]   Mikhail Heller and Aleksandr M. Nekrich, *Utopia in Power: The History of the Soviet Union from 1917 to the Present* (New York: Simon & Schuster, 1986), 502.

[521]   Johnson, *History of the Jews*, op. cit., 526.

[522]   Heller and Nekrich, op. cit.

[523]   Benjamin Pinkus, *The Jews of the Soviet Union: The History of a National Minority* (Cambridge: Cambridge University Press, 1988), 171.

organizing pogroms against the Jews in Russia.[524] The Soviet propaganda mill further charged that Zionists in the 1930s had met with Italy's Fascist leader Benito Mussolini and broached the possibility of Italian protection for a Jewish state.[525]

These accusations were designed to turn the Soviet public against the Jews as Stalin began to move against this "reactionary national movement" within his own domains. When the first Israeli ambassador to the Soviet Union, Golda Meir, visited a Moscow synagogue on Yom Kippur, October 13, 1948, a massive crowd of Jews greeted her enthusiastically. This only deepened Stalin's suspicions that the Jews were a subversive element with divided loyalties. In November 1948, according to historian Benjamin Pinkus, Stalin began "the liquidation of Jewish culture in the Soviet Union."[526] The Jews would become indistinguishable from all other citizens of the Soviet Union, no longer enjoying anything that would render them distinctive within the great workers' collective.

This involved the closing of Jewish-oriented theaters, museums, and, indeed, all Jewish institutions aside from synagogues. Pinkus, however, suggests that this simply may not have been considered necessary: "The already depressed situation of the Jewish religion in the Soviet Union—in terms of number of synagogues functioning (about 100 in the entire country), the number of rabbis, and the number of worshippers—probably made the authorities consider it of too little importance to justify a strict anti-religious campaign."[527] Also, having a few rabbis available to participate in postwar "peace" organizations was useful for propaganda, and having Jews worship in synagogues

---

[524]   Ibid., 171–2.
[525]   Ibid., 172.
[526]   Ibid., 202.
[527]   Ibid., 208.

made surveillance easier than it would have been if they had been meeting in private homes.[528]

"MURDERERS IN WHITE COATS"

After the destruction of the Jewish Anti-Fascist Committee, anti-Jewish propaganda began to be a common feature in the Soviet press. The Jews were portrayed as scheming exploiters who evaded military service and sponged off the hardworking non-Jewish citizenry.[529] In December 1952, Stalin added to the propaganda by announcing to the Politburo: "Every Jewish nationalist is the agent of the American intelligence service. Jewish nationalists think that their nation was saved by the USA... They think they are indebted to the Americans. Among doctors, there are many Jewish nationalists."[530]

On January 13, 1953, all this propaganda having suitably prepared the ground, the Soviet newspapers announced that authorities had uncovered a counterrevolutionary plot of Jewish doctors; the plotters had already murdered two prominent Communist Party members and planned to murder the chief officers of the Red Army under the guise of providing them medical care.[531]

One Soviet publication ran a banner article entitled "Murderers in White Coats."[532] The flagship Soviet newspaper *Pravda* wrote on that day that "the majority of the participants of the terrorist group...were bought by American intelligence. They were recruited by a branch-office of American intelligence—the international Jewish bourgeois-

---

[528] Ibid.

[529] Ibid., 141–2.

[530] Mark Regev, "Stalin and the Creation of Israel: The Soviet Tyrant's Inadvertent Zionism – Opinion," *Jerusalem Post*, May 5, 2023.

[531] Pinkus, op. cit., 179.

[532] Heller and Nekrich, op. cit., 503.

nationalist organization called 'Joint' [that is, the American Jewish Joint Distribution Committee, a relief organization]. The filthy face of this Zionist spy organization, covering up their vicious actions under the mask of charity, is now completely revealed."[533]

Stalin planned to use this fabricated plot as a pretext for a purge of some of the top Communist Party officials, including Molotov. These men were not Jewish, but Stalin planned to use the claim that the whole plot centered around Jewish doctors committing murder under the appearance of medical treatment as a further pretext, allowing him to exile the Jews from the major Soviet cities into gulags in the desolate Soviet Far East.[534] Not only Jewish doctors, but lawyers, shop managers, and others were accused of being part of the plot, along with a handful of non-Jews who were apparently only accused in order to make the claims appear less of an exercise in crude Jew-hatred than they actually were.[535] The whole thing, the Soviet press proclaimed, was a "Zionist-American" effort to do nothing less than to bring down the socialist state.[536] Stalin was determined, telling Khrushchev: "The good workers at the factory should be given clubs so they can beat the hell out of those Jews."[537] He told his subordinates to "beat, beat and beat again" in order to wring concessions out of the accused doctors at their show trial.[538]

The show trial, according to researcher A. Mark Clarfield, "was meant to initiate a carefully constructed plan in which almost all of the Soviet Union's two million Jews, nearly all of whom were survivors of the Holocaust, were to be transported to the Gulag—in cattle

---

[533] Lawrence Bush, "January 12: Mikhoels and the Doctors Plot," *Jewish Currents*, January 12, 2010.

[534] Pinkus, op. cit., 180.

[535] Ibid., 178.

[536] Ibid., 181.

[537] Lawrence W. Reed, "The Night of the Murdered Poets," American Institute for Economic Research, August 16, 2022.

[538] Ibid.

cars. Between the January announcement and Stalin's death a month and a half later it became clear that careful plans had been laid for the transfer and 'concentration' of Soviet Jews."[539]

Only Stalin's death on March 5, 1953, forestalled all this and prevented what could very well have been the extermination of Soviet Jewry at the hands of the international socialists, eight years after the end of the National Socialist devastation of the Jews of Europe. Both National Socialism and international socialism were intrinsically hostile to the Jews, as both were totalitarian systems that were dedicated to the exaltation of the collective: the master race on the one hand and the proletariat on the other. There was no place in either system for a people that stubbornly maintained its own practices, perspectives, and priorities.

In both National Socialist Germany and the Soviet Union, the same accusations that marked earlier forms of antisemitism appeared yet again: the Jews are saboteurs, working to destroy the system. They are a corrosive influence, breaking down the unity and cohesion of the larger society. They are the enemies of what society at large values as good, and they will never be able to fit in or accept the values of the majority.

And both followed this line of thinking out to the conclusion that this criminal element had to be eradicated from society.

---

[539]   A. Mark Clarfield, "The Soviet 'Doctors' Plot'—50 Years On," *The BMJ*, December 21, 2002.

PART II

THE CHARGES

The ugly recrudescence of Jew-hatred today draws upon all these well-springs. In the wake of the October 7 massacres, Christian antisemitism, Islamic antisemitism, and the antisemitism of the collectivists of various kinds have all reappeared and made it clear that despite appearances to the contrary, they had never actually been eradicated. They had all been beneath the surface, and not so very far beneath, waiting for an opportunity to reassert themselves.

Now, that opportunity had come. Social media enabled the rapid dissemination of numerous features of the ancient hatreds: blood libels, allegations of the rape and abuse of children, and all manner of claims that the Jews may appear to adhere to the moral standards of the wider society, but they were secretly up to no good, and working in various ways to subvert and destroy that society. They were the killers of Christ, the killers of the prophets, the enemies of God, and the stubborn unassimilable people who would not give up their distinctive practices and join the collectivist paradise.

To consider and answer all the charges against the Jews would require not only a book of many volumes, but a blog or magazine where new charges could be constantly rebutted. Some of the charges are simply unanswerable because they rely, without, of course, offering any evidence, on assertions that the worst things that the Jews are doing are all in secret or are the work of secret societies who are pulling the levers of the world from safely behind the scenes.

That sort of charge could be levied against any individual or group and, by its very nature, cannot be answered. It would be a most inefficient secret society that did its nefarious deeds in the open, where they could be readily perceived by the discerning.

Yet some of the most destructive and influential charges that have recently reappeared can and must be answered. It's a matter of simple justice to combat lies whenever they circulate.

Chapter Seven

AN ABSURD, UGLY, AND IMMORAL BOOK?

IT'S THE JEWS' FAULT

Throughout history, attackers of Jews explained that their victims were justifiably brutalized because of the claims made by the believers in the various forms of Jew-hatred we have examined. The Jews were justly attacked, the attackers contended, because their laws are different from those of every other people and because they involve repugnant practices. The Jews killed Christ. The Jews are the enemies of the Muslims. The Jews are the opponents of the master race and saboteurs of the National Socialist order. The Jews are the capitalists and saboteurs of the socialist order.

These accusations come from non-Jewish sources: understandings of the Christian and Islamic scriptures that have been and, in many instances, remain mainstream, and the political and social analyses of

Karl Marx and Adolf Hitler. Many who have hated Jews throughout history and considered them to be a malignant force in society claim that they would have had no animus against Jews at all, but that the Jews had an animus against them. Jews, they contend, hate non-Jews and are bound to do so by their own sacred texts. Non-Jews, consequently, need to be informed, and it's only natural, they insist, that they would return hatred for hatred.

We have seen that Antiochus Epiphanes commanded that the Jews' sacred books, "by which they were taught to hate all other nations, should be sprinkled with the broth made of the swine's flesh."[540] Antiochus was one of many throughout the ages who have contended that the Jews' sacred books teach them to hate all other nations. For centuries, claims have circulated that the sacred literature of the Jews contains invective against non-Jews that makes manifestations of Christian and Islamic antisemitism look mild. The Jews, or so goes the claim, are taught that they are superior to non-Jews in every way; indeed, they are the only true humans, while the non-Jews are animals who are to be exploited, enslaved, and manipulated for the benefit of the Jews. These claims center around the voluminous body of literature that forms the centerpiece of Judaism for the last fifteen hundred years and more: the Talmud.

To enter into the arena of criticism of the Talmud is to descend into a twilight world of sweeping claims, wild exaggerations, willful misunderstandings, forced misreadings, falsehoods, fabrications, and all manner of crackpottery. One must sift through not only numerous conclusions drawn from what it says, but a dizzying number of claims that are based upon what it does not actually say. Yet the Talmud has been the focus of anti-Jewish polemic, and the justification for anti-Jewish violence, for centuries, going back to the Talmud trial in Paris in 1240.

---

[540]   Diodorus Siculus, Books 34 & 35, 1, http://attalus.org/translate/diodorus34.html.

That trial was by no means the last time that high governmental authorities denigrated the Talmud. In 1844, Czar Nicholas I ordered Vladimir Ivanovich Dal, a lexicographer in the Russian Ministry of Domestic Affairs, to investigate the Damascus Affair, in which Jews in that city were accused of murdering a Christian and a Muslim in 1840 in order to mix their blood into the Passover matzohs. Dal produced a report, *A Note About Ritual Murders of Babies and How These Jews Use the Babies' Blood*, which has since become revered and highly recommended among antisemites and to which we will return in discussing the blood libels.[541]

"UTTERLY VICIOUS FANATICISM"

One antisemitic website, AntiMatrix.org, offers online versions of books and other material that the "powers of evil are trying to block and suppress, and for years at that."[542] The site, with its chaotic presentation and breathless prose, has the appearance of having been put together and maintained by a person or group in the severe grip of paranoia and likely other derangements as well. Nevertheless, Jew-haters today revere it and refer to it frequently, for it contains a repository of antisemitic literature from throughout the ages.

This repository includes an English version of Dal's report, although it is not always clear whether it is Dal speaking or the frenzied editors of AntiMatrix.org. Whoever the author may be, the assertion is made (in large red type) that "the Talmud contains the incredibly absurd, ugly and immoral weaving of the most bizarre

---

[541] Dal's book is reprinted at the antisemitic e-book depository, AntiMatrix.org. We will return to Dal when we discuss the blood libel in chapter six.

[542] "NWO, ZioNazi, Illuminati, Freemason, Secret Societies Collection," AntiMatrix, https://antimatrix.org/TOC_Books.html.

concoctions of fanaticism."[543] He says that the Talmud justifies the ritual murders of Christians and that "to this day," what it includes "remains a secret, inaccessible to us," for "all the existing copies of it are incomplete and dangerous places obscured with the intent to mystify, with extreme cunning, as, for example, that sometimes, according only to the rules, known only to initiates in the Kabbalistic mysteries, one should not read the words as written, though they have meaning, but to rearrange the letters [Hebrew symbols], and thus derive completely different meaning."[544]

Even what can be known about it, he says, makes it clear that "the Talmud is still so rich in pointless, bizarre and disgusting to humanity utterly vicious fanaticism, that, of course, there exists no barbaric violence it would not allow the Jews to commit against the Christian."[545] AntiMatrix.org refers to "probably the most terrible document in history—the main laws of Talmud as collected in *Shulchan Aruch*," a compendium of Jewish law.[546] Even if these claims originate with the hysterics at this website, they are representative of widespread suspicion of the Talmud, which began to appear openly once again on social media after October 7.

E. Michael Jones, who gives the initial impression of being more sober and scholarly than the wide-eyed editors of the antisemitic e-book site, but who certainly has little or no disagreement with them and who sees Jews as "the people who killed Christ and [as] enemies

---

[543] Vladimir Ivanovich Dal, *A Note about Ritual Murders of Babies and How These Jews Use the Babies' Blood* (Moscow: Ministry of Domestic Affairs, 1844), as presented at https://antimatrix.org/Convert/Books/Dahl/Ritual_Murders/Dahl_Ritual_Murders_En.html.

[544] Ibid.

[545] Ibid.

[546] Ibid.

of the entire human race," says that the Talmud "became the essence of the redefinition of Judaism as anti-Christian."[547]

WHAT THE TALMUD ACTUALLY IS

From all this (and there is much more in this vein), one would get the impression that the Talmud is an occult tome with the primary purpose of counseling all manner of immorality and seething with hateful invective against Gentile society, and particularly Christianity. Scholars of the Talmud, unless they are familiar with such charges, might find the real Talmud difficult to recognize in the way antisemites describe it.

Leave the world of Jew-hatred and reacquaint oneself with the light of day, and the Talmud is spoken of in terms that sound as if a completely different body of literature is being discussed. The Talmud is actually an extremely extensive compendium of Jewish knowledge, encompassing law and many other matters, with rabbis across generations engaging in discussions and grappling in differing ways with biblical texts and many other issues.

The Talmud is massive, comprising thirty-five volumes in a 1952 English edition, eighteen in a 1961 version, and twenty-two volumes in a 1989 edition. Rabbi Noson Weisz, in his foreword to a popular introduction to the Talmud, *The Complete Idiot's Guide to the Talmud*, marvels at the Talmud's comprehensiveness and breadth: "Not only does the Talmud contain the entirety of Jewish law, from ritual law, to family laws to torts; it is also a work of ethics, philosophy, biography, literature, history, and folktales. But that is not all. To fully appreciate

---

[547]   E. Michael Jones, X, February 3, 2024, https://twitter.com/EMichaelJones1/status/1753845338773832039; E. Michael Jones, *The Jewish Revolutionary Spirit and Its Impact on World History* (South Bend, Indiana: Fidelity Press, 2015), 50.

its genius you also have to realize that the Sages compiled a work that contains all this information and is still suited to all age groups and all levels of scholarship."[548]

Rabbi Aaron Parry, author of *The Complete Idiot's Guide to the Talmud*, asserts that "the Talmud truly stands apart as one of the most unique and fascinating written works known to humankind. Part religious laws, part wise sayings, and part stories, it presents ancient teachings and beliefs that are as fresh and inspiring today as they were centuries ago."[549]

The gulf between the ugly, hateful book that is depicted in anti-Jewish literature and this treasury of timeless wisdom couldn't be wider. Far from being a hate screed against non-Jews or a manual for how to subvert their societies, another popular introduction to the Talmud explains that "the Talmud, and its contemporary companion, the Midrash, were originally oral discussions that brought to bear the legal and homiletical interpretations of the postbiblical Rabbis, whose goal was to help their people make the Torah a more usable and understandable document."[550]

The Torah is comprised of the five books of Moses that stand at the beginning of the Jewish and Christian scriptures. Parry explains: "Not one book, but instead a number of volumes, the Talmud is considered the most influential document in the history of Judaism. Of course, the 24 books of Hebrew scriptures—and especially the first five books of Moses that comprise what is known in the Jewish faith as the Torah or the Pentateuch—are vitally essential. But without the

---

[548] Rabbi Noson Weisz, "Foreword," in Rabbi Aaron Parry, *The Complete Idiot's Guide to Talmud* (New York: Penguin Random House, 2004), Kindle edition, loc. 306.

[549] Ibid., 2.

[550] Rabbi Dov Peretz Elkins, *The Wisdom of Judaism: An Introduction to the Values of the Talmud* (Woodstock, Vermont: Jewish Lights Publishing, 2007), Kindle edition, loc. 118.

Talmud, we have no way of knowing how to interpret and apply the laws of the Torah."[551]

Also, Parry continues, "Jewish tradition holds that the Talmud is the 'oral Torah,' or a verbal explanation of the laws that God gave to Moses on Mt. Sinai, and that Moses taught to others. Just about everyone is familiar with the story of how Moses received the Ten Commandments from God, but what is lesser known about this story is that Moses and God had a good chat on that mountain that ranged far beyond what could be inscribed on the tablets that he brought with him when he climbed back down. It is this information, transmitted orally from God to Moses, and then from Moses to the generations that followed him, that is the basis for the Talmud."[552]

One principal reason why it was considered necessary to commit this oral Torah to writing after it had been transmitted by word of mouth for centuries is because of the destruction of the Jewish temple in Jerusalem in 70CE, at the conclusion of the Jewish war against Roman rule that had gone on for four years. Rabbi Chananya Weissman explains: "The oral teachings of the Talmud were given to Moshe [Moses] at Mount Sinai, and were only written down later to preserve them in the face of persecution, which threatened the continued transmission of these oral teachings. These teachings were written in a work called the Mishna—and the sages of the Mishna lived during the times of the temple! The Talmud is an elaboration and elucidation of the Mishna, since continued persecution and deterioration of Torah knowledge and understanding of the Mishna necessitated this."[553]

Persecutions of the Jews in the fourth century and thereafter made this task all the more urgent. An initial compendium, the Jerusalem

---

[551] Parry, op. cit., 3.
[552] Ibid., 4.
[553] Rabbi Chananya Weissman, email to the author, March 5, 2024.

Talmud, appeared in that century; the Babylonian Talmud, which is far more extensive and detailed, followed about a century later and is what most people are referring to when they speak of "the Talmud." The Talmud is made up of the Mishnah, a compendium of the oral Torah compiled toward the end of the second century CE and the beginning of the third, and the Gemara, a commentary on the Mishnah that frequently discusses passages from the Hebrew scriptures, that is, what Christians know as the Old Testament.

WHAT THE TALMUD ISN'T

Critics of the Talmud often commit the fundamental error of not realizing what kind of material they're reading. A person reads a news article in a different way from how he reads a comic book; when reading the former, he is seeking information, while when reading the latter, he is seeking entertainment. If Batman says something in the comic book about the state of the world, the reader is unlikely to approach it as seriously as he would a statement from the president of the United States in a news article, because he knows what genre of literature he is reading.

Mistaking genres can lead to ludicrous errors and blind alleys. If an archaeologist twenty centuries from now mistook a restaurant menu for the scriptures of a vanished civilization, he might reasonably conclude that the people of this civilization worshipped various food items. If the same confused archaeologist came across a comic book, he might think that Batman was the god of this people and that the stories of his exploits in Gotham City were holy writ.

The Talmud is often misread because it encompasses a large variety of genres. Not all of its statements are laws that all Jews are required to follow, and not all of the statements in it are considered to be beliefs that all Jews must hold. The Talmud contains legal precepts, and Jewish law is derived in large part from it. However, the Talmud and Jewish law are not identical. Not everything in the Talmud is Jewish law, and not everything in Jewish law is in the Talmud. The Talmud contains history, theology, geography, medicine, and more, but it is not primarily a work of any of those areas, either. As it is a series of conversations between rabbis, including conversations among rabbis across the centuries, as their various opinions on a point are brought together in a single passage, it contains much that is controverted and rejected within the Talmud itself. It does not issue dictates that are binding upon all Jews, except when it is discussing what is acknowledged to be divine law.

Jewish sources acknowledge that the Talmud is a product of the time and place in which it was written. Even Orthodox Jews acknowledge that the rabbis who deliberate in the Talmud were wrong on occasion; one notable example is the fact that, like the best scientific minds of their day, they believed in spontaneous generation. They discuss, for example, a being that is half flesh and half dirt and that does not reproduce but simply springs into being. They assume that such beings exist.[554]

This does not mean that all Jews must accept this and believe that such beings exist. Nor does it invalidate the rabbis' other statements, any more than it invalidates the thinking of anyone from prescientific ages. It does, however, indicate the hazards of assuming that if something is written in the Talmud, therefore all Jews accept it and follow it. Jews today, like everyone else, do not believe in spontaneous generation, and its presence in the Talmud doesn't change that.

In order to understand the Talmud properly, the reader must have a full understanding of the genre of what he is reading. Many passages

---

[554] "Chullin 127a (Part II) - Spontaneous Generation," Talmudology, April 3, 2019, https://www.talmudology.com/jeremybrownmdgmailcom/2017/10/14/sanhedrin-91-spontaneous-generation-rbaf8.

that are taken to be approval of immoral behavior actually aren't discussing the moral character of an act at all, but the civil or criminal liability attached to it. Those who hate Jews often take passages that don't make clear the moral evaluation of an act as evidence that the Talmud doesn't consider the act to be wrong, when actually that issue is simply not being discussed in that particular passage.

The Talmud is also not a quick-reference guide. It is the record of an extensive exercise in Socratic thought; thus, it is full of apparent contradictions and posited arguments that are later rejected. It often remains cryptic even in translation, which is why the main text is surrounded by commentary and citations to the Torah, markings on what constitutes the law (halachah), and more.

In the Talmud, there is usually more than meets the eye, and one can't simply glean the meaning from a cursory look at the text. In yeshivas, students can spend weeks studying a single page. Those who produce lists of allegedly hateful quotes from the Talmud never demonstrate any awareness of the status of the texts they quote in Jewish law or any idea of what the Talmud itself really is.

A NEW FORM OF JUDAISM?

Foes of the Talmud, however, claim that it would be incorrect to accept this picture of the Talmud as a compendium of biblical commentary and related wisdom. They insist that however much commentary on the scriptures there may be in the Talmud, there is a tremendous chasm between the Hebrew Bible and the rabbinic literature. They claim that Jews do not follow their own scriptures at all, but rather the Talmud. Antisemites insist that the Talmud teaches principles and values that are different from, and frequently opposed to, the teaching of the scriptures. They maintain that the Judaism of the rabbis cannot even be said to be the same religion as biblical Judaism.

Going even further, opponents of the Talmud often assert that it exalts the teachings of the rabbis above those of the scripture. Eitan Bar, a convert from Judaism to Christianity and a vociferous critic of the Talmud and Judaism in general, states that in rabbinic tradition, "studying the Mishna and the Talmud will grant you favor, but learning the holy of holies—the Bible—will gain you absolutely nothing!"[555] The Talmud itself, however, contradicts this idea, noting amid a discussion of what to do when an animal falls into a dyke that "[the avoidance of] suffering of dumb animals is a Biblical [law], so the Biblical law comes and supersedes the [interdict] of the Rabbis."[556]

Those who hate the Talmud see what they regard as the disjunction between the Judaism of the Bible and the Judaism of the rabbis whose teachings make up the Talmud as evidence of the latter's evil. In seeing the Talmud as "the essence of the redefinition of Judaism as anti-Christian," E. Michael Jones is working from a common assumption among Christian foes of the Talmud: were it not for the Talmud, Jews would follow the plain words of their scriptures, and that would lead them to embrace Christ and become Christians.[557] Jones and others who agree with him thus see the Talmud as evil in itself, in providing an alternative interpretation of Judaism that constitutes a massive impediment to Jews' converting to Christianity.

In response to claims that the Talmud represents a departure from biblical Judaism, Rabbi Chananya Weissman asks a rhetorical question: "What is the law according to 'Biblical Judaism' if someone caused his fellow to lose exactly 45% of his vision, since it's impossible to blind the criminal exactly that amount? Too little would be

---

555 Eitan Bar with Golan Broshi, *Rabbinic Judaism Debunked* (Independently published, 2019), 19.

556 Babylonian Talmud: Tractate Shabbath 128b, H. Freedman, trans., https://halakhah.com/shabbath/shabbath_128.html.

557 E. Michael Jones, X, February 3, 2024, https://twitter.com/EMichaelJones1/status/1753845338773832039; E. Michael Jones, *The Jewish Revolutionary Spirit and Its Impact on World History* (South Bend, Indiana: Fidelity Press, 2015), 50.

injustice to the victim, and too much would be injustice to the criminal. And what if a blind person blinds others? I can provide endless examples, but this should suffice to torpedo the notion that 'Biblical Judaism' could possibly exist without a DIVINE understanding of the written word that was transmitted orally, which they inaccurately refer to as 'Rabbinic Judaism.' You simply cannot have one without the other."[558]

However, there is much more to the hatred of the Talmud than just an alleged discrepancy between it and the Hebrew scriptures. The Talmud, according to those who sound the alarm about it, contains numerous teachings that are so evil and repulsive that the mass burning of volumes of it in Paris in 1240, as well as later attempts to suppress and ban it, did not spring from irrational prejudice, but were entirely justified. After October 7, it became easy to find lists of these alleged terrible Talmudic teachings on social media. Antisemites gleefully posted them as if they were the key to why Hamas decided to massacre Israelis on that day and why they were justified in doing so.

BLACK HATRED OF HUMANITY

These kinds of charges against the Talmud go back centuries, as the 1240 trial demonstrates, and have persisted. In 1991, General Moustafa Tlass, who was identified as a "Member of the Syrian Academy," published in Damascus a book entitled *The Matzo of Zion*, discussing the 1840 Damascus blood libel. Tlass contended that "the Egyptian authorities in Cairo and Damascus were very concerned about this horrible crime" and that the French consul in Damascus took

---

558 Rabbi Chananya Weissman, op. cit.

particular interest because the victim was a subject of the Kingdom of France.[559]

Tlass states that "the investigation revealed serious matters that surpassed the crime itself as to the nature and motives connected with the Jewish teaching, prescribed by the Talmud, which contained destructive deviations guided by black hatred of humanity and all other religions equally, and together."[560] When this became known, Tlass asserts, "the French Consul in Damascus sent a translation from the Talmud"; he doesn't say where he sent it, but apparently he meant that it was sent to the governing authorities in Paris.[561]

The Talmud passage that the French consul supposedly sent said this:

1. There is nothing said or done in Christian Churches which is not different from the truth, and not different from what the unbelievers practice. The duty of the Jew is the destruction of these Churches. The Christian Bible is nothing but a belief of Great Sins; therefore, the duty of the Jew is to burn it, regardless of the presence of God's name in it.

2. It is the duty of the Jew to curse the Christians three times daily, and pray that God may destroy them all, especially their Kings and Rulers. This is the Law, and its faithful observance falls upon the leaders of this belief, especially those whose duty it is to urge the curse of the Christians. God has ordered the Jewish People to put their hands on Christian wealth by all means possible, it matters not whether they use trick, theft, or interest charge.

---

[559] Moustafa Tlass, *Matzo of Zion* (Damascus: Dar Tlas, 1991), https://archive.org/stream/MatzoOfZion_201903/Matzo%20of%20Zion_djvu.txt.
[560] Ibid.
[561] Ibid.

3. It is the duty of the Jews to consider the Christians as beasts and to treat them as such. If a Jew sees a Christian on the edge of a cliff, he should push him or throw him to the bottom.[562]

According to Tlass, "the French Consul explained that there are some Talmudic references to the Muslims, which are even more severe than those for the Christians; and that he refrained from translating them due to his fear of Muslim anger over them."[563]

No references are given to the source of these alleged quotations. Neither the French consul, apparently, nor Tlass himself provided any indication of where these statements could be found in the Talmud. Meanwhile, Tlass's assertion that the Talmud contains even more incendiary material about Muslims is remarkable, as the Talmud was compiled at least two centuries before the advent of Islam.

Fabricated quotations, with false attributions to accompany them, have been common in attacks on the Talmud for centuries. Writing in 1939, as hatred of Jews was engulfing Europe, a prominent Conservative rabbi in New York, Ben Zion Bokser, traced modern claims regarding the evils of the Talmud back to seventeenth-century Germany and pointed out that numerous collections of the allegedly evil quotations from the Talmud simply aren't in the book:

> The Talmud baiters occasionally support their assertions with elaborate quotations. It is not always easy to trace these quotations to their sources. The titles of the works cited are often so grossly misspelled that it is difficult to recognize them. Yalkut is cited as "Jektut;" Yad as "Jak;" Nedarim as "Nadarine." Occasionally, the titles as cited appear altogether fictitious, such as "Gad. Shas.," "Rabbi Ismael," "Rabbi

---

Chambar," et al., "Tract Mechilla." Frequently, the works quoted are the well known but no volume, page, chapter or verse is indicated, such as a general reference to "SzaolothUtszabot, the Book of Jore Dia 17." Shaalot Utshubot simply means "responsa" and it applies to the correspondence of the rabbis on religious questions. The New York Public Library lists in its catalogue hundreds of such volumes of responsa.[564]

LYING ABOUT THE TALMUD'S CONTENTS

One such list of proof texts, however, that purports to demonstrate the evil teachings of the Talmud seals itself off from charges that the Talmud quotations are fabricated, misquoted, or even taken out of context by claiming that the Talmud commands Jews to lie to non-Jews about its contents: "If the Gentiles knew that the Talmud teach [sic] Jews to destroy them they would kill us openly. Never communicate the Talmud with Gentiles."

This claim is attributed to *"Libbre David 37,"* but there is just one problem: Rabbi Gil Student, a defender of the Talmud, notes that "while it is *possible* that the book *Libbre David* existed, I have not been able to find it, even with the help of a librarian from Yeshiva University's Gottesman Library. It was certainly never a mainstream book. In fact, it is strictly prohibited to lie about the contents of the Talmud."[565]

---

[564]   Ben Zion Bokser, "Talmudic Forgeries: A Case Study in Anti-Jewish Propaganda," *Contemporary Jewish Record*, July-August 1939, 15, https://www.bjpa.org/content/upload/bjpa/2_ar/2_Articles_July-August_1939.pdf.

[565]   Gil Student, "It Is Forbidden to Lie about the Talmud," The Real Truth About the Talmud, https://www.angelfire.com/mt/talmud/lie.html.

Writing in defense of the Jews, Judaism, and the Talmud in the early decades of the twentieth century, the Austrian rabbi Joseph S. Bloch traces the claim that Jews must lie to Gentiles about the contents of the Talmud to "a pamphlet (number 5) originating in Mecklenburg," apparently in the latter part of the nineteenth century. He provides a fuller quotation: "It is written in Libre David, Whenever a Gentile asks a Jew for information about a passage in the rabbinical writings, it is the duty of the Jew to expound it falsely; for if the Gentiles knew what we were teaching against them, would they not kill us all?"[566] Like Gil Student long afterward, however, Bloch can find no such book as *Libre David*. A 2018 article on antisemitic claims suggests that "it could be referring to the Book of Psalms, as 'liber' is book in Latin and most of the psalms are attributed to King David, but there is still no text there matching this 'quotation.'"[567]

Bloch, however, states that what was meant was a book named *Dibre David*. Bloch notes that "there are, it is true, three Hebrew books of this title."[568] He adds, however, that another researcher "obtained all the three books and declares briefly and to the point: there is nothing of the kind to be found in any of them."[569] The antisemitic literature is repeating a charge based on a fabrication from a source whose name they have obscured with a typographical error.

Hardcore critics of the Talmud, however, claim that material of this kind really can be, or once could be, found within its many volumes, but was removed on the orders of medieval Christian authorities who wanted to blunt the Talmud's power to incite Jews to acts of subversion and attacks of Christians, or was hidden so as

---

[566] Josef S. Bloch, *Israel and the Nations*, trans. anon. (Skokie, Illinois: Varda Books, 2001), 4.

[567] Daniel Lipson, "Into the Depths of Evil: How the Nazis 'Recruited' the Talmud for Anti-Semitic Propaganda," The Librarians, January 29, 2018, https://blog.nli.org.il/en/nazisandthetalmud/.

[568] Bloch, op. cit.

[569] Ibid.

to allay suspicions about the Jews' good intentions. However, those who believe, along with E. Michael Jones, that the Jews in the aggregate are the "enemies of the entire human race" contend that such passages continue to circulate among Jews, hidden in the recesses of secret books that Jews are forbidden on pain of death to share with non-Jews.[570]

In discussing the 1840 blood libel in Damascus, Tlass quotes a rabbi from that time who had converted to Islam explaining that if a Jew "speaks ill about the Jews, or causes harm to any of them, or insults the Jewish Religion, then for sure he must be killed. This is done even today in spite of their weak position because they consider him an enemy of their religion. There is no sin offering for this offence except death. The Jewish Religion relies on this practice in these days."[571] The converted rabbi explained that this was why he could not tell the truth about the incident in which the Jews killed the Christian and Muslim for their blood until he had embraced Islam: "For this reason I did not confess the truth, and I was unable to confess until I had declared my conversion to Islam."[572]

TEACHINGS INSPIRE ACTIONS

Does the Talmud really contain such secret teachings that Jews are forbidden on pain of death to reveal? There is no way to prove definitively that it doesn't, for anyone who points out that no available edition of the Talmud contains the passages the French consul quoted, or any others like them, will simply be dismissed as impossibly naïve

---

[570] E. Michael Jones, X, February 3, 2024, https://twitter.com/EMichaelJones1/status/1753845338773832039.

[571] Tlass, op. cit.

[572] Ibid.

or in the pay of the Zionists and reminded of the Jews' dishonesty and secrecy.

There is, however, one primary obstacle to accepting this scenario: Jews don't act this way. We don't see Jews destroying churches or burning Christian Bibles. We hear nothing of Jews cursing Christians three times daily or pushing Christians off cliffs. Those who consider the Jews to be the enemies of the entire human race might reply that they are not generally in a position to do such things and prefer indirect methods over direct ones, that is, undermining churches by enticing young Christians with pornography and other sources of immorality and impugning the Bible with historical-critical analysis, to say nothing of simple ridicule.

Yet if the Talmud commands so straightforwardly that Jews behave this way toward Christians, it would be only reasonable to expect that at least some Jews, somewhere, would opt for the more direct approach and simply bomb a church or set fire to a New Testament or murder a Christian simply because he was a Christian. By way of analogy, consider the Qur'an. I have elucidated in several books, notably *The Critical Qur'an*, *The History of Jihad*, and *Muhammad: A Critical Biography*, the fact that the holy book of Islam and the words and deeds of the central figure of the Islamic religion contain a great deal of material that calls for Muslims to do violence against non-Muslims. Over the years, however, as I have pointed this out not just in books, but also in a large number of articles, video debates, and live presentations, numerous people have confronted me on many occasions, claiming that what I am saying is not true.

Whether I am lying or simply ignorant is a matter of some debate, but it is not difficult to find both Muslims and non-Muslims, including many academics who are highly regarded as "experts" on Islam and the Qur'an, who say that I have gotten Islam all wrong and that it is at its core a religion of peace. They claim that I am taking

Qur'an passages out of context, ignoring ones that counsel peace and coexistence, and portraying Muhammad as a man of war when he was, in reality, a kind of proto-Gandhi, a man who did his utmost to establish friendly and harmonious relations between peoples.

The Islamic apologist Karen Armstrong, whose rose-colored version of Islam became immensely popular in the wake of the September 11, 2001 jihad attacks, declared in her biography of Muhammad that "the very idea that Muhammad would have found anything to be optimistic about in the carnage committed in his name on September 11 is an obscenity, because, as I try to show in these pages, Muhammad spent most of his life trying to stop that kind of indiscriminate slaughter.... Muhammad eventually abjured violence and pursued a daring, inspired policy of non-violence that was worthy of Gandhi."[573]

Karen Armstrong wrote those words in 1992. Since then, we've had the 9/11 attacks, followed by nearly forty-five thousand violent jihad attacks worldwide.[574] There have been numerous Muslims who, in committing these acts of violence, made it abundantly clear that Islam's teachings of violence were their motivation by shouting "Allahu akbar" during their attack. This means "Allah is greater" and is a declaration of the superiority of the god of Islam over other deities, as manifested by the attack on unbelievers that is at hand. 9/11 hijacker Mohamed Atta reminded himself just before the attack to "shout, 'Allahu akbar,' because this strikes fear in the hearts of the non-believers."[575]

While imprisoned at Guantánamo Bay and still awaiting trial, Khalid Sheikh Mohammed and other 9/11 plotters penned a document in March 2009 entitled "The Islamic Response to the

---

[573] Karen Armstrong, *Muhammad: A Biography of the Prophet* (San Francisco: Harper San Francisco, 1992), 5.
[574] See thereligionofpeace.com for a listing of those attacks and an ongoing count.
[575] "Last Words of a Terrorist," *Guardian*, September 30, 2001.

Government's Nine Accusations."[576] Calling themselves the "9/11 Shura Council" (a shura is a consultative assembly), they filed this document with the Guantánamo military commission, answering the charges that had been made against them regarding the 9/11 attacks. They admitted their involvement in planning those attacks and made it clear that the 9/11 attacks were all about Islam: "Many thanks to God for his kind gesture, and choosing us to perform the act of Jihad for his cause and to defend Islam and Muslims. Therefore, killing you and fighting you, destroying you and terrorizing you, responding back to your attacks, are all considered to be great legitimate duty in our religion."[577]

They were by no means alone in seeing Islam in this way. Two years before they wrote this document, a Taliban leader named Baitullah Mehsud declared that "Allah on 480 occasions in the Holy Koran extols Muslims to wage jihad. We only fulfil God's orders. Only jihad can bring peace to the world. We will continue our struggle until foreign troops are thrown out. Then we will attack them in the US and Britain until they either accept Islam or agree to pay jazia."[578] "Jazia," or jizya, is the Qur'an-mandated tax on subjugated "people of the book" (that is, mainly Jews and Christians).[579] In May 2013, a Muslim in Britain named Michael Mujaheed Adebolajo beheaded a British soldier, Drummer Lee Rigby, on a London street. Then, bloody cleaver in hand, Adebolajo approached an individual who was filming and explained: "We are forced by the Qur'an, in Sura

---

[576] Khalid Sheikh Mohammed, Walid bin Attash, Ramzi bin As-Shibh, Ali Abd al-Aziz Ali, and Mustafa Ahmed al-Hawsawi, "The Islamic Response to the Government's Nine Accusations," Jihad Watch, March 11, 2009.

[577] Ibid.

[578] "Pakistan Taliban Vow More Violence," BBC, January 29, 2007.

[579] Qur'an 9:29.

At-Tawba, through many ayah [verses] in the Qur'an, we must fight them as they fight us."[580]

There are literally hundreds, if not thousands, of other readily available accounts of Muslims justifying acts of violence (their own and those of others) by invoking the Qur'an and the teachings of Muhammad. Those who invoke Muhammad's example in performing Gandhiesque gestures of nonviolence are considerably more difficult to find. Accordingly, it is now quite clear to any objective observer that what I have been contending all these years about Islam is correct, and that what Armstrong claimed is wrong. I point this out to emphasize that when a religion contains certain teachings, some believers in that religion will act upon those teachings. If those teachings are obscure passages found only in long-forgotten books, the number of believers who act upon them, and even know they exist, will be small, whereas if those teachings form a central element of the traditions of the religion, then many believers will act upon them.

The analogy should now be clear. If the essence of the Talmud were to articulate Judaism as anti-Christian, and if Jews were explicitly directed within it to destroy churches and kill Christians, we would expect to see at least some Jews doing this. We generally do not. Accordingly, the likelihood that such secret teachings exist is slim to none.

Aside from the possible existence of secret teachings, however, there are charges against the Talmud based on what it actually says.

---

[580] Paul Vernon Angus Stott, *British Jihadism: The Detail and the Denial*, A thesis submitted to the degree of Doctor of Philosophy. University of East Anglia School of Politics, Philosophy, Language and Communication Studies, 30 April 2015, 184, https://ueaeprints.uea.ac.uk/id/eprint/53460/1/British_Jihadism_The_Detail_and_The_Denial.pdf   file:///Users/Robert1/Documents/My%20Documents/Jihad%20Watch/British_Jihadism_The_Detail_and_the_Deni.pdf.

NON-JEWS ARE SUBHUMANS?

There are, however, other apparently disturbing passages that actually do appear in the Talmud and are not the inventions of antisemites. These passages seem to vindicate all the antisemites' contention that the massive compendium is really as pernicious as they claim. The Talmud is charged with going much further than the New Testament or the Qur'an in its hatred for the outsider: it even states, goes the claim, that non-Jews are subhuman.

The evidence is in a Talmudic passage that states clearly that "heathens," or Gentiles, are not "men":

> Our Rabbis have taught: He who pours the oil of anointing over cattle or vessels is not guilty; if over heathens or the dead, he is not guilty. The law relating to cattle and vessels is right, for it is written: Upon the flesh of man [*adam*] shall it not be poured; and cattle and vessels are not man. Also with regard to the dead, [it is plausible] that he is exempt, since after death one is called corpse and not man. But why is one exempt in the case of heathens; are they not in the category of *adam*?—No, it is written: And you my sheep, the sheep of my pasture, are *adam* [man]: You are called *adam* but heathens are not called *adam*.[581]

In another, a Jewish priest is asked: "Are you not a priest? Why then do you stand in a cemetery?"[582] The priest replies that there is no

---

[581] Babylonian Talmud: Tractate Krithoth 6b, trans. anon., https://halakhah.com/pdf/kodoshim/Krithoth.pdf. Language slightly modernized for clarity. I am indebted to Gil Student's "The Real Truth about the Talmud" site for these discussions of controversial Talmudic passages: https://www.angelfire.com/mt/talmud/man.html.

[582] Babylonian Talmud: Tractate Baba Mezi'a 114b, H. Freedman, trans., https://halakhah.com/babamezia/babamezia_114.html. Language modernized for clarity.

problem, for it is not a Jewish cemetery: "Has the Master not studied the laws of purity? For it has been taught: R. Simeon b. Yohai said: The graves of Gentiles do not defile, for it is written, *And ye my flock, the flock of my pastures, are men*; only you are designated *men*."[583]

These passages are quite clear in stating that non-Jews are not men, that is, not human beings, although they do not actually say that they are inferior or subhuman. One could hold that they leave open the possibility that non-Jews could be considered to be greater, rather than lesser, than Jews.

Other passages, meanwhile, appear to contradict those that deny the status of "man" to the Gentiles. One says that "a heathen can own land in the Land of Israel so fully as to have the right of digging in it pits, ditches and caves, as it says, The heavens are the heavens of the Lord, but the earth he gave to the sons of man [*bnei Adam*]."[584]

Gil Student explains that these passages can be reconciled with one another when one understands the distinctions between *adam*, *bnei Adam*, and *haAdam*, which appears in another passage that demonstrates that non-Jews are assumed to be human beings in the Talmud. "The Jews," Student explains, "as a unified nation, are one organic entity. We are obligated to treat each other as close family members and are responsible for each other's actions. When the Talmud sees the Hebrew word *Adam*, it sees an allusion to Adam of Genesis 1–5, who was at one time the only person. The Talmud understands this as referring to the Jewish people who are an organic unit like one person. Gentiles do not have this organic national bond with each other and are therefore excluded from this concept."[585] However, "other terms referring to people, *Bnei Adam* (sons of Adam) or *HaAdam* (the

---

583   Ibid.
584   Babylonian Talmud, Tractate Gittin 47a, Maurice Simon, trans. https://halakhah.com/pdf/nashim/Gittin.pdf.
585   Gil Student, "Gentiles Are Human," The Real Truth about the Talmud, https://www.angelfire.com/mt/talmud/man.html.

man), are understood to refer to the species homo sapien of which gentiles are obviously members just as Jews are."

The difference is made even clearer when one notes that the first two passages have to do with Jewish ritual practice, and the others with activities that are common to both Jews and non-Jews: "Thus, with regard to ritual impurity and holy oil, which are uniquely Jewish concepts, the Talmud sees an exclusion to all those who are not part of the organic Jewish nation. With regard to practical matters such as the purchase of land or individual matters such as spiritual status, gentiles are included. An understanding of *all* of the relevant passages in the Talmud shows that Gentiles are considered human but not Jewish and the accusations against the Talmud are false."[586]

Rabbi Chananya Weissman notes that the claim that the Talmud teaches that non-Jews are animals "is deliberately taken completely out of context. There are numerous instances where the same Talmud specifically refers to gentiles as 'Adam,' as noted on the spot by the commentaries. There is no contradiction. In this and other aspects of law, gentiles are not equated with Jews, as derived from a specific Torah teaching. In these cases, which generally deal with spiritual considerations, in a comparison between Jews and gentiles, only Jews are considered 'Adam.' All the rest of the time, the word 'Adam' referred to all human beings, Jew and gentile alike, as, in fact, we all come from Adam."[587]

And yet a different passage states that "an Egyptian," which is generally understood as meaning all non-Jews, "has no father."[588] The passage immediately denies that this is because of the Egyptians' "excessive indulgence in carnal gratification," to the extent that a woman would not know who the father of her child was. Rather, the

---

[586] Ibid.

[587] Rabbi Chananya Weissman, op. cit.

[588] Babylonian Talmud, Tractate Yevamoth 98a, Israel W. Slotki, trans. https://halakhah.com/pdf/nashim/Yevamoth.pdf.

passage is discussing converts to Judaism and explaining that they do not maintain the same relations with their non-Jewish family that they had before. That is a common sentiment regarding converts to many religions, and there are varying interpretations of its implications within Judaism.

The passage, however, goes on to state that "the All Merciful declared their children to be legally fatherless, for [so indeed it is also] written, Whose flesh is as the flesh of asses, and whose issue is like the issue of horses."[589] In a list of proof texts claiming to demonstrate the evil of the Talmud, this is rendered as "All children of Goyim are animals," with the citation "Yebamoth 98a."

That is the reference for the Talmud's statement that "an Egyptian has no father," and at first glance, it does indeed seem to suggest that non-Jews are like animals, for their "flesh is as the flesh of asses." Another passage, however, explicitly rules out this interpretation:

> Rab Judah said: It is forbidden to recite the Shema in face of a naked heathen [Gentile]. Why do you say a heathen? The same applies even to an Israelite!—In the case of an Israelite there is no question to him that it is forbidden, but this had to be stated in the case of a heathen. For you might have thought that since Scripture says of them, Whose flesh is as the flesh of asses and whose issue is as the issue of horses, therefore he is just like a mere ass. Hence we are told that their flesh also is called 'nakedness', as it says. And they saw not their father's nakedness.[590]

---

589   Ibid.
590   Babylonian Talmud, Tractate Berachot 25b, Maurice Simon, trans. https://halakhah.com/pdf/zeraim/Berachoth.pdf.

This passage, like the previous one, appears to apply the scriptural passage "whose flesh is as the flesh of asses" to Gentiles, but this one explicitly rules out the interpretation that a Gentile is "just like a mere ass," as it stipulates that one must not recite the Shema ("Hear, O Israel, the Lord your God, the Lord is one") in front of a naked person, whether a Jew or a Gentile.[591] Thus, the antisemites' claim that the Talmud states that non-Jews are not human, but animals, is false. The Talmud is referring to people who are animalistic in their behavior, whose "flesh is as the flesh of asses, and whose issue is like the issue of horses," but there is no indication that this refers to every last non-Jew.

Yet Rabbi Weissman emphasizes: "It does not require a scholar to know that Jews view gentiles very much as human beings, which is reflected across the board in Jewish law. We are allowed to slaughter animals for our consumption or other benefits, but one who slaughters a gentile is a murderer. The Talmud is filled with admonishments to treat all people, gentiles included, with respect and decency, and Torah-true Jews take this very seriously."[592]

This doesn't mean that human beings cannot become animalistic: "At the same time, those who willfully defy God's laws can sink to the lowest of levels, at which point referring to them as animals would be an insult to animals. The Talmud feigns no respect for idolators or other immoral people, Jewish or gentile, but to suggest that decent gentiles are viewed as subhuman is a complete lie and distortion of Talmudic sources."[593] Thus, "a gentile who keeps the Torah (the parts that pertain to him) can reach great spiritual heights, and earns a share in the world to come. Judaism is the only 'religion' that promises

---

[591] Ezekiel 23:20.
[592] Rabbi Chananya Weissman, op. cit.
[593] Ibid.

anyone and everyone eternal reward without predicating this on join-ing the religion."[594]

KILL THEM WHEREVER YOU FIND THEM?

Yet there is worse. For centuries, those who have warned that the Talmud is dangerous have pointed to one passage in particular. In 1240, it was a central focus of the trial of the Talmud in Paris, and those who claim in our own day that Jews constitute a serious threat to the peace and stability of the world cite it frequently. The Talmud states: "Kill the best of the Gentiles."[595]

Taken in isolation, this appears to confirm all the worst claims about the Jews' alleged inveterate hatred of non-Jews and determi-nation to destroy them. There, in one succinct sentence, is the entire genocidal imperative. Yet here again, the reality is less lurid and less threatening. During the 1240 Talmud trial, the man who had been responsible for the Talmud being scrutinized in this way, Nicholas Donin, a convert from Judaism to Christianity, cited this passage. In response, Rabbi Yechiel of Paris asked him if he knew where to find this passage in the Talmud. When Donin admitted that he did not, the rabbi showed him that in the Talmud's minor tractate Soferim, the passage did not say simply, "Kill the best of the Gentiles," but "Kill the best of the Gentiles in time of war."[596]

The offending statement comes in the context of a discussion among rabbis of a passage from the Book of Exodus regarding Pha-raoh's pursuit of the fleeing Israelites: "When the king of Egypt was told that the people had fled, the mind of Pharaoh and his servants

[594] Ibid.
[595] Babylonian Talmud, Tractate Soferim 15:10, *The William Davidson Talmud* (Araha, Cohen, Soncino Press, 1965), https://www.sefaria.org/Tractate_Soferim.15.10?lang=bi.
[596] Bloch, op. cit., 204.

was changed toward the people, and they said, 'What is this we have done, that we have let Israel go from serving us?' So he made ready his chariot and took his army with him, and took six hundred picked chariots and all the other chariots of Egypt with officers over all of them. And the LORD hardened the heart of Pharaoh king of Egypt and he pursued the people of Israel as they went forth defiantly."[597]

Those discussing the passage ask where the horses came from to pull these six hundred chariots that Pharaoh sent out to pursue the Israelites. They couldn't have come from Pharaoh himself, for Exodus says before this: "Behold, the hand of the LORD will fall with a very severe plague upon your cattle which are in the field, the horses, the asses, the camels, the herds, and the flocks."[598] They couldn't have come from the Israelites, for they took their animals with them when they left Egypt: "Our livestock also must go with us; not a hoof shall be left behind, for we must take of them to serve the LORD our God, and we do not know with what we must serve the LORD until we arrive there."[599]

The conclusion follows that they came from the Egyptians who feared God and protected their animals from the plagues. Exodus says: "Then he who feared the word of the LORD among the servants of Pharaoh made his slaves and his livestock flee into the houses."[600] The Egyptians who were disposed to serve the Lord nonetheless supplied Pharaoh with horses so that he could pursue the Israelites. The commentary thus continues: "We find, then, that the cattle driven off by those who feared the word of the L–rd proved to be an impediment

---

[597]   Exodus 14:5–8.
[598]   Exodus 9:3.
[599]   Exodus 10:26.
[600]   Exodus 9:20.

to Israel—whence R. Shimon says: 'the best of the gentiles—kill! The best of the serpents—crush its head!'"[601]

The conclusion is that they came from the God-fearing Egyptians, and so even the Egyptians who revered the God of the Jews to the extent of taking the plagues seriously must be fought if they attack.

The point of the story is thus not to exhort Jews to kill non-Jews wholesale, but to emphasize that when attacked, one should not hesitate to fight against even those among the attackers whom one may wish to spare. It is a call to fight when attacked even against those among the attackers whom the Jews might regard well and respect. It is not a call for Jews to murder non-Jews wholesale, and here again, the behavior of Jews throughout history demonstrates that it has not been understood as such.

For, while those who hate and fear the Jews will claim that this exhortation manifests itself in subversive behavior that undermines Gentile society and results in the long run in the deaths of non-Jews, in any community, some will inevitably not be patient enough to let the subversion play out. The Qur'an directs Muslims to "kill them wherever you find them." Muslim Brotherhood-linked organizations in the West have been accused of working to undermine and subvert Western societies. They do this in order to bring about the ultimate subjugation and death of non-Muslims. However, many Muslims have always been willing to take a more direct approach, attacking non-Muslims at random. Today, even on the streets in France and elsewhere in Europe, knife-wielding jihadis attack and sometimes kill non-Muslims at random in order to receive Allah's rewards for fulfilling his command.[602]

---

[601]   Mekhilta DeRabbi Yishmael, Tractate Vayehi Beshalach 2, Rabbi Shraga Silverstein, trans., https://www.sefaria.org/Mekhilta_DeRabbi_Yishmael%2C_Tractate_Vayehi_Beshalach.2?lang=bi&with=all&lang2=en.

[602]   Qur'an 2:191, 4:89, cf. 9:5.

If Jews, in the same way, understood this bald statement, "the best of the gentiles—kill!," divorced from its context, to mean simply that Jews should kill Gentiles who are perfectly peaceful, minding their own business and not waging war against Jews, why don't we see it happening? It would be entirely reasonable to expect that if such a statement were widely regarded among Jews as a command, at least some Jews would behave in the way all too many Muslims have done and begin attacking random non-Jews.

The Talmudic statement is clearly about not holding back in fighting when responding to aggression, but purveyors of moral equivalence will invoke a handful of Jews who have allegedly committed terror attacks in recent years. It is difficult, if not impossible, to find even one among these cases in which the details aren't hotly controverted. There is simply no case at all of a Jew committing gratuitous violence and ascribing it to the teachings of the Talmud. That glaring fact, when compared to the more than forty-four thousand jihad attacks worldwide since September 11, 2001 (and there were many before that date), most of which were committed by Muslims who explicitly invoked the Qur'an or Allah. This demonstrates the massive difference between the teachings of the Qur'an, so full of calls to violence against non-Muslims, and of the Talmud, which utterly lacks exhortations to violence.

While there is no Qur'anic passage, or any teaching in all of the Islamic corpus, calling for infidels to be treated with respect as persons of equal dignity before Allah, there are numerous passages in the Talmud that do exactly this. One states that "even an idolater who studies the Torah is equal to a High Priest."[603] This idea is derived from the Torah, which states: "You shall therefore keep my statutes and

---

[603] Babylonian Talmud: Tractate Avodah Zarah 3a, A. Mishcon, trans., https://halakhah.com/pdf/nezikin/Avodah_Zarah.pdf.

my ordinances, by doing which a man shall live: I am the LORD."[604]
The Talmud explains: "It does not say 'If a Priest, Levite, or Israelite
do, he shall live by them,' but 'a man' [*haAdam*]; here, then, you can
learn that even a heathen who studies the Torah is equal to a High
Priest!"[605] This passage also demonstrates the falsehood of claims that
the Talmud does not regard non-Jews as human beings at all.

Yet even if the Talmud does not actually regard Gentiles as subhuman, it does seem to devalue their lives. One passage states: "With
regard to bloodshed, if a gentile murders another gentile, or a gentile
murders a Jew, he is liable. If a Jew murders a gentile, he is exempt."[606]
This appears disturbing indeed, but once again, it would be unwise
to take this statement at face value as if it were a simple matter of a
law that is binding upon all Jews.

The key to properly understanding the passage is the fact that it
comes in a section of the Talmud entitled "Sanhedrin," which was the
supreme judicial tribunal for Jews. This passage is about the question
of what penalty is to be administered in particular cases, not of the
morality of the act itself. It also involves an issue of jurisdiction. A
Gentile who kills a Gentile will be tried in the courts of the land. A
Gentile who kills a Jew should also be tried in those courts. Amid the
Gentile persecution of Jews, however, a Jew who was accused of killing
a Gentile could not be assured of a just hearing in the Gentile courts,
as we have seen in blood libel trials. This passage is not saying that
Jews who murder Gentiles should suffer no penalty, but that those
who were accused in this way should not be tried in Gentile courts.

Another translation renders the passages this way: "For murder,
whether of a Cuthean by a Cuthean, or of an Israelite by a Cuthean,
punishment is incurred; but of a Cuthean by an Israelite, there is

---

604   Leviticus 18:5.
605   Avodah Zarah 3a, op. cit.
606   Babylonian Talmud: Tractate Sanhedrin 57a, William Davidson Edition, https://www.
       sefaria.org/Sanhedrin.57a.16?lang=en&with=About&lang2=en.

no death penalty."[607] This translation sheds further light upon what is actually being stated here. "Cutheans" are Samaritans, who accept the Torah but whose understanding of it differs tremendously from how it is understood in Judaism, and who have faced accusations of idolatry. The word "Cuthean" is also often taken to refer not only to Gentiles, but to any idolater, even one who is Jewish. The Talmud itself notes differing opinions on this among the rabbis. One Jewish scholar says of the Samaritans that "there were Tannaim [rabbinic sages] who considered them Jews in many respects and others who saw them as gentiles. In a discussion regarding *teruma* (tithes), we read: 'Rebbi said: "A Cuthean is like a gentile." Rabbi Shimon Ben Gamliel said: "A Cuthean is considered a Jew"' (*Tosefta Terumot* 4:10, 4:12)."[608]

If a Cuthean can be considered a Jew, then the antisemites' view of the passage regarding murder is destroyed. This is not a declaration that Jews who murder Gentiles are not committing any wrongdoing. Given that a Cuthean could be an idolatrous Jew, it is impossible to see this passage as evidence that Judaism devalues the lives of non-Jews.

There is no indication in the Talmud or any Jewish tradition that killing Gentiles is not prohibited as part of the blanket prohibition of murder, which is one of the commandments Jews and Christians believe that Moses brought down from Mount Sinai. Instructions for waging war do not amount to such an exemption. Neither does a discussion of judicial jurisdiction in murder cases involving non-Jewish victims.

---

[607] Babylonian Talmud: Tractate Sanhedrin 57a, H. Freedman, trans., https://halakhah.com/pdf/nezikin/Sanhedrin.pdf.

[608] Rav Alex Israel, "*Sefer Melakhim Bet*: The Second Book of Kings," The Israel Koschitzky Torat Har Etzion, January 19, 2016, https://etzion.org.il/en/tanakh/neviim/sefer-melakhim-bet/melakhim-b-17-shomronim.

Chapter Eight

CONDONING
IMMORALITY?

STEALING FROM NON-JEWS IS PERMITTED?

Yet even if the Talmud teaches that non-Jews' lives are to be respected, foes of the Talmud maintain that Jews are not required to show them any other form of respect; they are permitted, for example, to steal from non-Jews.

The Talmud does indeed take up this question, asking: "Is then the robbery of a heathen permissible?"[609] Here again, the "heathen" is the non-Jew. Immediately after this question is raised, the Talmud answers it: no, robbing Gentiles is not permissible. Rabbi Akiva, one of the foremost Jewish scholars of the second century CE, is

---

[609] Babylonian Talmud: Tractate Baba Kama 113a, E. W. Kirzner, trans., https://halakhah.com/pdf/nezikin/Baba_Kama.pdf.

quoted saying that "the robbery of a heathen is forbidden." He gives a full explanation based on the Torah, which states: "If a stranger or sojourner with you becomes rich, and your brother beside him becomes poor and sells himself to the stranger or sojourner with you, or to a member of the stranger's family, then after he is sold he may be redeemed; one of his brothers may redeem him."[610] This, says Rabbi Akiva, "implies that he could not withdraw and leave him" without paying the money to redeem the man who had sold himself into slavery.[611] The stranger, that is, the non-Jew, cannot simply be robbed.

Yet the Talmud also says that "withholding of a laborer's wage" is forbidden when it involves "one Cuthean from another, or a Cuthean from an Israelite"; however, "an Israelite from a Cuthean is permitted."[612] Yet at the same time, another tractate says of righteous Gentiles: "The prohibitions *you shall not do him wrong, you shall not oppress* and *the wages of a hired servant shall not abide with you all night* apply to him."[613] How can these passages be reconciled? Gil Student explains that the passages regarding withholding wages from workers do not "touch upon the issue of whether a worker is paid; they deal solely with WHEN a worker is paid." Workers must be paid promptly. Student continues:

> The commandments specify that a worker must be paid within that day/night period and that the employer is prohibited from delaying payment. For example, a babysitter who watches children at night must be paid before sunrise of the next day. Similarly, a shoemaker who gives you your shoes during the day

610 Leviticus 25:47–8.
611 Baba Kama 113b, op. cit.
612 Sanhedrin 57a, op. cit.
613 Tractate Gerim 3, *The Minor Tractates of the Talmud*, A. Cohen, trans. (London: Soncino Press, 1965), https://www.sefaria.org/Tractate_Gerim.3.4?lang=bi&with=About&lang2=en. Language slightly modernized for clarity.

must be paid before sunset of that day (Talmud Bava Metzia 110b; R. Yisrael Meir HaCohen Kagan, *Ahavat Chesed*, 1:9:1-2). Even without these commandments, or if the time period has expired, a worker must still receive his wages. If not, the employer is guilty of theft (Talmud Bava Metzia 111a; *Ahavat Chesed*, 1:10:14). These commandments only determine WHEN an employee must be paid.[614]

It is important to recall at this point that the Talmud states that in the opinion of some of the rabbis, the Cutheans could be regarded as Jews. That means that this passage is not even about Jewish relations with non-Jews at all, but about the interaction of religious Jews with those who are not observant, as well as with non-Jews. Gil Student continues: "We therefore see that the Talmud states that the commandments prohibiting holding back a worker's wages do not apply to idolaters, Jewish or gentile. What remains unstated in this passage but is implicit in other passages is that an employer must still pay an idolater his fair wages. He only need not go the extra mile and pay him immediately if there was no pre-arranged payment schedule."[615]

This hardly amounts to a nefarious blanket permission to steal from non-Jews.

The Talmud enjoins Jews to engage in fair dealings with all. A compendium of Jewish law says flatly: "It's forbidden to steal or exploit (even) any amount, whether from a Jew or a non-Jew."[616] There is no equivocation or unclarity in that. The Talmud also forbids Jews from selling non-kosher meat to Gentiles, because they might assume it is

---

[614] Gil Student, "Paying Gentiles' Wages," The Real Truth about the Talmud, https://www.angelfire.com/mt/talmud/wages.html.

[615] Ibid.

[616] Shulchan Arukh, Choshen Mishpat 359, https://www.sefaria.org/Shulchan_Arukh%2C_Choshen_Mishpat.359.1?lang=bi.

kosher, and it is not permitted to deceive them: "And for two reasons they said, a man should not sell to a gentile animals that have become nevelah or terefah [that is, non-kosher]: first because he is deceiving him, and secondly because he in turn might sell it to another Israelite."[617] If deceiving Gentiles is forbidden, it is hard to sustain the idea that stealing from them is permitted.

GENTILE SLAVES?

On April 19, 2024, an imam preached a sermon at Masjid Al-Iman in Fort Lauderdale, Florida; the sermon was livestreamed on the mosque's Facebook page. The imam, whom the mosque did not identify, lamented the alleged misdeeds of the Israelis in Gaza and continued: "We will mention what the Jews believe," he stated, "because you wonder: How come? Why are they such a breed of human beings? It is simply because they are indoctrinated that way. That is their creed."[618]

The imam was, of course, referring to the book that antisemites love to hate. "I will give you the proof," he continued, "from two passages from the Talmud, which is one of the books that the Zionists refer to…. 'Allah created the foreigner, the non-Jew…'—listen to this—'in human form so that they would be suitable to serve the Jews.' This message goes to those who bow—from amongst this Islamic nation—to the Zionists, to the Jews. This is how they look at

---

617   Babylonian Talmud: Tractate Chullin 94a, trans. anon., https://halakhah.com/pdf/kodoshim/Chullin.pdf.

618   "Fort Lauderdale, Florida Friday Sermon: Why Are the Jews Such a Breed of Humans? Their Talmudic Creed Makes It an Honor for Them to Shoot Gazan Babies in Their Incubators; They View Non-Jews as Worthless Animals," MEMRI, April 19, 2024.

you. This is how they see you, as an animal that is in the form of a human being, [created] just to serve them."[619]

This belief was, he said, playing out in Gaza: "We are talking about babies in the incubators in the [Gaza] hospitals—shooting everybody. That's why, because in their creed, we're all animals, and we are worthless. It is an honor for them, and they will be raised in the ranks if they do that."[620] This idea is based on fabricated Talmud quotes that circulates widely these days, such as this one: "When the Messiah comes every Jew will have 2800 Gentile slaves." This is attributed to "Simeon Haddarsen, fol. 56-D," which does not exist.[621]

There is a Talmud passage that states this: "Once the Messiah comes, all the nations will be subservient to the Jewish people, and they will help them prepare whatever is needed for Shabbat."[622] This is, however, about the Messianic age, not daily life now, and is widely interpreted as meaning that the Gentiles will help the Jews serve in a priestly capacity ("help them prepare whatever is needed for Shabbat"), not that they will be slaves in the common understanding of the word.

The imam, however, was not disposed to see any of this as benign and continued: "Now you wonder why they go, they fly from Brooklyn…from under the tunnels there is an airline that goes underground…. I'm joking. They go from under the tunnels straight to Palestine. To do what? To steal the land. Why? Because for them it is permissible to steal from someone who is not a Jew."[623] This we have already seen to be false. Nevertheless, the imam's sermon illus-

---

[619] Ibid.
[620] Ibid.
[621] Nezir Katan, "More Anti-Talmudic Rhetoric: A False Narrative," Katnut d'Katnut, September 4, 2020, https://aronbengilad.blogspot.com/2020/09/more-anti-talmudic-rhetoric-false.html.
[622] Babylonian Talmud: Tractate Eruvin 43b, https://www.sefaria.org/Eruvin.43b.7?lang=bi.
[623] "Fort Lauderdale, Florida Friday Sermon," op. cit.

trated how widespread the idea that the Israelis' supposedly abhorrent behavior is theologically based, and specifically derived from the Talmud, has become.

PEDOPHILIA AND CHILD TRAFFICKING?

The Talmud is also charged with justifying sexual intercourse with non-Jewish girls as young as three years old, thus providing a theological justification for the trafficking and rape of children. Yet this charge is as baseless as it is lurid. One passage used to justify it comes in the course of a discussion about how Jewish men are prohibited from having sexual relations with non-Jewish women, which should cause no offense as many religions and cultures have restrictions upon marriage with outsiders. It is observed that "the Biblical ordinance against such association refers to an [Israelite] married woman; [the Biblical King] David came and extended the law to association with an unmarried woman; and the disciples of the Schools of Shammai and Hillel came and extended it still further to association with a heathen woman."[624]

Then the discussion turns to the question of the age at which these restrictions begin. One of the rabbis states: "It is therefore to be concluded that a heathen girl [communicates defilement] from the age of three years and one day, for inasmuch as she is then capable of the sexual act she likewise defiles by a flux."[625]

Bokser notes that this passage, although it is used to support the claim that the Talmud justifies pedophilia, actually teaches just the opposite:

---

[624] Babylonian Talmud: Tractate Avodah Zarah 36b, Abraham Cohen, trans., https://halakhah. com/zarah/index.html.
[625] Ibid., 37a.

Another charge also supported with the formidable evidence of direct "quotation" is that the Talmud holds non-Jews in contempt, and encourages Jews to abuse them. "A gentile girl who is three years old can be violated," one Talmud baiter quotes from Abodah Zarah 37a. What the passage does say is the very opposite. It applies the customary modesties expected between Jewish boys and Jewish girls to the mixed relationships of Jewish boys and non-Jewish girls; it declares that these modesties must be observed after the girl passes her third birthday. To explain the importance of these modesties at so early an age the Talmud adds the comment that after her third birthday the girl might be subject to intimacies of a sexual character. It is this explanatory comment which the baiters of the Talmud have torn out of its context and distorted into an alleged sanction for immorality.[626]

Indeed. This Talmudic passage is a stipulation regarding the nature of the sin that would be committed in such a case, not the fact that it is a sin at all. The Talmud is not saying that one may have sexual intercourse with non-Jewish girls before they turn three years and one day old; it is saying that on top of the enormity of the rape of a child, one is also religiously defiled if the girl has reached that age. Rabbi Student explains: "Nowhere is the Talmud permitting such behavior. Sex outside of a marriage is strictly forbidden (Maimonides, *Mishneh Torah*, Hilchot Ishut 1:4, Hilchot Na'arah Betulah 2:17; *Shulchan Aruch*, Even HaEzer 26:1, 177:5) as is this obvious case of

---

[626]   Bokser, op. cit., 15-6.

child abuse. The Talmud is only discussing ex post facto what would happen if such a case arose."[627]

Not only is such behavior prohibited, but the rabbis speak strongly against any kind of sexual impurity, including masturbation. An illuminating discussion of this issue turns on an interpretation of this biblical passage: "And when you spread forth your hands, I will hide My eyes from you; even when you make many prayers, I will not hear; your hands are full of blood."[628] One rabbi explains: "These are those men who commit adultery with the hand, by masturbating. Likewise, the school of Rabbi Yishmael taught: When it is stated in the Ten Commandments: 'You shall not commit adultery' (Exodus 20:13), this means that there shall not be adultery among you, whether you masturbate by hand or whether with one's foot."[629] The same passage goes on to excoriate those who "marry minor girls who are not yet capable of bearing children," for such marriages delay the Messiah's coming.[630]

Bloch likewise points out that according to *Shulchan Aruch*, a widely consulted manual of Jewish law, "a Jew having intercourse with a non-Jewess is liable to the punishment of 39 stripes; if he did it without having in view marriage or a lasting relation the punishment is doubled; if he lives with her in concubinage it is trebled. Besides, the offender is reminded of the Divine punishment, viz. that he will die without offspring. According to Sanhedrin 82b, the ravisher of a non-Jewess is liable to the curse of God."[631]

Rabbi Weissman states: "Nowhere does the Talmud or any Torah source permit violating anyone sexually. A husband is not even allowed

---

[627] Gil Student, "The Talmud Does Not Permit Sex with a Three Year Old," The Real Truth about the Talmud, http://talmud.faithweb.com/articles/three.html.

[628] Isaiah 1:15.

[629] Babylonian Talmud, Tractate Niddah, 13b, trans. anon., https://www.sefaria.org/Niddah.13b.

[630] Ibid.

[631] Bloch, op. cit., 289.

to be with his wife against her will—not just forcibly against her will, God forbid, but even without appeasing her first. According to the Talmud (based as always on derivations from the written Torah) men and women are not even allowed to be secluded together, let alone touch or engage in relations outside of marriage."[632] He points out the inconsistency of the antisemites' accusations: "The same people who feign horror that a Jewish man will not shake a woman's hand or sit next to her on cramped planes, accusing him of being insensitive, sexist, and prudish, turn around and pretend these same men are lascivious predators!"[633]

This passage, Rabbi Weissman explains, "is in no way a statement about the attitude of Jews toward gentiles. It is a legal source (one of several) which teaches the principle that a girl's hymen will regenerate up to the age of three, which means that she retains her legal status as a virgin. In addition, the spiritual impurity from 'flux' is clearly noted in the written Torah, and the sages of the Talmud merely explain that this phenomenon applies to females of any age. This is not a license to have intercourse with someone younger than that—which is self-understood by everyone except cherry-pickers hunting for something, anything to grossly distort."[634]

Are we then to believe that the same group of authorities who take such a severe view of masturbation, fornication, adultery, rape, and child marriage, and specifically speak of non-Jews in connection with all this, also cheerfully approve of the defilement of non-Jewish girls who are less than three years and one day old? Some who are convinced that the Talmud is the evil handbook of a group that is the perennial enemy of all that is good will have no trouble thinking this, but those who are more reasonable will see the absurdity of this.

---

[632] Rabbi Chananya Weissman, email to author, March 6, 2024.
[633] Ibid.
[634] Ibid.

Another passage that haters of the Talmud invoke in order to claim that the rabbis permit, and even encourage, the rape of small children is this: "One passage that haters of the Talmud adduce as evidence has a rabbi stating: "When a grown-up man has intercourse with a little girl it is nothing, for when the girl is less than this, it is as if one puts the finger into the eye; but when a small boy has intercourse with a grown-up woman he makes her as 'a girl who is injured by a piece of wood.' and [with regard to the case of] 'a girl injured by a piece of wood.' itself, there is the difference of opinion between R. Meir and the Sages."[635]

It seems at first glance to be supremely callous, and indeed, criminal, to say that "when a grown-up man has intercourse with a little girl it is nothing," but here again, the import of the passages is not what the antisemites claim it to be. The discussion in which this statement appears is about dowries. It is not at all about what acts are permitted or forbidden. Thus, when it is said that "when a grown-up man has intercourse with a little girl it is nothing," it is not saying that this act is of no importance, with no moral evaluation or any opprobrium attached to it. It is saying that a girl who has been subjected to this can still be considered a virgin when it comes to questions of the dowry, which is different for virgins and non-virgins.[636]

Rabbi Weissman explains that this, too, "is a legalistic statement, not a philosophical or ideological statement, which is clear both from the context and general Jewish law. 'It is as if one puts a finger into the eye' is nothing more than a metaphor for legalistic purposes; the Talmud is stating that the girl's legal status as a virgin has not been affected by the act. It is no way a justification for the act; the criminal will still be punished, but the girl's status remains unchanged.

[635] Babylonian Talmud: Tractate Kethuboth 11a, Samuel Daiches, trans., https://halakhah. com/pdf/nashim/Kethuboth.pdf.
[636] Student, "The Talmud Does Not Permit Sex with a Three Year Old," op. cit.

Conversely, an adult woman would be 'damaged goods' in regards to her 'value' on the marriage market. One should also note that the second part of the passage refers to the small boy as the aggressor, which clearly indicates that it is *only* the legal status of the woman as a result of the intercourse that is under discussion, not the permissibility of the act itself."[637]

Judaism clearly does not regard these passages the way that the Talmud's detractors do, as it does not permit marriages to small children. Rabbi David Novak of the Union for Traditional Judaism explains that "although child marriages were quite common in biblical and early rabbinic times for whatever reasons, already in the late Tanaitic period (2nd century C.E.) there was growing disapproval of this practice."[638] In the third century CE, "an actual rabbinic decree was issued either in the name of the Babylonian authority Rav or the Palestinian authority Rabbi Eleazar: 'It is forbidden (*asur*) for one to contract a marriage for his daughter when she is still a minor (*ketanah*) until she is mature and can say "it is X whom I want."'"[639]

Once again also, the most significant proof that the Talmud's foes are willfully twisting what the book actually teaches is the fact that child marriage is not a common phenomenon in Jewish communities. The organization Girls Not Brides, which is dedicated to calling attention to and ending the phenomenon of child marriage, notes that such marriages are illegal in Israel, but they "reportedly still take place under the radar." In 2016, the Israeli Knesset's Law and Justice Committee published a report stating that "716 child marriages took

---

[637] Rabbi Chananya Weissman, op. cit.

[638] Rabbi David Novak, "Concerning the Marriage of a Minor Girl," Union for Traditional Judaism, https://utj.org/viewpoints/responsa/concerning-the-marriage-of-a-minor-girl/.

[639] Ibid.

place between 2014 and 2015."[640] There are about a million and a half girls under eighteen in Israel out of a population of nine million. If one thousand were married as children, that would amount to 0.0001 percent of the total population. Also, as there are two million Muslim Arabs in Israel, these 716 girls cannot all be assumed to be Jews.

To put that number in perspective, consider the fact that there are about ten million girls under eighteen in Afghanistan, and Girls Not Brides estimates that 28 percent of them are married before they turn nineteen. That's nearly three million girls out of a population of forty million people, or 0.75 percent of the total population.

In Israel, the children in question are generally post-pubescent. Girls Not Brides reports that "child marriages are prevalent in the Haredi (Jewish ultra-Orthodox) community and Arab groups living in Israel. In Hasidic customs, the sons of distinguished rabbis often marry young in order to minimise the time between puberty and the wedding to prevent them from engaging in inappropriate thoughts."[641] This establishes that even the child marriages that take place among Haredi Jews involve post-pubescent girls. No one is talking about marriage to three-year-olds.

Some who traffic in these lists of Talmud proof texts will brush all this aside, pointing out that the problem is not so much marrying children, but that the Talmud gives license for the mistreatment of non-Jewish girls from an extremely young age, thus leading to rampant child trafficking. Yet there is frequently less to this than meets the eye. When a tunnel was discovered under the Chabad headquarters in Brooklyn, New York, in December 2023, complete with a soiled mattress and a broken high chair, wild rumors flew about a massive network of tunnels being used for child trafficking. The only thing

---

[640]   "Israel," GirlsNotBrides.org, https://www.girlsnotbrides.org/learning-resources/child-marriage-atlas/regions-and-countries/israel/#:~:text=Religion%3A%20Child%20marriages%20are%20prevalent,from%20engaging%20in%20inappropriate%20thoughts.

[641]   "Israel," GirlsNotBrides.org, op. cit.

that was lacking was any actual evidence of any child trafficking, or of any other illegal activity.[642]

While there are criminals and perverts in all cultures and groups, it is a recurring tendency of antisemites to claim that the actions of Jewish individuals demonstrate the existence of a worldwide Jewish imperative to subvert and destroy non-Jewish society. The antisemites do not explain why they believe that Jews scrupulously follow the Talmud when it supposedly tells them to kill, steal from, and rape Gentiles with impunity, while steadfastly ignoring its many passages directing them to treat people with dignity and respect.

EIGHT GENDERS

While some of the charges against the Talmud are quite ancient, a new one has appeared in recent years: the Talmud, we're told, provides justification for today's fashionable gender madness by teaching that there are no fewer than eight genders. This is supposedly all part of the larger Jewish effort to subvert and destroy Gentile society.

This claim apparently originated among leftist Jews, although Jew-haters have eagerly picked it up. In November 2015, the Jewish Telegraphic Agency (JTA) published an article entitled "The 8 Genders of the Talmud," which began by noting that "the Jewish obligation to observe commandments is traditionally divided along male/female lines: men pray three times daily, while women don't have to; men put on tefillin, while women do not," and then delivered the punch line: "But what if we told you that the foundation for all this was wrong? That Judaism recognized not two, but as many as

---

[642] Sofia Ahmed and Jeff Cercone, "Antisemitic Claims about Brooklyn Synagogue Tunnel Spread on Social Media," PolitiFact, January 12, 2024.

eight genders?"[643] The article goes on to explain that "the Mishnah describes half a dozen categories that are between male and female, such as *saris* or *ailonit*—the terms refer to a non-reproductive version of the male or female body, respectively—and categories that refer to ambiguous or indeterminate gender."[644] Then the claim is made: "these terms seem to provide the refreshing view that a binary view of gender in Judaism is relatively recent."[645]

This view has become popular in circles that find it affirming of their own choices. In October 2022, a Jewish writer went through the Talmud's alleged teaching about eight genders and concluded that "the rabbis never question that a variety of different kinds of nonbinary bodies exist in the world. And for some rabbis, being born into a particular body is akin to saying that a person's body was created by God. We see statements that assert that the born eunuch was created by the 'hand of heaven.'"[646]

This is, however, an example of reading into a text what one wishes to find there. The Talmud doesn't actually delineate six or eight genders at all. A writer who went through the Talmudic passages that are used to buttress the claim that the Talmud teaches eight genders found that the Talmud says nothing of the kind. One of the supposed eight genders *tumtum*, "lacking sexual characteristics," is not a "distinct gender category," but is actually "a doubt concerning whether the *individual* in question is a male or a female."[647] The other categories beyond male and female are likewise all males or females who have a deformity, have suffered an injury, or are otherwise unable to

643 Leah Falk, "The 8 Genders of the Talmud," Jewish Telegraphic Agency, November 9, 2015.
644 Ibid.
645 Ibid.
646 Max Strassfeld, "Turning to the Talmud to Find Gender Diversity that Speaks to Today," *The Revealer*, October 6, 2022.
647 "How Many Genders Are Actually in the Talmud?," Boshes HaBayis, July 25, 2022. https://bosheshabayis.com/posts/talmudic_genders/.

function normally as men or women. This does not, however, create any new genders, and the author thus concludes:

> Reading modern ideas into the Torah is nothing new and is often an integral part of how Torah is learned throughout the generations. What is particularly frustrating about this instance is not modern ideas about gender being read into the Talmud, but the thin textual support upon which these readings are based and then presented to unwitting readers of JTA and other publications as fact. The Talmud does in fact acknowledge diversity in sexual characteristics and even the inability of the gender binary to completely encompass the reality of human sexual function. The claim of 6 (or 8) Talmudic genders however, requires reading Talmudic sources extremely liberally (perhaps even dishonestly) to reach a predetermined conclusion and does a disservice to the actual conversation there is to be had about the Talmudic view of sex and gender.[648]

WHAT ABOUT JESUS?

Numerous critics of the Talmud point to passages within it that depict Jesus Christ in a negative light. It's not certain that all the passages that are often taken to refer to Jesus are really talking about him at all. There are a handful of passages that discuss a personage named Jesus, or variants on that same, but it is not an open-and-shut certainty that all or even any of these are about the Jesus of the New Testament.

---

[648]   Ibid.

Rabbi Student points out that "it is important to keep in mind that there are many people in the Talmud with the same names. R. Aaron Hyman in his biographical work on the sages of the Talmud, *Toldot Tannaim VeAmoraim*, lists 14 Hillels, 61 Elazars, and 71 Hunas. Josephus lists approximately twenty different men named Jesus, at least ten of whom lived in the same time as the famous Jesus."[649]

In his fascinating and groundbreaking book *Jesus in the Talmud*, the contemporary scholar Peter Schäfer discusses passages from the Talmud that have been taken as referring to Jesus, carefully analyzing each and presenting a case for whether or not each one actually refers to Jesus Christ, and what its implications are.[650] Some Talmudic stories, however, are unmistakably about Jesus Christ and have caused horror and anger among Christians for centuries. Schäfer notes that one Talmudic passage states:

> It was taught in a *baraita* [oral tradition] that Rabbi Eliezer said to the Rabbis: Didn't the infamous ben Stada take magic spells out of Egypt in a scratch on his flesh? They said to him: He was a fool, and you cannot cite proof from a fool. That is not the way that most people write. Incidentally, the Gemara asks: Why did they call him ben Stada, when he was the son of Pandeira? Rav Ḥisda said: His mother's husband, who acted as his father, was named Stada, but the one who had relations with his mother and fathered him was named Pandeira. The Gemara asks: Wasn't his mother's husband Pappos ben Yehuda? Rather, his mother was named Stada and he was named ben Stada after her. The Gemara asks: But wasn't his mother

649   Gil Student, "The Jesus Narrative in the Talmud," The Real Truth about the Talmud, https://www.angelfire.com/mt/talmud/jesusnarr.html.
650   Peter Schäfer, *Jesus in the Talmud* (Princeton, New Jersey: Princeton University Press, 2007).

Miriam, who braided women's hair? The Gemara explains: That is not a contradiction. Rather, Stada was merely a nickname, as they say in Pumbedita: This one strayed [*setat da*] from her husband."[651]

From this passage, we learn that there was a certain Ben Stada whose mother's name was Miriam, and who worked magic spells that he learned in Egypt. Miriam was a hairdresser and an adulteress, and Ben Stada's real father was named Pandeira. There is no indication in the Talmudic text that any of this has anything to do with Jesus of Nazareth, although his mother's name was Miriam (the Hebrew form of the name Mary) also, and he was renowned for working miracles.

Confirmation that this passage is indeed about Jesus Christ, or was at least widely understood as being about him, comes from the pagan Greek philosopher Celsus, who wrote a polemic against Christianity in the second century CE. Celsus's work is lost, but the Christian theologian Origen wrote a lengthy reply to his charges, in the course of which he quoted Celsus extensively. Describing one of Celsus's arguments against Christianity, Origen writes:

And since, in imitation of a rhetorician training a pupil, he introduces a Jew, who enters into a personal discussion with Jesus, and speaks in a very childish manner, altogether unworthy of the grey hairs of a philosopher, let me endeavor, to the best of my ability, to examine his statements, and show that he does not maintain, throughout the discussion, the consistency due to the character of a Jew. For he represents him disputing with Jesus, and confuting Him, as he thinks, on many points; and in the first place, he accuses

---

[651] Babylonian Talmud, Tractate Shabbat 104b, William Davidson Edition, https://www.sefaria.org/Shabbat.104b.5?lang=bi&with=About&lang2=en; Schäfer, op. cit., Kindle edition, 34.

Him of having invented his birth from a virgin, and upbraids Him with being born in a certain Jewish village, of a poor woman of the country, who gained her subsistence by spinning, and who was turned out of doors by her husband, a carpenter by trade, because she was convicted of adultery; that after being driven away by her husband, and wandering about for a time, she disgracefully gave birth to Jesus, an illegitimate child, who having hired himself out as a servant in Egypt on account of his poverty, and having there acquired some miraculous powers, on which the Egyptians greatly pride themselves, returned to his own country, highly elated on account of them, and by means of these proclaimed himself a God.[652]

The Jew whom Celsus invokes says several things that correspond to the Talmud text: Jesus is described as illegitimate, with an adulterous mother, although in Celsus's version, she is a spinner rather than a hairdresser. Jesus has miraculous powers, which he picked up in Egypt. Origen goes on to describe more of what Celsus conveys from his Jewish source about Jesus. Schäfer points out that in doing so, Celsus removes any ambiguity about who is actually being discussed in the Talmudic passage about Miriam the adulterous hairdresser:

But let us now return to where the Jew is introduced, speaking of the mother of Jesus, and saying that when she was pregnant she was turned out of doors by the carpenter to whom she had been betrothed,

---

[652]   Origen, Contra Celsum, I.28, Frederick Crombie, trans. From *Ante-Nicene Fathers*, Vol. 4. Alexander Roberts, James Donaldson, and A. Cleveland Coxe, eds. (Buffalo, NY: Christian Literature Publishing Co., 1885.) Revised and edited for New Advent by Kevin Knight. http://www.newadvent.org/fathers/04161.htm.

as having been guilty of adultery, and that she bore a child to a certain soldier named Panthera; and let us see whether those who have blindly concocted these fables about the adultery of the Virgin with Panthera, and her rejection by the carpenter, did not invent these stories to overturn His miraculous conception by the Holy Ghost: for they could have falsified the history in a different manner, on account of its extremely miraculous character, and not have admitted, as it were against their will, that Jesus was born of no ordinary human marriage.[653]

Celsus's soldier named Panthera is clearly the Pandeira who is Ben Stada's real father in the Talmud. Thus, the Talmud is saying that Jesus was not born of a virgin, but of an adulteress, and that he did not work miracles by the power of God, or much less because he was God incarnate, but because he had mastered some magic tricks in Egypt.

Gil Student, however, maintains that this passage is not about Jesus Christ at all, for three reasons:

1. Mary Magdalene was not Jesus' mother. Neither was Mary a hairdresser.
2. Jesus' step-father was Joseph. Ben Stada's step-father was Pappos Ben Yehudah.
3. Pappos Ben Yehudah is a known figure from other places in talmudic literature. The Mechilta Beshalach (Vayehi ch. 6) has him discussing Torah with Rabbi Akiva and Talmud Berachot 61b has Pappos Ben Yehudah being captured and killed by Romans along with Rabbi Akiva. Rabbi Akiva lived during the second half of the first century and the first half of

---

[653] Origen, op. cit., I, 32; Schäfer, op. cit., 38–9.

the second century. He died in the year 134. If Pappos Ben Yehudah was a contemporary of Rabbi Akiva's, he must have been born well after Jesus' death and certainly could not be his father.[654]

If it is about Jesus of Nazareth, this passage is an obvious rejoinder to and mockery of the Christian doctrine of the virgin birth. Contrary to the Christian narrative, it asserts instead that Jesus was not born of a virgin, but has no earthly father in the conventional sense only because he was born of adultery. Schäfer, however, contends that the Talmud is also making a theological point:

> This story of the adulterous mother and her bastard son is the perfect counternarrative to the New Testament's claim that Jesus was born from a virgin betrothed to a descendant of the house of David. Against the New Testament story (with its inherent inconsistency between "husband" and "betrothed") the Talmud concocts its drastic counternarrative of the adulteress and her bastard son (presumably from a Roman soldier), demonstrating the complete absurdity of any Davidic (and hence Messianic) claim. As a bastard, Jesus belongs to the community of Israel only in a limited sense. One of the restrictions of his status implies that he cannot enter a legitimate marriage with a Jewish woman and father Jewish children—let alone found a congregation that claims to be the "new Israel."[655]

---

[654] Gil Student, "The Jesus Narrative in the Talmud," The Real Truth about the Talmud, https://www.angelfire.com/mt/talmud/jesusnarr.html.

[655] Schäfer, op. cit., 141.

Thus, in the Talmud, Jesus is not only not a miracle worker and not the Messiah; he is arguably not even Jewish. Nor does the polemic end with that. Another Talmudic passage states:

On Passover Eve they hung the corpse of Jesus the Nazarene after they killed him by way of stoning. And a crier went out before him for forty days, publicly proclaiming: Jesus the Nazarene is going out to be stoned because he practiced sorcery, incited people to idol worship, and led the Jewish people astray. Anyone who knows of a reason to acquit him should come forward and teach it on his behalf. And the court did not find a reason to acquit him, and so they stoned him and hung his corpse on Passover eve. Ulla said: And how can you understand this proof? Was Jesus the Nazarene worthy of conducting a search for a reason to acquit him? He was an inciter to idol worship, and the Merciful One states with regard to an inciter to idol worship: "Neither shall you spare, neither shall you conceal him" (Deuteronomy 13:9). Rather, Jesus was different, as he had close ties with the government, and the gentile authorities were interested in his acquittal. Consequently, the court gave him every opportunity to clear himself, so that it could not be claimed that he was falsely convicted.[656]

This adds to the charges of adultery for his mother and fakery or sorcery for Jesus himself the new charge of leading the Jewish people astray by tempting them to worship idols. It does depict Jesus being hanged just before Passover, as the Gospel of John depicts him as

---

[656] Babylonian Talmud, Tractate Sanhedrin 43a, William Davidson Edition, https://www.sefaria.org/Sanhedrin.43a.20-26?lang=en&with=About&lang2=en; Schäfer, op. cit., 96.

being crucified on the day of preparation, that is, the day before the beginning of Passover.[657]

There are a handful of other Talmudic passages that Schäfer determines are references to Jesus. By far, the most frequently cited in antisemitic literature is one that depicts notorious sinners being punished in hell with punishments befitting the crimes they committed while alive. It depicts a necromancer, Onkelos bar Kalonikos, nephew of the Roman emperor Titus, who was responsible for the destruction of the Temple in 70 CE. Onkelos raises Titus from the dead and asks him a series of questions, including: "What is the punishment of that man in the next world?," with "that man," the Talmud tells us, being "a euphemism for Titus himself."[658] Titus replies: "That which he decreed against himself, as he undergoes the following: Every day his ashes are gathered, and they judge him, and they burn him, and they scatter him over the seven seas."[659] He burned the Temple, so he himself is burned.

Onkelos then raises Balaam from the grave and asks him the same question: what is his punishment in the next world? Balaam answers: "He is cooked in boiling semen, as he caused Israel to engage in licentious behavior with the daughters of Moab."[660] Onkelos then raises Jesus of Nazareth from the dead and asks him the same question as well. Jesus is depicted as responding: "He is punished with boiling excrement. As the Master said: Anyone who mocks the words of the Sages will be sentenced to boiling excrement. And this was his sin, as he mocked the words of the Sages."[661]

---

[657] John 19:31.

[658] Babylonian Talmud, Tractate Gittin, 57a, William Davidson Edition, https://www.sefaria.org/Gittin.56b.18-57a.13?lang=en; Schäfer, op. cit., 122–5.

[659] Ibid.

[660] Ibid.

[661] Ibid.

The Talmud does not explain how this punishment is fitting, as are those of Titus and Balaam. Peter Schäfer speculates that it is because of the Christian doctrine and practice of the Eucharist, in which the faithful consume the body and blood of Christ. Jesus says, "he who eats my flesh and drinks my blood has eternal life, and I will raise him up at the last day."[662] When the Pharisees rebuke Jesus because his disciples do not perform the ritual washing of their hands before they eat, Jesus says: "Do you not see that whatever goes into the mouth passes into the stomach, and so passes on? But what comes out of the mouth proceeds from the heart, and this defiles a man. For out of the heart come evil thoughts, murder, adultery, fornication, theft, false witness, slander. These are what defile a man; but to eat with unwashed hands does not defile a man."[663]

Schäfer suggests that the Talmud depicts Jesus suffering in boiling excrement in hell as a response to this idea: "The rabbinic counternarrative about Jesus' punishment would then ironically invert his attack on the Pharisaic purity laws by having him sit in excrement and teaching him (as well as his followers) the lesson: you believe that only what comes out of the mouth defiles, well, you will sit forever in your own excrement and will finally understand that also what goes into the mouth and comes out of the stomach defiles."[664]

Whatever the significance of the punishment might be, the Talmud oddly follows it up with this: "The Gemara comments: Come and see the difference between the sinners of Israel and the prophets of the nations of the world. As Balaam, who was a prophet, wished Israel harm, whereas Jesus the Nazarene, who was a Jewish sinner, sought their well-being."[665]

---

[662] John 6:54.
[663] Matthew 15:17–20.
[664] Schäfer, op. cit., 133.
[665] Gittin, 57a, op. cit.

Still, after depicting someone as sitting in boiling excrement in hell, it is hardly mitigating to observe that he meant well. And if the Jews are such blasphemers, many Christians have said since October 7, how can any Christian ally with them in good conscience?

Yet once again, it must be stated: the Talmud is not binding upon Jews in every detail. There is no obligation that Jews must even believe that Jesus of Nazareth is punished this way. Gil Student, among others, doesn't even believe that this passage refers to the Jesus of Christianity at all. He says that the "Yeshu," or Jesus, who is referred to in this story, was "most likely a prominent sectarian of the early first century BCE who deviated from rabbinic tradition and created his own religion combining Hellenistic paganism with Judaism. While Yeshu may be the proto-Jesus some scholars point to as inspiring the early Christians, he is definitely not the man who was crucified in Jerusalem in the year 33 CE."[666]

Despite the lack of certainty or unanimity about whether the passage about Jesus in hell refers to Jesus Christ at all, it has, along with other Talmudic passages that are often understood as referring to Jesus of Nazareth, gone viral after Hamas's October 7 massacre. The response to expressions of support for Israel not infrequently takes the form of statements to the effect of "You'll reconsider your support for Israel after you see what the Talmud says about Jesus and his mother." One Orthodox Christian priest stated: "To see this Zionist state allied with the United States of America, a Knesset that is full of, the vast majority who think Jesus Christ was a false rabbi, properly executed for his blasphemy, and this is our chief ally? For what? For what?"[667]

Obviously, the United States is, with its First Amendment provision that Congress shall make no law respecting the establishment of

---

[666] Gil Student, "Jesus in the Talmud," The Real Truth about the Talmud, https://www.angelfire.com/mt/talmud/jesus.html.

[667] Thaddeus Patrick, X, April 30, 2024, https://twitter.com/jacfalcon/status/1785468882683318584.

a religion, not a Christian state. The US does not conclude alliances only with Christian states, but the priest's disgust toward Israel is clearly based, at least in part, upon the Jews' rejection of Christ. He doesn't refer to the Talmud's statements about Jesus, but they would no doubt only reinforce his disgust. It has become common since October 7 for quotations from the Qur'an about the Jews, or the Muslim holy book's exhortations to jihad violence, to be met with calls to look into what the Talmud says about Jesus and Mary.

Indeed, the harshness of the Talmudic passages has led some Christians to believe that Islam is closer to Christianity than Judaism, and more charitable toward it, for the Qur'an reveres Jesus as a prophet of Allah, although it sharply rebukes those who believe in the divinity of Christ and who say that he is the Son of God, one of the Trinity, and that he was crucified. The Qur'an says that those who call Jesus the Son of God are under Allah's curse.[668]

This is better than saying that Jesus is suffering tortures in hell only in that it is reserving this fate for his followers, not for the central figure of Christianity himself, and that the suffering of hell is not described or even mentioned. Yet Allah's curse lands one there, and so in the final analysis, hell is hell.

Ultimately, however, no one should be surprised or even particularly offended that the Talmud contains anti-Christian material. If the rabbis who participated in the conversations that the Talmud records and those who compiled, copied, and preserved the Talmud had believed the Christians' case for the contention that Jesus was the Jewish Messiah, they would have become Christians. It should also be remembered that the Talmud's polemic against Christianity cannot be taken in isolation or understood as some gratuitous attack against the meek and mild followers of the gentle Savior. On the contrary,

---

[668] Qur'an 9:30.

the Talmud was compiled at a time of rising tensions between Jews and Christians.

The Babylonian Talmud was first published in the fifth century CE, in the decades following Augustine of Hippo saying that the Jews were suffering from "madness," John Chrysostom calling their festivals an "abomination" that God himself hated, and Ambrose of Milan applauding a mob's destruction of a synagogue. Chrysostom said that "the synagogue is not only a brothel and a theater; it also is a den of robbers and a lodging for wild beasts."[669]

Whether one will find that less offensive than the Talmud's statements about Jesus will depend on one's own point of view. Christians throughout the ages have persecuted Jews for killing their Messiah and Savior, while simultaneously teaching that it was not any group in particular, but the sins of every human being that put him on the cross.

From the Jewish standpoint, the charge of deicide is as offensive as the Talmudic picture of Jesus as a false Messiah who is punished for his imposture is from a Christian one. Each of what are often referred to as the three great Abrahamic religions regards the others as false and misguided. And even if the most disparaging of these stories does indeed refer to Jesus of Nazareth, this has never been understood among Jews as giving them a license to mistreat Christians, any more than the Christian charge of deicide should have led Christians to think that they had a license to be uncharitable to Jews. In the latter case, however, it all too often did.

It is also important to bear in mind that as the Babylonian Talmud was being compiled, Christians were persecuting Jews, not the other way around. Christian polemicists who profess shock, horror, and indignation at the Talmud's depiction of Jesus without considering the Christian polemic against Jews coupled with Christian

---

[669] John Chrysostom, *Against the Jews*, trans. unknown, Homily 1, III.1.

persecution of Jews should remember Jesus's exhortation: "Physician, heal yourself."[670]

This is even clearer in light of the fact that some Christians have treated post-Christian religious claims in exactly the same way that the Talmud treats Jesus Christ. In Dante's *Divine Comedy*, one of the people Dante encounters in hell is none other than the Islamic prophet Muhammad:

> Even a wine-cask, that has lost a stave in the middle or the end, does not yawn as widely, as a spirit I saw, cleft from the chin down to the part that gives out the foulest sound: the entrails hung between his legs: the organs appeared, and the miserable gut that makes excrement of what is swallowed.
>
> While I stood looking wholly at him, he gazed at me, and opened his chest with his hands, saying: 'See how I tear myself: see how Mahomet is ripped! In front of me, Ali goes, weeping, his face split from chin to scalp, and all the others you see here, were sowers of scandal and schism in their lifetimes: so they are cleft like this. There is a devil behind who tears us cruelly like this, reapplying his sword blade to each of this crowd, when they have wandered round the sad road, since the wounds heal before any reach him again.[671]

Muhammad and Ali are split open from the chin to the anus because they were "sowers of scandal and schism." Dante certainly isn't the Talmud; he is in no sense an authoritative Christian source, but in his depiction of Muhammad, he reflects the common Christian

---

[670] Luke 4:23.
[671] Dante Alighieri, *Inferno*, Canto XXVIII, A. S. Kline, trans., 2000, https://www.poetryintranslation.com/PITBR/Italian/DantInf22to28.php.

belief of his day regarding the prophet of Islam. A fresco depicting Muhammad in hell, as per Dante's description, remains to this day in the church of San Petronio in Bologna, Italy, although it is difficult to approach, not well-lighted, and under constant guard, so as to prevent Islamic jihadists from destroying it.

Nowadays, with so many Christian clerics eager to affirm their respect and love for the prophet of Islam, it is easy to find Christians who will disavow Dante and call for the removal of the fresco from the church, or at the very least, insist that not all Christians think of Muhammad that way. That is undeniable, just as it is undeniable that not all Jews accept the Talmud's passages of anti-Christian polemic as articles of faith.

Still, that polemic in the Talmud is unfortunate. It is as unfortunate as the anti-Jewish polemic in patristic Christian literature. Both have helped create a climate of suspicion and misunderstanding where there could have been mutual respect. It is, perhaps, human nature that those who differ in belief will criticize the beliefs of others, and that is perfectly understandable. Those who do this, however, should have the intellectual consistency and generosity not to cry foul when the same thing is done to their own beliefs. Also, it must be borne in mind that while antisemites insist that the Talmud influences Jewish behavior in all manner of fields, most Jews have not studied the Talmud and are unfamiliar with its contents. Many do not even have a clear idea of what it is. They certainly do not take random statements as immutable divine commands that must be obeyed. The idea that Jewish behavior is heavily influenced by the Talmud is itself an antisemitic myth and ridiculous on its face.

As long as passages criticizing the other religions are not presented as pretexts to justify violent or immoral behavior against the adherents of the other religions, there is no reason for them to impede friendly relations or the obligations of charity between people of the differing faiths. As Thomas Jefferson famously put it, "It does me no injury for my neighbour to say there are twenty gods, or no god. It neither picks my pocket nor breaks my leg."[672] Nor does our neighbor's belief in a different God or religion free us from the obligation of charity toward him. The Talmud's passages about Jesus have been represented as an indication of the deep and abiding hatred that every individual Jew has for the central figure of Christianity, and not only for him, but for his followers and for the civilization they made. There is no foundation for this assumption.

---

[672]   Thomas Jefferson, *Notes on the State of Virginia* (Philadelphia: Prichard and Hall, 1788), 169.

Chapter Nine

BLOOD LIBELS

SACRIFICING A CHILD

In the eyes of some, it is always the Jews' fault. If the Talmud doesn't actually teach Jews to subvert and destroy non-Jewish society, the rationale for persecuting them must be found elsewhere.

One common theme that runs through all the accusations against Jews throughout history is the claim that they deserve what they have suffered because they have committed such heinous crimes. Examining the causes of Germany's defeat in World War I, Hitler declared: "If we pass all the causes of the German collapse in review, the ultimate and most decisive remains the failure to recognize the racial problem and especially the Jewish menace."[673] Even as Germany lay in ruins and Hitler was preparing to commit suicide, he still blamed

---

[673]   Hitler, *Mein Kampf,* op. cit., 327.

the Jews: "If the nations of Europe are once more to be treated only as collections of stocks and shares of these international conspirators in money and finance, then those who carry the real guilt for the murderous struggle, this people will also be held responsible: the Jews!"[674]

The Holocaust was the result of this kind of diagnosis. And after the jihad attacks on October 7, 2023, leftist and Muslim spokesmen in the West insisted that the Hamas massacre of 1,200 Israelis was justified "resistance" after decades of alleged Israeli occupation and oppression.

Both Hitler and the Hamas apologists followed a long-established pattern. For centuries in Europe, persecutions of the Jews found justification in claims that they had committed unspeakable acts, including the ritual sacrifice of Christian children.

These claims had their roots, as we have seen, in pre-Christian allegations going back to Antiochus IV Epiphanes and possibly even before that, to Damocritus. Those charges, however, involved the Jews engaging in the blood sacrifice of an adult. The fifth-century ecclesiastical historian Socrates Scholasticus seems to have recorded the first claim that Jews had killed a Christian child. Socrates states that in fifth-century Syria, near Antioch where John Chrysostom taught that "the synagogue is not only a brothel and a theater; it is also a den of robbers and a lodging for wild beasts," and that the Jews "renewed their malevolent and impious practices against the Christians, and drew down upon themselves deserved punishment":

> At a place named Inmestar, situated between Chalcis
> and Antioch in Syria, the Jews were amusing them-
> selves in their usual way with a variety of sports. In
> this way they indulged in many absurdities, and at

---

674 "Adolf Hitler: Political Testament (April 29, 1945)," Jewish Virtual Library, https://www.jewishvirtuallibrary.org/hitler-s-political-testament-april-1945.

length impelled by drunkenness they were guilty of scoffing at Christians and even Christ himself; and in derision of the cross and those who put their trust in the Crucified One, they seized a Christian boy, and having bound him to a cross, began to laugh and sneer at him. But in a little while becoming so transported with fury, they scourged the child until he died under their hands. This conduct occasioned a sharp conflict between them and the Christians; and as soon as the emperors were informed of the circumstance, they issued orders to the governor of the province to find out and punish the delinquents. And thus the Jewish inhabitants of this place paid the penalty for the wickedness they had committed in their impious sport.[675]

In Socrates's history, this immediately follows a similar story in which Christians are the perpetrators:

There was a woman at Alexandria named Hypatia, daughter of the philosopher Theon, who made such attainments in literature and science, as to far surpass all the philosophers of her own time. Having succeeded to the school of Plato and Plotinus, she explained the principles of philosophy to her auditors, many of whom came from a distance to receive her instructions. On account of the self-possession and ease of manner, which she had acquired in

---

[675] Socrates Scholasticus, *Church History*, A.C. Zenos, trans. From *Nicene and Post-Nicene Fathers, Second Series*, Vol. 2, Philip Schaff and Henry Wace, eds. (Buffalo, New York: Christian Literature Publishing Co., 1890), VII, 16. Revised and edited for New Advent by Kevin Knight, http://www.newadvent.org/fathers/26017.htm.

consequence of the cultivation of her mind, she not infrequently appeared in public in the presence of the magistrates. Neither did she feel abashed in coming to an assembly of men. For all men on account of her extraordinary dignity and virtue admired her the more.

Yet even she fell a victim to the political jealousy which at that time prevailed. For as she had frequent interviews with Orestes, it was calumniously reported among the Christian populace, that it was she who prevented Orestes from being reconciled to the bishop. Some of them therefore, hurried away by a fierce and bigoted zeal, whose ringleader was a reader named Peter, waylaid her returning home, and dragging her from her carriage, they took her to the church called *Cæsareum*, where they completely stripped her, and then murdered her with tiles. After tearing her body in pieces, they took her mangled limbs to a place called Cinaron, and there burnt them. This affair brought not the least opprobrium, not only upon Cyril, but also upon the whole Alexandrian church. And surely nothing can be farther from the spirit of Christianity than the allowance of massacres, fights, and transactions of that sort. This happened in the month of March during Lent, in the fourth year of Cyril's episcopate, under the tenth consulate of Honorius, and the sixth of Theodosius.[676]

The differences between the stories are as intriguing as the similarities. In both, the mobs are carried away with hatred for a rival

---

[676]   Ibid., VII. 15.

faith and commit murder as a result. Socrates, however, takes care to note that of the killing of the pagan philosopher Hypatia, "surely nothing can be farther from the spirit of Christianity than the allowance of massacres, fights, and transactions of that sort." Yet he says nothing of the kind about Judaism, thereby leaving the impression that the torture and murder of a little Christian boy did not violate the teachings of the perpetrators' religion.

It is also striking, however, that Socrates is quite specific about the time and place where Hypatia was murdered, noting even the month when the murder happened, the names of the relevant officials at the time, and the name of the church where it took place. On the other hand, he doesn't offer anything comparable to that wealth of detail about the Jews' alleged murder of the Christian boy. He says that it took place in Inmestar, a town so insignificant that there is virtually nothing else said about it in history beyond this incident itself, and he doesn't name the governor of the province who was supposedly given the responsibility of identifying and punishing those who were guilty of this crime.

Socrates's story of Jews crucifying a Christian boy is so vague that it is impossible to confirm and likewise impossible to refute; it is scarcely more than a rumor, and could have been just that, a story devised in order to justify the persecution of Jews.

Certainly, the blood libel accounts of the Middle Ages had that character.

BLOOD MIXED INTO MATZOHS?

One of the first of these comes from twelfth-century England, where "the perfidious Jews" (as they were styled in the Church's liturgy for Good Friday) were said to have sacrificed a child, a pure and innocent

Christian baby, in order to demonstrate their hatred for God and his Christ and to satisfy the requirements of their blood rituals.

The first and largest hole in this narrative is the fact that the Jews have no such rituals. The blood libel stories most commonly involve the Jews draining the blood from their victim in order to mix it into their Passover matzohs. The Torah, however, clearly forbids the consumption of blood: "For the life of the flesh is in the blood; and I have given it for you upon the altar to make atonement for your souls; for it is the blood that makes atonement, by reason of the life. Therefore I have said to the people of Israel, No person among you shall eat blood, neither shall any stranger who sojourns among you eat blood."[677]

Many modern purveyors of Jew-hatred, however, insist that it doesn't matter what the Torah says, for as we have seen, they maintain that Jews, after the destruction of the temple in Jerusalem, don't follow the Torah anyway. They insist that the religion of the rabbis, the Judaism of the Talmud, is quite different from the Judaism of the Torah. Yet this argument gets them nowhere closer to their goal, for the Talmud, like the Torah, nowhere allows for blood sacrifice of any kind, much less human sacrifice. Even opponents of contemporary Judaism agree: Eitan Bar writes that in the absence of the temple, the rabbis replaced the system of animal sacrifice that the Torah delineates not with some new system of blood sacrifice, but with their teachings: "if the Sinai covenant was based on the blood of the sacrifices, the rabbis' 'new covenant' was established upon the rabbis and their traditions."[678] Not on new blood sacrifices.

Rabbi Chananya Weissman notes in reference to the Torah passage that "Tanach (the written Torah, what you call the Bible or Old

---

[677] Leviticus 17:11–2.
[678] Bar, op. cit., 18.

Testament) clearly forbids eating blood in the strongest of terms."[679] In fact, "there is not a single statement to the contrary anywhere in the Talmud or rabbinic literature (in fact, those who accuse Jews of eating the blood of gentiles provide no source, and claim it is hidden, while still claiming the Talmud somehow justifies it). It is quite clear from the Torah that the sum total of the ingredients of matza are flour and water. Jews were eating matza on Pesach long before Christians and Muslims even existed. The laws of matza (and the puzzling absence of any reddish color that could resemble blood) have never changed, and cannot change. No one has the power to change them."[680]

Even a seventeenth-century convert from Judaism to Christianity, Friedrich Albrecht Christiani, affirmed the same thing at a time when such charges were all too common:

> Although there is indeed a general slander against the Jews, that they follow after Christian children, and when they have got hold of them, stab them horribly, extract the blood from them, using it with certain ceremonies as a remedy...I am able, as a born Jew (who without boasting, know well all their customs, having myself practised, or at any rate seen with my eyes, most of them) to asseverate by God, that the whole time I was connected with Judaism, I never heard among them of such dealings with Christian children, much less that they had ever had Christian blood or had ever used it in the aforesaid manner.[681]

---

[679]   Rabbi Chananya Weissman, op. cit.

[680]   Ibid.

[681]   Hannah R. Johnson, *Blood Libel: The Ritual Murder Accusation at the Limit of Jewish History* (Ann Arbor: The University of Michigan Press, 2012), 50.

Also, in virtually every case, there was no evidence adduced to support them, or that evidence consisted of confessions obtained under torture. Yet it is also true that no members of any religious group have ever followed the teachings of their religion with one-hundred-percent fidelity; however, if some group of Jews at some point were found actually to have killed a Christian child, this would not mean what the European Christians in the twelfth century and thereafter took it to mean, that the killers were acting in accord with the actual teachings of Judaism and that the Jews as a whole were guilty and thus deserved collective punishment. It would, instead, be the act of a group of criminals. Such an act would carry no larger significance than any other criminal act; people who commit such acts can be found among every group on the planet.

It cannot be honestly maintained that any form of Judaism allows for human sacrifice or for the ingestion of the blood of the victim. Nevertheless, there was intense hostility between Jews and Christians, which is understandable in light of the rhetoric of John Chrysostom, Augustine, and others and the license to plunder and kill Jews that the words of Ambrose of Milan and, much later, Martin Luther, once again among others, provided. This made for an environment in medieval Europe in which Jews frequently served as convenient scapegoats, and pretexts to brutalize them were all too readily found.

NOT EVERYONE BELIEVED THESE STORIES

Even throughout the Middle Ages, many Christians didn't believe claims that Jews sacrificed Christian children in bloody secret rituals and then consumed their blood in matzoh. As we have seen, Pope Gregory X (1271–6) was one of several popes who condemned the blood libels. "Even as it is not allowed to the Jews in their assemblies presumptuously to undertake for themselves more than that which is permitted them by law," Gregory wrote, "even so they ought not to suffer any disadvantage in those [privileges] which have been granted them."[682]

The pope expressed annoyance that they persisted in not becoming Christian but added that "inasmuch as they have made an appeal for our protection and help, we therefore admit their petition and offer them the shield of our protection through the clemency of Christian piety. In so doing we follow in the footsteps of our predecessors of blessed memory, the popes of Rome Calixtus, Eugene, Alexander, Clement, Celestine, Innocent, and Honorius."[683]

As we have also seen, Gregory declared the invalidity of Christian testimony against Jews in blood libel cases and then pointed out that many blood libel claims arose from Christians who wanted to bring harm to Jews:

> Since it happens occasionally that some Christians lose their Christian children, the Jews are accused by their enemies of secretly carrying off and killing these same Christian children and of making sacrifices of the heart and blood of these very children. It happens, too, that the parents of these children or some other Christian enemies of these Jews, secretly hide these very children in order that they may be able to injure these Jews, and in order that they may be able to extort from them a certain amount of money by redeeming them from their straits.
>
> And most falsely do these Christians claim that the Jews have secretly and furtively carried away these

---

682   Pope Gregory X, "Letter on Jews, (1271–76) - Against the Blood Libel," Internet Medieval History Sourcebook, https://sourcebooks.fordham.edu/source/g10-jews.asp.

683   Ibid.

children and killed them, and that the Jews offer sacrifice from the heart and blood of these children, since their law in this matter precisely and expressly forbids Jews to sacrifice, eat, or drink the blood, or to eat the flesh of animals having claws. This has been demonstrated many times at our court by Jews converted to the Christian faith: nevertheless, very many Jews are often seized and detained unjustly because of this.

We decree, therefore, that Christians need not be obeyed against Jews in a case or situation of this type, and we order that Jews seized under such a silly pretext be freed from imprisonment, and that they shall not be arrested henceforth on such a miserable pretext, unless—which we do not believe—they be caught in the commission of the crime. We decree that no Christian shall stir up anything new against them, but that they should be maintained in that status and position in which they were in the time of our predecessors, from antiquity till now.[684]

In the thirteenth century, a pope was acknowledging that some Christians fabricated blood libel claims against Jews in order to do them harm. Yet after October 7, Jew-haters have revived ancient blood libel claims and take the fact that there was a large number of accusations as evidence that the Jews must have been guilty of doing this at least on *some* occasions; with so much smoke, they claim, there must have been fire. Today's antisemites would do well to read and ponder the words of Pope Gregory X, and also to remember that they were issued only after many Jews who were completely innocent of the

---

[684]   Ibid.

charges leveled against them had been victimized and even killed over such claims. It is also noteworthy that the Christian behavior Pope Gregory discusses—extorting money from them on the basis of false accusations—would be imitated by others even centuries later, particularly the National Socialist regime in twentieth-century Germany.

Yet even after Pope Gregory issued this extraordinary acknowledgment of Christian persecution of Jews, blood libel allegations continued. Over a century later, the English poet Geoffrey Chaucer wrote "The Prioress' Tale," one of his *Canterbury Tales*. It depicts Satan inciting Jews to murder a Christian child who sang a hymn to the Blessed Virgin as he made his way through the Jewish ghetto. Even after the Jews kill him, the boy is miraculously enabled to continue singing.

MOCKERY OF CHRIST'S CRUCIFIXION

The twelfth-century *Peterborough Chronicle*, one of the *Anglo-Saxon Chronicles*, contains this entry for the year 1137:

> Now we will relate in part what happened in King Stephen's time. In his reign the Jews of Norwich bought a Christian child before Easter, and tortured him after the same manner as our Lord was tortured; and on Good Friday hanged him on a cross, in mockery of our Lord, and afterwards buried him. They supposed that it would be concealed, but our Lord showed that he was a holy martyr. And the monks took him, and buried him with high honor in the minster. And

through our Lord he works wonderful and manifold miracles, and is called St. William.[685]

This was the earliest account of St. William of Norwich, the accusation of ritual murder of a Christian child to be leveled against the Jews in medieval Europe. Images of little William's "martyrdom" proliferated in churches in and around Norwich. The accounts of that "martyrdom" echo the claim that the ecclesiastical historian Socrates Scholasticus made centuries earlier, that the Jews tortured their young victim by hanging him on a cross.

This in itself is an indication that we are not in the realm of soberly reported history. As if it weren't enough to claim that the Jews mix blood in the matzohs, the gratuitous detail is added that they mock the crucifixion of Christ while obtaining that blood. This became a common element of these stories: blood libels from Gloucester, England, in 1168; Blois, France, 1171; and Saragossa, Spain, in 1182 contain this feature, as do many thirteenth-century accounts.[686]

Around 1255, the English chronicler Matthew Paris represents the Jewish sacrifice, including the crucifixion, of a Christian child as a full-blown Jewish ritual, to which Jews are summoned by being told that "a sacrifice" was about to take place. This account of the murder of the boy who became known as "Little Saint Hugh of Lincoln" not only includes the Jews mocking the crucifixion of Christ but also repeats Apion's ancient claims against the Jews:

> In this same year, about the time of the festival of
> the apostles Peter and Paul, the Jews of Lincoln stole
> a boy of eight years of age, whose name was Hugh;

---

685 "*The Anglo-Saxon Chronicle*, Part 7: A.D. 1102–1154, Online Medieval and Classical Library Release #17," The Medieval and Classical Literature Library, http://www.mcllibrary. org/Anglo/part7.html. Language slightly modernized.

686 Haim Hillel Ben-Sasson and Dina Porat, "Blood Libel," *Encyclopedia Judaica*, op. cit., III, 775.

and, having shut him up in a room quite out of the way, where they fed him on milk and other childish nourishment, they sent to almost all the cities of England where the Jews lived, and summoned some of their sect from each city to be present at a sacrifice to take place at Lincoln; for they had, as they stated, a boy hidden for the purpose of being crucified. In accordance with the summons, a great many of them came to Lincoln, and on assembling, they at once appointed a Jew of Lincoln as judge, to take the place of Pilate, by whose sentence, and with the concurrence of all, the boy was subjected to divers tortures. They beat him till blood flowed and he was quite livid, they crowned him with thorns, derided him, and spat upon him. Moreover, he was pierced by each of them with a wood knife, was made to drink gall, was overwhelmed with approaches and blasphemies, and was repeatedly called Jesus the false prophet by his tormentors, who surrounded him, grinding and gnashing their teeth. After tormenting him in divers ways, they crucified him, and pierced him to the heart with a lance. After the boy had expired, they took his body down from the cross and disembowelled it; for what reason we do not know, but it was asserted to be for the purpose of practising magical operations.[687]

As in Apion's account, the victim is first fattened up before being sacrificed, although why this is done remains unclear; even these wild stories don't contain accusations of cannibalism. Matthew of Paris

---

[687] Matthew Paris, *Matthew Paris's English History*, J. A. Giles, trans. (London: Henry G. Bohn, 1854), III, 138–9.

even has a Jew confess to the whole thing. "There was present at this scene," notes Matthew, "one John of Lexington, a man of learning, prudent and discreet, and he thus addressed the people: 'We have already learned,' said he, 'that the Jews have not hesitated to attempt such proceedings as a reproach and taunt to our Lord Jesus Christ, who was crucified.'" How he learned this, John does not say, and the only evidence for it is repeated accusations.

John of Lexington then proceeds to threaten a Jew with dismemberment and death unless he confesses, and his unfortunate captive duly does so:

> ...then addressing a Jew who had been seized upon, and the one whose house the boy had gone into whilst at play, and who was therefore an object of greater suspicion than the others, he said to him: "Wretched man, do you not know that a speedy death awaits you? Not all the gold of England will avail to ransom you, and save you from your fate. However, I will tell you, undeserving as you are, how you may preserve your life and prevent your limbs from being mutilated. Both of these I will guarantee to you, if you will without fear or hesitation disclose to me, without any falsehood, all that has happened on this occasion."
>
> The Jew, whose name was Copin, thinking he had found a means of escape, then said, "My lord John, if by your deeds you will repay me for my statements, I will reveal wonderful things to you." Then, being urged on and encouraged by the eloquence of John to do so, he continued: "What the Christians say is true; for almost every year the Jews crucify a boy as

an insult to the name of Jesus. But one is not found every year, for they only carry on these proceedings privately, and in out of the way places."[688]

Here we see revived the pre-Christian claim of Apion that the Jews engage in human sacrifice on a regular basis. Meanwhile, the claim that the Jews would capture and crucify Christian children became so common that it even made its way into the legal code of Spain in 1263, *Siete Partidas*: "We have heard it said that in certain places on Good Friday the Jews do steal children and set them on the cross in a mocking manner."[689] Yet even here, when it was given the solemn affirmation of appearing in a code of law, it did not rise above the level of hearsay: "We have heard it said…"

Yet blood libel accounts frequently contained the claim that the Jews had ritually crucified their victim. These claims constitute one of the reasons why these stories don't ring true: there is no point to the detail that the Jews mocked the crucifixion even within the parameters of the blood libel charges themselves. The crucifixion mockery is not represented as part of some ritual or as some required element involved in obtaining blood for matzohs.

This element of the blood libel stories seems added in solely in order to horrify Christians and emphasize to them that the Jews are their enemies and hate all that they hold most dear. This was another instance of projection, for it was the Christians who were filled with hatred toward the Jews and committing acts of violence against them, not the other way around. Among many Christians, Jews were despised and regarded as evil, while the evil that was done to the Jews as a result of that perception was not regarded as evil. The blood libel stories are the work of Christians, written in order to incite hatred

---

[688]   Ibid., 139.
[689]   Ben-Sasson and Porat, "Blood Libel," *Encyclopedia Judaica*, op. cit.

of Jews among those who read them. In that, they were certainly successful.

SIMON OF TRENT

Historian Ronnie Po-Chia Hsia notes that in fifteenth-century southern Germany, there were several blood libel allegations, including one that was discovered to be a hoax at the time:

> 1430 Ravensburg: Several Jews were executed when a dead child was discovered in the cellar of their house.

> 1440 Meran: A Christian planted a dead child in the house of a Jew, but the plot was uncovered by the captain of the town.

> 1440 Landshut: Fifty-five Jews were burned on a ritual murder charge.

> 1461 Trent: Blond Gretchen's missing son was found in Samuel's shed.

> 1461 Pfullendorf: Jews were condemned to death for alleged child murder.

> 1470 Endingen: Jews were accused of the alleged murder of a Christian family and burned to death.

> 1473 Trent: When the body of the missing Eysenposch child was found, Bishop Hinderbach ordered it to be examined for cut marks.

1475 Regensburg: rumors of a blood libel in the town
reached the Jews of Brixen.[690]

This is a social contagion. Human beings are imitative, and so
when one group sees the Jews being blamed and persecuted, they
come up with accusations of their own. The accusations fed upon one
another, fanned by a Franciscan preacher, Bernardine da Feltre, who
visited Trent in March 1475 and preached a series of Lenten sermons
warning against the evils of the Jews. On April 2, 1475, Good Friday, a three-year-old boy named Simon was found dead in the cellar
of a prominent Jew named Samuel in the northern Italian city of
Trent. The subsequent trial invoked several of these earlier incidents
in support of the central claim that the Jews had murdered Simon in
order to use his blood in their rituals. One of those who testified was,
according to Hsia, "a German woman, Margaritha, nicknamed 'the
blond Gretchen.'"[691]

Through a translator, as she spoke only German, Blond Gretchen
recounted that back in 1461, fourteen years before the present proceedings, her son Joachim, who wasn't even three years old, went
missing on Good Friday, just as Simon had. She looked everywhere
for him but could not find him. Finally, she obtained permission from
the local bishop (who was responsible for the protection of the local
Jews) to search Samuel's house. She didn't find Joachim there, but
Hsia notes that "she noticed a secret place in Samuel's shed."[692] The
next day, however, she heard Joachim calling for her and returned in
the company of the local priest to Samuel's shed, where, she said, she
found Joachim alive and unharmed. Nevertheless, the boy died two

690 R. P-Chia Hsia, *Trent 1475: Stories of a Ritual Murder Trial* (New Haven, Connecticut: Yale University Press, 1992), 92–3.
691 Ibid., 31.
692 Ibid., 32.

months after this; Blond Gretchen added that Samuel had denied any knowledge of how the boy had gotten into his shed.[693]

Did Joachim's death have anything to do with Samuel? Whether it did or not, this curious incident from fourteen years before would now help to seal his fate and that of the Jewish community in Trent. At the time that little Simon's body was found, the practice of judicial torture was well-established in Trent, as elsewhere in Europe, and taken for granted as a reliable means of extracting the truth from recalcitrant witnesses. The arms of those who were brought in for questioning were bound behind their backs, and they were hoisted up on a device known as the strappada, pulled up on ropes by pulleys; if they didn't give the answers that their questioners wanted, they would be dropped down suddenly from great heights, or whipped, or weights were attached to their feet.

Those who scoff at the efficacy of such methods in eliciting the desired response have never been forced to endure them. The desired response, however, is not necessarily even remotely congruent with the actual truth. The fifteenth-century trial records in the case of Simon of Trent make that clear. Of one Jew of Trent, Seligman, it is said: "the podestà [the civil magistrate of the city], seeing that he did not want to reveal the truth, ordered him to be stripped, bound, and hoisted up."[694] At that, Seligman panicked and provided the story the podestà wanted to hear: he named the Jew who had murdered Simon and described how it had been done, although his testimony did not coincide with that exacted from other members of the Jewish community later.

Others, however, held out longer. Joaff, another Jew of Trent, had been the one who brought the dead body of Simon out of the water. After hoisting Joaff up on the ropes, the podestà "asked him how the

---

693   Ibid.
694   Ibid., 35.

child got there in the first place." Despite the pain he was enduring, Joaff, Hsia notes, "insisted that the Jews were framed."[695] Joaff even told the podestà: "It is not true that Jews kill Christian children. He has only heard this charge from Christians."[696]

Samuel likewise endured as much as he could, and even while being tortured, he asked the magistrates what gave them the idea that the Jews used the blood of Christians in their rituals:

> On the strappada, he said he knew "the blond Gretchen" but denied she had ever accused him of kidnapping her son. Stating he had never done anything wrong, Samuel told the magistrates they were doing him an injustice. Left dangling in the air, he asked the podesta where he had read or learnt that Christian blood was useful in Jewish rites. Giovanni de Salis answered he learnt it from the Jews and asked for "the truth, the truth!" The scribe recorded the following scene:

> He [Samuel] answered: He has said it and they are torturing him unjustly. At that, it was ordered to make him jump two or three arm's length. So there he hung and said: "God the Helper and Truth help me!" And after he had been hanging for two-thirds of an hour, it was ordered to let him down and return him to prison.[697]

Finally, under even more severe torture, Samuel confessed to murdering Simon. Likewise under torture, another one of the Jews of Trent "explained that Jews used blood to celebrate Passover when

---

695   Ibid., 37.
696   Ibid.
697   Ibid., 40.

the Red Sea turned into blood and destroyed the Egyptian army."[698] There was no truth to that, but the authorities of Trent neither knew that nor cared. Now they not only had the confession of the supposed perpetrator, but the theological justification within Judaism that indicted the entire community.

The entire community was duly punished. Samuel and fourteen other members of the Jewish community in Trent, that is, all the men of the community, were burned at the stake. The women of the community were imprisoned for three years and released only after the pope intervened on their behalf.

That was, however, not even close to the end of the matter. Amid questions that the trial had been irregular even by the standards of the day, Pope Sixtus IV ordered a full investigation. On June 20, 1478, he issued a papal bull declaring his approval of the proceedings. Hsia states that "the commission of cardinals, who had diligently examined all pertinent records, concluded that the trial was conducted in conformity with legal procedure."[699] Sixtus did, however, warn the local bishop not to allow "any Christian, on this or any other occasion, without papal judgment, to kill or mutilate Jews, or extort money from them, or to prevent them from practicing their rites as permitted by law."[700]

Yet even this gesture of magnanimity was only partial. During the controversy, many Jewish children had been taken from their mothers to be raised as Christians. Sixtus had no problem with this, but he asked that the local bishop, Johannes Hinderbach, allow children of Jewish women who had been baptized to return to their mothers. The only way they could get their children back was to become Christian.

---

698   Ibid., 41.
699   Ibid., 127.
700   Ibid.

The pope's admonition that there be no violence against Jews was frequently ignored. Hsia notes that "in 1478, ritual murder accusations were raised against the Jews of Reggio and Mantua; in 1479, in Arena, near Milan, a trial was conducted; in 1480, several Jews living at Portobuffuola near Treviso were executed on the charge of child kidnapping; the same year, a similar accusation was heard in Verona. The chain of anti-Jewish events was manifest in Vicenza: from the report of the alleged murder of Simon in 1475, to the Lenten sermons of the Franciscan Nicholas in 1476, leading to the termination of all contracts with Jewish moneylenders in 1479, concluding with the expulsion of all Jews in 1486."[701]

Bishop Hinderbach, meanwhile, began an initiative that would make the memory of Simon of Trent endure for centuries. He began to popularize the idea that three-year-old Simon of Trent was a child martyr, murdered by the haters of Christ out of their entrenched enmity toward God. Other alleged victims of Jewish ritual murder had been venerated as saints before Simon, but Simon's cult grew larger and more rapidly than the others.

Hundreds of miracles were attributed to little Simon's intercession. All over northern Italy, churches began to feature paintings and frescoes of the holy toddler, to the extent that on November 4, 1475, the Doge of Venice, Pietro Mocenigo, ordered a halt to it all in order to prevent massacres of the Jews in his domains. He ordered that "no person of any condition may dare or presume in any place to depict or have depicted, or buy or sell [images] of that little boy called Simon of Trent who was killed, as they say, by the Jews, or to preach about him in either public or to write in print anything about these miracles."[702]

---

[701] Ibid., 128–9.

[702] Jeanette Kohl, "A Murder, a Mummy, and a Bust: The Newly Discovered Portrait of Simon of Trent at the Getty," *Getty Research Journal*, 10 (10), 39, 2018.

The doge's order was to no avail. Devotion to Simon, featuring the little boy in poses that resembled those of the Christ Child, continued to spread in northern Italy and beyond. Trent became a popular pilgrimage site. In 1588, over one hundred years after the boy's body had been found, Pope Sixtus V beatified him. Blessed Simon of Trent, as he was then called, became known as Simon, the patron of victims of kidnapping and torture. Bernardine da Feltre, the Franciscan preacher who had whipped up anti-Jewish sentiment in Trent just before Simon's body was found and became a leading proponent of the cult of Simon after the trial, was likewise beatified in 1654.

THE ROMAN CATHOLIC CHURCH AFFIRMS BLOOD LIBELS

Despite papal condemnations of blood libel charges from Pope Gregory X and others, in the beatification of Simon of Trent, the Roman Catholic Church thus gave the full weight of its authority to the idea that Jews, on occasion, committed ritual murder of Christian children. The guilt of Samuel of Trent had been exacted under torture, and the whole premise that Simon had been ritually killed was based on a false claim about Jewish belief and practice; nevertheless, Simon was now a holy figure, a miracle worker, the recipient of the petitions of the faithful, and a repository of their hopes. Roman Catholics who beseeched his prayers or his aid didn't trouble themselves with doubts about whether the whole incident really happened; they trusted the Church to tell the truth about such matters. The legend, born in hatred and torture, had become fact.

Even in the late nineteenth century, the Roman Catholic Church kept alive the notion that Jews sometimes killed Christian children for their blood. Between December 1880 and April 1884, the Vatican biweekly *Civiltà Cattolica* published thirty-six furiously antisemitic articles, and some revived old blood libel charges against the Jews. An article that appeared in June 1881 actually claimed that the Talmud itself commanded Jews to kill Christians.[703]

In October 1883, *Civiltà Cattolica* ran a story about Eszter Solymosi, a fourteen-year-old Catholic girl who had been found dead in the village of Tiszaeszlar, Hungary. Fifteen Jews were put on trial on charges that they had ritually murdered young Eszter in order to obtain her blood; *Civiltà Cattolica* endorsed the proceedings and stated that Jews were "required, in view of their piety, religion and rite to kill Christians and take their blood for their own liturgical and sacramental rites."[704]

That wasn't all. In a January 8, 1884 article, *Civiltà Cattolica* claimed that Jews were "using Christian blood in Jewish rites in contemporary synagogues."[705] In another article that was published on January 23, 1884, the same publication stated that Jews "ritually extract blood" from adults as well as children and mixed the blood not only in Passover matzohs, but in cake that was sold to Christians.[706] The same issue contained three full articles on this supposed practice of the Jews. One claimed, with the all-caps hysteria of a twentieth-century tabloid, that "ALL JEWS need Christian blood every seven years."[707] Another added that a Christian child seized for his or her blood "should be no older than thirteen years old."[708] The third explained that this "blood is needed for Passover."[709]

The Vatican daily *L'Osservatore Romano* was no better. In July 1892, it stated, "It has already been established by many

---

[703] Gomes, "The Vatican's Mouthpieces," op. cit.
[704] Ibid.
[705] Ibid.
[706] Ibid.
[707] Ibid.
[708] Ibid.
[709] Ibid.

unimpeachable witnesses that Jews practice ritual homicides so that they can use Christian blood in making their Passover matzah."[710] In 1898, when the novel *Dracula* was published and was gaining a great deal of attention, the paper said that Jews were vampires, as they thirsted for the blood of Christians.[711] A year later, *L'Osservatore Romano* ran an article entitled "A new ritual murder" after the body of a seven-year-old boy in Hungary was discovered; his throat had been slit.[712] Several weeks later, it published another article, entitled "Jewish ritual murder," in which it addressed "certain" Jews: "Don't throw oil on the fire.... Content yourselves...with the Christians' money but stop shedding and sucking their blood."[713] When several ritual murder cases were found to be baseless and the accused Jews acquitted, *L'Osservatore Romano* claimed that in every case, wealthy Jews had bought off the judges and charged that "the judiciary is entirely in the synagogue's control."[714]

The Church did, however, eventually get around to telling the truth about Simon of Trent. On November 1, 1965, it withdrew "martyr" status from Simon of Trent and declared that the Jews of Trent had been innocent of his death. This came a week after Pope Paul VI had promulgated the decree of the Second Vatican Council stating that the Jews were not guilty of charges of deicide.[715]

This was a generous gesture. How many Jews, however, had suffered violence, harassment, discrimination, or worse in the 490 years between the death of Simon of Trent and that declaration because

[710] Ibid.
[711] Ibid.
[712] Ibid.
[713] Ibid.
[714] Ibid.
[715] "Vatican Annuls Ritual Murder Charge; Declares Jews 'innocent,'" Jewish Telegraphic Agency, November 1, 1965, https://www.jta.org/archive/vatican-annuls-ritual-murder-charge-declares-jews-innocent.

some Roman Catholics and other Christians believed that they were enemies of God who engaged in ritual murder?

THE DAMASCUS AFFAIR

In February 1840, Jews in Damascus were accused of the ritual murder of Tommaso al-Capuci, an Italian Roman Catholic monk, and his Muslim servant. This became the occasion for a convergence of Christian and Islamic antisemitism. According to *The Matzo of Zion*, which was published in Syria and accepts all the allegations against the Jews as axiomatically true, "the Consul General of Egypt wrote to the French Foreign Minister, on April 2, 1840: 'I find myself obliged to present to you a copy of a report, which was sent to Mohammad Ali [the ruler of Egypt] and prepared by a Rabbi who was converted to Islam, that reveals to us the truth that human blood is necessary for the Jewish celebration of Yom Kippur. This strange discovery helps us understand the disappearance of large numbers of people without any knowledge of their fate, and certain Greek slaves bought by the Jews during the war may have disappeared for this reason."[716]

The consul general's source was not above reproach. He or his family may have been threatened, or he may have harbored bitterness toward his former coreligionists and been anxious to defame them.

A number of Jews, however, confessed to these murders, although their confessions were exacted by torture. There was great interest in this case in Europe, with the French consul in Damascus reporting back to Paris. Historian Jonathan Frankel points out that in the reports the consul submitted in February and March 1840, he "made no mention of the violent measures being employed, referring only… to the application of 'an appropriate degree of severity.' Obviously,

---

[716]   Tlass, *The Matzo of Zion*, op. cit.

though, torture was the fuel that alone provided the investigation with its momentum." Frankel observes that this is a recurring phenomenon throughout history: "In this respect, the Damascus affair was essentially no different from hundreds of other such chapters that occur throughout medieval and modern history, involving the ritual-murder cases, of course, but also people accused wholesale of satanism (heretics, witches) or treason (the most notable instances in recent years being the Stalinist show trials). For varying reasons, depending on the time and place, brute force was cloaked in the mantle of justice in order to prove imagined crimes."[717]

All too often, the victims of such treatment have been Jews, with the accusations themselves being taken as ipso facto proof of guilt. In the Damascus case, the Jews of Europe appealed to Muhammad Ali, who, after numerous entreaties, freed the Jews who had been falsely accused and not yet executed. They then obtained a denunciation of the blood libels from the Ottoman sultan himself. There was, however, always an irreducible number of people who would not be convinced by any volume of evidence that these kinds of charges were false.

WHY DID ANYONE BELIEVE THESE CLAIMS?

Haters of Jews today maintain that the sheer number of stories of ritual murder is evidence of their authenticity. Why would so very many people, across so many centuries and such an enormous expanse of territory, claim that Jews were engaging in the ritual murder of Christian children in order to obtain their blood to mix into their Passover

---

[717] Jonathan Frankel, *The Damascus Affair: "Ritual Murder," Politics, and the Jews in 1840* (Cambridge: Cambridge University Press, 1997), 38.

matzoh if at least some of the accusations weren't true? Why would false claims without any basis in reality persist for so very long?

The answer is actually quite clear. Jews in Europe were the objects of hatred and distrust, going back to the ancient charges against them emanating from Christian leaders. Accordingly, not only did suspicion fall on them virtually whenever the perpetrator of a crime was not obvious, but they were also vulnerable over the centuries to false charges from accusers who knew that their accusations would be believed and accepted over the word of a Jew.

One notable example of unscrupulous people scapegoating and victimizing the Jews was the case of a twenty-one-year-old woman named Giuditta Castilliero, who in June 1855 vanished from her aunt's home in Badia, a town in northern Italy that was then part of the Kingdom of Lombardy-Venetia, a client state of the Austrian Empire. Castilliero made a dramatic reappearance on June 25, eight days after her disappearance, and announced, to considerable alarm among the local people, that she had been kidnapped by Jews who had planned to sacrifice her but had managed to get away before they could carry out their nefarious plans.

The Jews, Castilliero told the rapt Badians, had transported her to Verona, where she had been prepared for sacrifice along with a poor, terrified little girl whose ultimate fate she did not know. The Jews opened a vein in one of Castilliero's arms and collected her blood in a basin; she dramatically showed her audience six wounds in her arm. Ultimately, however, one of their servants, a Catholic, had helped her escape.

Having heard Castilliero's story, the Badians determined that one of the local Jews, a prominent thirty-eight-year-old businessman and moneylender named Caliman Ravenna, must have been one of her kidnappers. Castilliero gave a deposition under oath. While Ravenna insisted on his innocence, the local magistrate believed Castilliero's claims, and Ravenna, along with several other Jews who supposedly had acted as his accomplices, was duly charged with public violence. Specifically, the charge was that the Jews had kidnapped Castilliero in order to subject her to ritual murder, purportedly in accord with the "religious superstition of the Jews."[718]

News traveled fast, as the local press assumed the truth of Castilliero's charges. On July 5, 1855, a local newspaper, *Annotatore friulano*, in nearby Udine told its readers about how a "young little peasant" had been brutalized and would have suffered worse if she had not escaped.[719] The Jews were not mentioned, but rumors had already spread far and wide about the case, and everyone knew who the perpetrator supposedly was. Jews in northern Italy began to be verbally abused and threatened.

Then, however, the tide began to turn. This was not medieval Europe, and Jews had some recourse when they were accused in this way. Jewish leaders did what they could to fight back, above all by explaining to anyone who would listen that there is no ritual murder in Judaism. The chief rabbi of Venice, Abraham Lattes, published a refutation of the charges in Veneto's influential paper *Gazzetta uffiziale di Venezia*, which ran it on the front page. The *Corriere Italiano*, an Italian paper in Vienna, accused the *Annotatore friulano* of promoting antisemitism.

The case ultimately fell apart, however, not because the Jews had fought back against the false charges, but because Giuditta Castilliero was caught lying. On July 9, 1855, she was arrested for stealing from

---

[718] Emanuele D'Antonio, "Jewish Self-Defense against the Blood Libel in Mid-Nineteenth Century Italy: The Badia Affair and Proceedings of the Castilliero Trial (1855–56)," *Quest. Issues in Contemporary Jewish History*, 14, December 2018, https://www.quest-cdecjournal.it/jewish-self-defense-against-the-blood-libel-in-mid-nineteenth-century-italy-the-badia-affair-and-proceedings-of-the-castilliero-trial-1855-56/. I am indebted to this article for the entire section on the Castilliero case in Badia.

[719] Ibid.

a family in Legnago. The family had hired her as a maid and then found that she had been purloining items from their home; the thefts took place during the eight days of her disappearance, while Ravenna and his accomplices were supposed to have been preparing her for ritual murder.

Castilliero was arrested for theft. The charges against Caliman Ravenna and the other Jews were dropped, and they were released from jail. Giuditta Castilliero confessed that she had fabricated the whole thing. She was further charged with slandering Ravenna and finally sentenced to six years in prison.

The case of Giuditta Castilliero is reminiscent of several modern-day cases that developed along quite similar lines. In Atlanta, in 1913, a thirteen-year-old girl named Mary Phagan was murdered. It was claimed that she had also been raped, although this was not defini-tively established. Leo Frank, the Jewish manager of the factory where she worked, was accused of the crime, found guilty, and sentenced to be hanged. During his trial, rumors flew that Judaism allowed men to rape non-Jewish women and only forbade them to rape women who were fellow Jews. Outside the courthouse, a mob chanted, "Hang the Jew."[720]

The day before Frank was to be executed, however, Georgia Governor John M. Slaton commuted his sentence to life imprison-ment, whereupon an enraged mob broke into the prison, carried Frank out, and lynched him. Two historians who closely examined the case in the 1950s concluded: "Leo Frank was the victim of one of the most shocking frame-ups ever perpetrated by American law-and-order officials."[721] Historians today generally agree that Frank was innocent and that his trial was a miscarriage of justice tainted by hatred of Jews. Frank was the only Jew ever to have been lynched in

---

[720] Donald E. Wilkes, "Politics, Prejudice and Perjury," *Flagpole Magazine*, March 1, 2000.
[721] Ibid.

the United States, and had he not been Jewish, he would likely not have been convicted at all. None of the men who lynched him were ever prosecuted or even arrested. Like Giuditta Castilliero, they were confirming the prejudices of their times.

The most notorious modern instance of this phenomenon is the case of Tawana Brawley. In 1987, Brawley, a black teenager in Dutchess County, New York, claimed that a group of white men had kidnapped and raped her, and finally smeared her with feces and left her by the side of a road in a plastic bag. A grand jury investigated her claims thoroughly and ultimately found that she had fabricated them, whereupon one of the accused, former Dutchess County prosecutor Steven Pagones, won a defamation suit against Brawley, her attorneys, and race hate agitator Al Sharpton.

Why did Brawley ever think she could get away with telling such a tale, which was as tall as it was incendiary? For the same reason that Giuditta Castilliero likely thought that she could get away with hers. With the American media extremely preoccupied with racism against blacks, it was all too ready to believe, and propagate, claims that powerful white men had victimized a young black woman; Brawley's story exactly fit the narrative the media was trying to propagate about American society. It was a mirror image of many others from earlier periods in American history, when blacks were falsely accused and convicted of crimes in an unmistakably racist atmosphere. As in medieval Europe, those who possessed judicial power were aligned with other powerful forces in society, and groups whom the people in power disliked, most notably the Jews, in all too many cases had no hope of getting a fair hearing in court.

In nineteenth-century Italy, when Giuditta Castilliero had to explain away her eight-day disappearance and deflect attention from scrutiny that might uncover her theft, she also had a ready scapegoat she could falsely accuse: once again, the most despised people in her area were the Jews. She knew that the political and ecclesiastical authorities already regarded them with distaste and that the Jewish community was essentially powerless against such charges, for judges and magistrates would not take the word of a Jew over that of a Christian. Also, although Castilliero herself may not have been aware of the fact, there were abundant precedents in European history of Jews being persecuted on the basis of confessions exacted through torture, particularly in the case of Simon of Trent, whose widespread veneration only demonstrated how much some Europeans wanted to believe stories such as the one Castilliero told. If she had told her tale just a century earlier, she might have gotten away with it.

ARIEL TOAFF

In 2007, an Italian Jewish historian in Israel, Ariel Toaff, delighted antisemites everywhere by publishing a book, *Pasque di sangue. Ebrei d'Europa e omicidi rituali* ("Passovers of Blood: The Jews of Europe and Ritual Murders"), in which he opened the door to the possibility that at least some of the ritual murder accusations had been true. Toaff based his case on the claim that some Jews in medieval Europe ignored the biblical prohibition on the ingestion of blood and used blood in various superstitious rituals:

> In fact, if we turn once again to the compendia of *segullot* [rituals or charms] in use among Jews of German origin, we will find a broad range of recipes providing for the oral ingestion of blood, both human and animal. These recipes are...sometimes complex in preparation, intended to cure ailments and bring about cures, as well as to protect and to cure. For Shabbatai Lipschütz, to arrest the excessive flow of

menstrual blood, it was advisable to dry before the fire and reduce into power a chicken feather soaked with the menstrual blood. The morning afterwards, a spoonful of that powder, diluted in wine and served up to the woman, on an empty stomach, was said to have infallibly produced the desired effect. Another secret medication, collected by Lipschütz and considered of extraordinary effectiveness on the basis of long tradition, was prescribed for women who wished to get pregnant. The recipe provided that a pinch of dried rabbit's blood be dissolved in wine and administered to the patient. As an alternative, a composite of worms and menstrual blood could be of great utility.[722]

Based on the existence of these folk practices, Toaff suggests that some of the stories about Jews kidnapping and killing Christian children in order to obtain their blood for Passover matzohs may have been true or have a basis in actual events. He did not, however, produce any evidence for any Jews, even heretical and irreligious Jews, actually advocating or approving of such a practice. Folk medicine was one thing, and ritual murder was quite another.

After his book caused a storm of controversy, Toaff initially stood his ground: "My research shows that in the Middle Ages, a group of fundamentalist Jews did not respect the biblical prohibition and used blood for healing. It is just one group of Jews, who belonged to the communities that suffered the severest persecution during the Crusades. From this trauma came a passion for revenge that in some cases led to responses, among them ritual murder of Christian children."[723]

---

[722] Ariel Toaff, *Blood Passover: The Jews of Europe and Ritual Murder*, Gian Marco Lucchese and Pietro Gianetti, trans. (Lucchese-Gianetti Editori LLC, 2014), 174.

[723] Alison Weir, "Israeli Organ Harvesting the New 'Blood Libel'?," *Arab News*, August 31, 2009.

Toaff was displaying fuzzy thinking, for "fundamentalist" is a term that is usually used for people who scrupulously observe all the tenets of their religion and admit of no mitigation of the literal meaning of various commands. If these Jews were "fundamentalist," they would not have disrespected the biblical prohibition.

Ultimately, Toaff recanted and withdrew his book, which was taken in some circles as clear evidence that he was telling the truth but that some powerful people didn't want those truths told. His book thus still circulates among Jew-haters, although they make more of it than is there. Even if everything that Toaff initially wrote were true, it would only definitively establish that some Jews contravened Jewish teaching and used blood in superstitious activities. This doesn't establish anything regarding even one claim of ritual murder of Christian or other non-Jewish children or adults. The charges of blood libel against Jews remain more revelatory of the mindset of the accusers than of the accused.

Chapter Ten

HOLOCAUST DENIAL

THE IMMENSE EVENT THAT NEVER HAPPENED

Two months after the October 7 jihad attacks, Syrian President Bashar al-Assad repeated the hoary charge that the Holocaust was a lie, fabricated for political purposes:

> There is no evidence that six million Jews were killed [in the Holocaust]. Perhaps there were holocausts, nobody denies this. True, there were concentration camps, but what shows you that this is a politicized issue, and is not a humanitarian issue, and is not real, how come we talk about these six millions, and not the 26 million Soviets who were killed in that war? Are those six millions more precious? The same acts were everywhere.

There was no method of torture or killing specific to the Jews. The Nazis used the same method everywhere. However, this issue was politicized, in order to falsify the truth, and later to prepare for the transfer of the Jews from Europe to other areas, or [rather] to Palestine. The Jews who came to Palestine are Khazar Jews, from east of the Caspian Sea. They were pagans who converted to Judaism in the eighth century. They emigrated to Europe, and from there, came to this region. They have nothing to do whatever with the [ancient] people of Israel.[724]

Assad's claims appealed to those who have declared the Jews to be a malignant force. E. Michael Jones, who is generally obscure but stands as one of the foremost intellectual lodestars of today's Jew-hatred, posted an article about Assad's statements on X (formerly Twitter), with the comment: "'Syria's Assad claims Holocaust was a lie fabricated to justify creation of Israel' I agree with Assad. #TheHolocaustNarrative."[725]

If the Holocaust didn't happen, or if far fewer than six million Jews were killed, then it stands as the biggest hoax ever perpetrated in the history of mankind, involving tens of thousands of people at all strata of society. It also blunts the force of the contention that Jews have been uniquely targeted for persecution both historically and today and supports the claim that the real problem is the Jews themselves, who perpetrated this massive hoax in order to gain the

---

[724] "Syrian President Bashar al-Assad: There Is No Evidence Six Million Jews Were Killed in the Holocaust; U.S. Financially Helped the Rise of Nazism between the Two World Wars," MEMRI, December 18, 2023.

[725] E. Michael Jones, X, December 20, 2023, https://twitter.com/EMichaelJones1/status/1737 556822746181716.

sympathy of the world and provide cover for their ongoing efforts at subversion and destruction.

It's understandable that Assad and Jones, who share a distaste for Jews and the claim that they are in various ways the cause of most or all of the world's ills, would gravitate to the idea that the mass murder of six million Jews in Europe during World War II was largely a fabrication for political purposes.

This charge, however, is as baseless as the others.

DEALING WITH THE DENIERS

Virtually every detail of the mass murder of Jews in Europe during World War II is now controverted, however spuriously. Rebutting each and every objection is impossible, for these objections multiply endlessly, and the rebuttals lead to further objections. Moreover, some contend that rebutting those who deny or minimize this enormous horror dignifies the debate itself over what would not be a disputed issue were it not for the widespread and deeply rooted hatred of the victims.

Many who have written about Holocaust denial have accordingly opted not to rebut the deniers point by point, which would inevitably be an incomplete effort in any case, but to point out the bad faith of those raising the objections and to expose them as National Socialist sympathizers. Those who deny the Holocaust in whole or part are almost invariably people who have demonstrated their distaste for Jews in other contexts; Holocaust denial is just one element of a whole constellation of charges against the Jews and often emanates from people who are openly or unmistakably National Socialists or admirers of Adolf Hitler. The subtext is that the Holocaust didn't happen but should have or that the National Socialists were merciful and generous toward the Jews, who were a genuinely subversive element in Hitler's Reich, and who repaid the Germans' magnanimity by scheming against the German state and fabricating the Holocaust narrative after the war.

There are inherent problems with this approach as well. Refusing to engage intellectually with Holocaust deniers, but instead being content to expose them as people who hold noxious views, has become a staple tactic of the contemporary Left and is used to silence and marginalize people who are speaking undeniable but unpopular truths by smearing them as akin to those who deny the Holocaust. The refusal to engage the arguments of Holocaust deniers has become an instrument in the hands of those who would shut down legitimate debate on pressing issues.

Refusing to answer the claims of Holocaust deniers risks leaving the unanswered claims to be discovered by those who don't know the truth and aren't aware of how the deniers are playing fast and loose with the facts. Holocaust survivors who could bear eyewitness testimony have now mostly died, and even most of those who knew survivors personally are now of advanced age. Particularly after October 7, denial has become a virtual cottage industry; while not dignifying the denial as a legitimate avenue of inquiry, it is important to make the general facts of the National Socialist genocide readily available and to point out some of the larger leaps of illogic among the deniers.

A third alternative to refutation and exposure has been presented in several countries: litigation and incarceration. Denial of the Holocaust is illegal in seventeen European countries, as well as Canada and Israel. This approach, however, is just as fraught with pitfalls as the other two. Once restrictions upon the freedom of speech are introduced in any context, no matter how justifiable and morally good, they can be used to restrict dissent from tyrannical authority and to silence discussion of topics the political elites wish to conceal.

Criminalizing denial, in whole or part, of what happened to the Jews of Europe during World War II also just gives ammunition to those who claim that the whole thing was a hoax. The deniers say that if the Holocaust is a matter of historical record, why can't it be examined, discussed openly, and questioned? Post-October 7 instant social media stars fan the flames of Jew-hatred by pointing out what they claim to be inconsistencies in the standard accounts of the Holocaust while insisting that they firmly believe in these supposed impossibilities because they'll go to jail if they don't. The idea that questioning the Holocaust could bring criminal penalties only reinforces the charge that those who say six million Jews were murdered in Europe have something to hide and that their claims cannot stand up to scrutiny.

FABRICATING A CASE

In fact, it is the claims of the deniers that do not stand up to scrutiny. Those who deny the Holocaust build their cases out of the thinnest of evidence. On November 22, 1944, an official of the International Committee of the Red Cross wrote a letter to an inquirer, informing him that a Red Cross "delegate" had been able to visit Auschwitz. "Our delegate told us," the official wrote, "that he had not been able to discover any trace of installations for exterminating civilian prisoners. This fact corroborates a report which we had already received from other sources, i.e., that for several months past there had been no further exterminations at Auschwitz. At all events, this is not a camp containing exclusively Jews."[726]

---

[726] International Committee of the Red Cross, Letter to Roswell McClelland, November 22, 1944, https://www.reddit.com/r/2ndYomKippurWar/comments/1867qzo/red_cross_letter_from_1944/?force_seo=1.

While this letter circulates today as if it proves definitively that there were no "installations for exterminating civilian prisoners" at Auschwitz, it actually only says that the Red Cross observer had been unable to find such facilities. Those who wish to claim that there were no facilities for mass murder at Auschwitz assume that the Red Cross observer was allowed full and unfettered access to the entire camp and that he was an indefatigable researcher who made sure he had determined exactly what was going on throughout the entire facility.

Even more damaging for the case that this letter proves that Auschwitz was not a killing center is the 1996 Red Cross admission that its officials knew about the Holocaust during World War II but said and did nothing. Red Cross archivist Georges Willemin said: "The International Committee of the Red Cross has shared responsibility for the silence of the world community."[727]

Randolph L. Braham, a professor of political science at City University of New York and author of a book entitled *The Politics of Genocide*, stated that "the International Red Cross feared that intervention in support of the Jews might jeopardize its traditional activities on behalf of prisoners of war."[728] Radu Ioanid of the United States Holocaust Memorial Museum added: "There is no doubt that the Red Cross let itself be used by the Nazis."[729] To illustrate this, Ioanid noted "positive reports" that the Red Cross had made after visiting the Theresienstadt camp and said that the observers were "clearly manipulated."[730]

Ioanid could also have mentioned the Auschwitz letter dated November 22, 1944. Yet it circulates widely as a hint to the reality behind the alleged grand Holocaust hoax.

---

[727]   Irvin Molotsky, "Red Cross Admits Knowing of the Holocaust During the War," *New York Times*, December 19, 1996.

[728]   Ibid.

[729]   Ibid.

[730]   Ibid.

THREE PROMINENT DENIERS

Holocaust denial is a subculture of its own, featuring people who have become stars among those who believe that the Jews are their misfortune and the murder of six million a hoax. While there are many who have denied the facts about the Holocaust in whole or part, and the field is constantly changing, three people have become particularly notorious for their espousal of these ideas and have come closest to making them mainstream: Ernst Zündel, Fred Leuchter, and David Irving.

Zündel, who died in 2017, was put on trial in Canada in 1984 for denying the Holocaust. The author of books including *The Hitler We Loved and Why*, Zündel eagerly took up the role of a martyr for the freedom of speech when he was tried, appearing in court wearing a hard hat with the legend "Freedom of Speech."[731] On the day he was sentenced, he walked up to the courtroom door carrying an eleven-foot cross, also emblazoned with "Freedom of Speech."[732] Zündel's trial often appeared to be more of a circus than a legal proceeding, with his attorney sneering at and insulting witnesses for the prosecution and even demanding that one Holocaust survivor give him the names of twenty relatives who had been killed in the camps.[733]

Zündel was convicted, thus only enhancing his martyr status and giving fuel to claims that those who opposed the deniers had to resort to legal silencing of their foes because the facts were not on their side. His conviction, however, was overturned on a technicality, where-upon he was tried again. Despite the farcical nature of his case and his willingness to play the clown (with a superabundance of grandiosity,

---

[731] Deborah Lipstadt, *Denying the Holocaust: The Growing Assault on Truth and Memory* (New York: Penguin Books, 1994), 159.

[732] Ibid.

[733] Ibid., 160.

he dubbed himself "the Gandhi of the right"), Zündel attracted the attention of a prolific revisionist historian, David Irving, who testified on his behalf at his second trial in 1988.[734]

Irving has called himself a "moderate fascist." [735] He has said that Rudolf Hess, Hitler's onetime second in command who flew to Britain in May 1941 on an unauthorized peace mission, should receive the Nobel Peace Prize. Irving has written numerous books about World War II, in which he seeks to overturn commonly accepted understandings of Hitler's motives and goals and, of course, of the nature and extent of the Holocaust.[736] Irving stated that he had been converted to extreme skepticism, if not outright denial, regarding the Holocaust by the work of Fred Leuchter. Leuchter surreptitiously spirited some brick fragments out of Auschwitz and subsequently wrote a report claiming that they contained no traces of cyanide and, thus, that there were no gas chambers at Auschwitz.

At Zündel's second trial, however, James Roth, the man who had actually tested the brickwork samples Leuchter brought back from Auschwitz, stated that Leuchter's conclusions were unfounded. "I went up to Toronto," Roth recounted, "on very short notice, not knowing any of the background, at all, of what was going on. They wanted somebody from the laboratory to say, yes, we analyzed these samples, yes, we produced this report on the analysis, and that's what I was there to do."[737] Yet all did not go according to plan. Roth continued: "I don't think the Leuchter results have any meaning. There's nothing in any of our data that says those surfaces were exposed or not."[738]

---

734 "Zundel Tells Immigration He's 'Gandhi of the Right,'" *Globe and Mail*, April 1, 2003.
735 Lipstadt, op. cit., 161.
736 Ibid.
737 Documentary film, *Mr. Death: The Rise and Fall of Fred A. Leuchter, Jr.*, May 12, 1999, transcript at https://www.errolmorris.com/film/mrd_transcript.html.
738 Ibid.

Roth wasn't even sure what the case was about or where Leuchter had obtained his specimens: "Even after I got off the stand, I didn't know where the samples came from. I didn't know which samples were which. And it was only at lunch that I found out, really, what the case involved. Hindsight being 20/20, the test was not the correct one to have been used for the analysis."[739] Roth explained that the methods he used to test the brick samples for the presence of cyanide actually worked against the possibility of cyanide being found:

> He presented us with rock samples anywhere from the size of your thumb up to half the size of your fist. We broke them up with a hammer so that we could get a sub-sample; we placed it in a flask, add concentrated sulfuric acid. It undergoes a reaction that produces a red-colored solution. It is the intensity of this red color that we can relate with cyanide concentration.
>
> You have to look at what happens to cyanide when it reacts with a wall. Where does it go? How far does it go? Cyanide is a surface reaction. It's probably not going to penetrate more than 10 microns. Human hair is 100 microns in diameter. Crush this sample up, I have just diluted that sample 10,000; 100,000 times. If you're going to go look for it, you're going to look on the surface only. There's no reason to go deep, because it's not going to be there. Which was the exposed surface? I didn't even have any idea. That's like analyzing paint on a wall by analyzing the timber that's behind it. If they go in with blinders on, they

---

[739]   Ibid.

will see what they want to see. What was he really
trying to do? What was he trying to prove?[740]

Then there was the fact that the cyanide whose absence Leuchter
was making so very much of had been used in the room in question
over fifty years before.

Nevertheless, Irving explained that Leuchter's findings transformed his view of the Holocaust: "He traveled abroad, probably
for the first time in his life, to Poland. He came back with these
earth-shattering results. The big point: there is no significant residue
of cyanide in the brickwork. That's what converted me. When I read
that in the report in the courtroom in Toronto, I became a hard-core
disbeliever."[741]

It was a massive exercise in people seeing what they wished to see.
Had they been willing instead to see the evidence that the Holocaust
actually happened, it would not have been hard to find.

PREDICTING THE MASS MURDER OF THE JEWS

Adolf Hitler predicted more than once that he would eradicate the
Jews of Europe. As far back as September 16, 1919, Hitler, then an
unknown agitator who had just begun to make a name for himself
among the antisemites of Germany, wrote in a private letter to a man
who had inquired about his political philosophy: "An antisemitism
based on purely emotional grounds will find its ultimate expression in
the form of the pogrom. An antisemitism based on reason, however,
must lead to systematic legal combating and elimination of the privileges of the Jews, that which distinguishes the Jews from the other
aliens who live among us (an Aliens Law). The ultimate objective [of

---

[740] Ibid.
[741] Ibid.

such legislation] must, however, be the irrevocable removal of the Jews in general."[742] Hitler disdained the idea of a pogrom that would kill only a certain number of Jews. He wanted them eradicated entirely.

Hitler apparently found these formulations pleasing, for he substantially repeated them at an April 6, 1920, meeting of the National Socialist German Workers Party: "We do not want to be the sort of emotional anti-Semites who create a pogrom mood. We are filled with the uncompromising determination to grasp this evil by the roots and tear it out in its entirety."[743] This threat, according to a record of the meeting, was met with "enthusiastic applause."

Much later, on January 21, 1939, Hitler made it clear that the intervening two decades had not changed his mind about grasping "this evil" and tearing it out "in its entirety." He told the Czech Foreign Minister Frantisek Chvalkovsky: "We are going to destroy the Jews. They are not going to get away with what they did on November 9, 1918," the day that the Jews, in Hitler's reckoning, had stabbed Germany in the back and compelled it to surrender in World War I. Hitler added ominously: "The day of reckoning has come."[744]

That was a private meeting, but just over a week later, Hitler proclaimed this threat before the entire world. On January 30, 1939, the sixth anniversary of his becoming chancellor of Germany, he said during a speech to the Reichstag:

> One thing I should like to say on this day which may be memorable for others as well as for us Germans: In the course of my life I have very often been a prophet, and have usually been ridiculed for it.

[742] "Adolf Hitler: First Anti-Semitic Writing (September 16, 1939)," Jewish Virtual Library, https://www.jewishvirtuallibrary.org/adolf-hitler-s-first-anti-semitic-writing.

[743] Volker Ullrich, *Hitler: Ascent 1889–1939*, Jefferson Chase, trans. (New York: Alfred A. Knopf, 2016), Kindle edition, loc. 18514.

[744] Lucy S. Dawidowicz, *The War Against the Jews 1933–1945* (New York: Bantam Books, 1975), 106.

During the time of my struggle for power it was in the first instance the Jewish race which only received my prophecies with laughter when I said that I would one day take over the leadership of the State, and with it that of the whole nation, and that I would then among many other things settle the Jewish problem. Their laughter was uproarious, but I think that for some time now they have been laughing on the other side of their face. Today I will once more be a prophet: If the international Jewish financiers in and outside Europe should succeed in plunging the nations once more into a world war, then the result will not be the Bolshevization of the earth, and thus the victory of Jewry, but the annihilation of the Jewish race in Europe![745]

This statement was well-known in the Third Reich. In September 1941, the National Socialists even distributed this extract from "Hitler's prophecy" as a wall poster to be displayed in homes, schools, offices, and the like: "If the international Jewish financiers in and outside Europe should succeed in plunging the nations once more into a world war, then the result will not be the victory of Jewry, but the annihilation of the Jewish race in Europe."[746]

Hitler himself referred several times thereafter to this "prophecy." On September 30, 1942, he declared: "On the first of September, 1939, we made two pronouncements in the Reichstag session of

[745] *The Speeches of Adolf Hitler, April 1922–August 1939*, Norman H. Baynes, ed. (London: Oxford University Press, 1942) I, 740–1.

[746] "Wenn Es Dem Internationalen Finanzjudentum Gelingen Sollte, Die Volker Noch Einmal In Einen Weltkrieg Zu Stuerzen, Dann Wird Das Ergebnis Nicht Der Sieg Des Judentums Sein, Sondern Die Vernichtung Der Juedischen Rasse In Europa," *Wochenspruch der NSDAP*, September 7–13, 1941, Hennepin County Library, https://digitalcollections.hclib. org/digital/collection/p17208coll3/id/315/rec/3.

that date: First, now that the Jews have forced this war upon us, no amount of military force and no length of time will ever be able to conquer us; and second, if Jewry is starting an international world war to eliminate the Aryan nations of Europe, then it won't be the Aryan nation which will be wiped out, but Jewry."[747]

The Führer's memory was faulty. He had not said this on September 1, 1939. On that day, he did indeed address the Reichstag on the occasion of the beginning of the war he had just begun in Europe, but he did not mention this "prophecy." However, in his 1942 statement, he remembered his prediction of the destruction of the Jewish people of Europe well enough.

On October 25, 1941, Hitler told his party comrades Heinrich Himmler and Reinhard Heydrich: "This criminal race has the two million dead of the World War on their conscience, and now hundreds of thousands. Let no one say to me: we cannot send them into the mire. Who concerns themselves about our men? It is good if preceding us is the terror that we are exterminating the Jews. The attempt to found a Jewish state will fail."[748] Hitler's boast that efforts to found a Jewish state would fail and that he would exterminate them instead was remarkable; eight decades later, Assad and Jones transformed this assertion into the claim that the Jews fabricated the idea that Hitler tried to exterminate them in order to create the justification for a Jewish state.

Those who deny that the Holocaust took place or claim that the number of Jews who were murdered was actually vastly smaller than is claimed are thus in the peculiar position of insisting that while

---

[747] "Adolf Hitler: Address at the Opening of the Winter Relief Campaign (September 30, 1942)," Jewish Virtual Library, https://www.jewishvirtuallibrary.org/adolf-hitler-address-at-the-opening-of-the-winter-relief-campaign-september-1942/.

[748] Ron Rosenbaum, *Explaining Hitler: The Search for the Origins of His Evil* (New York: Random House, 1998), 73.

Hitler *said* he would exterminate the Jews, he didn't take any steps actually to do so, at least on a large scale.

DISCUSSING THE EXTERMINA-
TION OF JEWS IN EUROPE

Empty braggarts have existed throughout history, but unfortunately, Hitler was not one of them. His followers got the message loud and clear and repeated it themselves. The German army, in 1939, issued a pamphlet for the troops entitled "The Jew in German History."[749] It declared:

> We Germans fight a twofold fight today. With regard to the non-Jewish peoples we want only to accomplish our vital interests. We respect them and conduct a chivalrous argument with them. But we fight world Jewry as one has to fight a poisonous parasite; we encounter in him not only the enemy of our people, but a plague of all peoples. The fight against Jewry is a moral fight for the purity and health of God-created humanity and for a new more just order in the world.[750]

One does not settle poisonous parasites in a different area or content oneself with restricting their activities in various ways; one eradicates them. The German General Franz Halder accordingly noted in his diary in September 1939 that among the goals of the war

---

[749] Dawidowicz, op. cit., 115.
[750] Ibid.

that had just begun was "Cleaning out: Jewry, intelligentsia, clergy, nobility."[751]

Shortly thereafter, Reinhard Heydrich, the commander of the Einsatzgruppen, National Socialist Germany's mobile paramilitary death squads that operated outside of the death camps, issued a directive entitled "The Jewish Question in the Occupied Territory."[752] In it, Heydrich "once more" told Einsatzgruppen leaders that "the planned overall measures (i.e., the final aim) are to be kept strictly secret."[753] SS officer Adolf Eichmann, one of the chief National Socialist leaders responsible for the logistics of the mass murder of Jews on such an immense scale during World War II, said at his 1961 trial that the phrase "final aim" referred to "physical extermination."[754]

Einsatzgruppen recruits were instructed that they were joining "the fight against vermin—that is, mainly the Jews and Communists," and were to struggle against "the terror of Jewish-Bolshevik dominion."[755] Halder entered some brief notes in his diary in late March 1941, after a meeting with Hitler, that the Führer had emphasized that "Communism extraordinary danger for future. We must disavow the point of view of soldierly comradeship. The Communist is not a comrade before and not a comrade after. It is a question of a war of destruction. If we don't conceive of it that way, then we will indeed beat the enemy, but in thirty years the Communist enemy will again confront us. We do not conduct war to conserve the enemy."[756] The war the National Socialists had started was to be a war of extermination, and in light of the fact that Hitler and his comrades often spoke of Communism as an invention of the Jews designed to subvert and

---

[751] Ibid.
[752] Ibid., 116.
[753] Ibid.
[754] Ibid.
[755] Ibid., 125.
[756] Ibid., 122.

destroy Aryan society, the targets for extermination would be not just Communists, but any and all Jews.

In the summer of 1941, Reichsführer-SS Heinrich Himmler told SS officer Rudolf Höss, the commandant of the Auschwitz concentration camp, "that the Führer had given the order for a Final Solution of the Jewish Question," and added that "we, the SS, must carry out that order."[757] Höss later recounted that Eichmann came to Auschwitz and discussed with him the "killing with showers of carbon monoxide while bathing, as was done with mental patients in some places in the Reich."[758] Eichmann also instructed Höss "about the methods of killing people with exhaust gases in trucks, which had previously been used in the East."[759]

The ultimate goal was widely known even outside of Auschwitz and the other death camps. SS-Sturmbannführer Rolf-Heinz Höppner, who headed the Central Migration Office in Posen, on September 2, 1941, addressed a memorandum to his staff, explaining that "after the conclusion of the war, there will need to be a significant resettlement of population segments unwanted for the Greater German Reich in various newly acquired areas of Germany."[760] After issuing various instructions for this eventuality, Höppner concluded: "What is essential, however, is to have complete clarity from the outset about the ultimate fate of these displaced ethnic groups unwanted in

---

[757] Ibid., 129.

[758] Ibid., 131.

[759] Ibid.

[760] "1941-09-02 Memorandum of SS-Sturmbannführer Höppner: 'The Ultimate Fate of These Displaced Ethnic Groups Unwanted in the Greater German Settlement Areas—Whether the Goal Is to Secure a Certain Life for Them Permanently or to Eradicate Them Entirely,'" Holocaust History Site, https://holocausthistory.site/memo-of-hoppner-of-2-september-1941-the-ultimate-fate-of-these-displaced-ethnic-groups-unwanted-in-the-greater-german-settlement-areas-whether-the-goal-is-to-secure-a-certain-life-for-the/.

the Greater German Settlement Areas—whether the goal is to secure a certain life for them permanently or to eradicate them entirely."[761]

Höppner himself favored the second choice, as he made clear in a memo to Eichmann dated July 16, 1941. "There is a danger this winter," Höppner wrote, "that the Jews may not all be able to be fed. It is seriously worth considering whether the most humane solution is not to eliminate the Jews, as far as they are not capable of working, by some quick-acting agent. In any case, this would be more pleasant than letting them starve. Furthermore, the proposal was made to sterilize all Jewish women in this camp who are still expecting children, so that with this generation, the Jewish problem is indeed completely solved."[762]

Plans were afoot to "solve" this "problem" much more quickly than within a generation. On January 20, 1942, in the Berlin quarter of Wannsee, Heydrich chaired a conference of SS officials and other concerned parties regarding a "Final Solution of the Jewish Question." Eichmann recalled that "the gentlemen were standing together, or sitting together and were discussing the subject quite bluntly, quite differently from the language which I had to use later in the record. During the conversation they minced no words about it at all…they spoke about methods of killing, about liquidation, about extermination…. After the conference, Heydrich, Müller [General Heinrich Müller, head of the Gestapo] and myself sat cozily around the fireplace. We had drinks. We had brandy. We sang songs."[763]

---

[761] Ibid.

[762] "1941-07-16 Letter of Höppner to Eichmann: '…To Eliminate the Jews, as Far as They Are Not Capable of Working, by Some Quick-Acting Agent,'" Holocaust History Site, https://holocausthistory.site/letter-of-rolf-heinz-hoppner-to-adolf-eichmann-of-16-july-1941/.

[763] Paul Roland, *Hitler and His Inner Circle: Chilling Profiles of the Evil Figures Behind the Third Reich* (London: Arcturus Publishing, 2021).

Even in his diary, National Socialist Propaganda Minister Josef Goebbels was more squeamish and reticent, writing on March 27, 1942, that "from the General Government [National Socialist-occupied Poland], starting at Lublin, the Jews are now being deported to the east. A fairly barbaric procedure not to be described in more detail is used, and there is not much left of the Jews themselves. In general, one can say that 60% of them have to be liquidated, while only 40% can still be used for work."[764] On October 9, 1942, Himmler issued a memorandum to his staff, directing that Jews who were being pressed into slave labor at German munitions factories were to be redeployed into "a few large Jewish concentration-camp enterprises," and that "even from there the Jews are someday to disappear, in accordance with the Führer's wishes."[765]

Just under a year later, on October 4, 1943, Himmler spoke frankly in a speech to SS officers:

> I also want to refer before you here, in complete frankness, to a really grave matter. Among ourselves, this once, it shall be uttered quite frankly; but in public we will never speak of it....
>
> I am referring to the evacuation of the Jews, the annihilation of the Jewish people. This is one of those things that are easily said. "The Jewish people is going to be annihilated," says every party member. "Sure, it's in our program, elimination of the Jews, annihilation—we'll take care of it." And then they all come trudging, eighty million worthy Germans, and

[764] Hans Metzner, "Seriously Now, Where Did The Jews 'Evacuated to The East' Go?," Holocaust Controversies, February 1, 2020, https://holocaustcontroversies.blogspot.com/2020/02/seriously-now-where-did-jews-evacuated.html.
[765] Dawidowicz, op. cit., 146.

each one has his one decent Jew. "Sure, the others are swine, but this one is an A-1 Jew." Of all those who talk this way, not one has seen it happen, not one has been through it. Most of you must know what it means to see a hundred corpses lie side by side, or five hundred, or a thousand. To have stuck this out and—excepting cases of human weakness—to have kept our integrity, this is what has made us hard. In our history, this is an unwritten and never-to-be-written page of glory....[766]

On March 16, 1946, Höss told two officers of the War Crimes Investigation Unit of the British Army of the Rhine: "I personally arranged on orders received from Himmler in May 1941 the gassing of two million persons between June-July 1941 and the end of 1943, during which time I was commandant of Auschwitz."[767] In all, 5,370,000 Jews and others whom the National Socialists considered enemies or undesirables were murdered in Auschwitz and the other National Socialist death camps.[768] Others were murdered outside those camps. The American Jewish Year Book for 1947 states: "The statistics on the Jewish population of Europe are based on the reports received by the JDC from their European sources. These figures reveal that there are in Europe today approximately 3,920,000 Jews out of a pre-war total of 9,740,000 in 1939."[769] That's a decrease of 5,820,000.

Hitler said he would do it. His National Socialist underlings discussed doing it. There is abundant evidence that it was done. Yet the

---

[766] Ibid., 149.

[767] Ibid., 148.

[768] Ibid., 149.

[769] *American Jewish Year Book, Volume 29 (5708) 1947–1948*, Harry Schneiderman and Morris Fine, eds. (Philadelphia: Jewish Publication Society of America, 1947), 734.

claims have persisted that the whole thing is a hoax, "the Holohoax," fabricated in order to further the aims of Zionism.

THE NATIONAL SOCIALISTS' ACTIONS WERE KNOWN

At the time that the Holocaust was going on, Hitler's aspirations were widely known. On August 8, 1942, a Jewish refugee from National Socialist-occupied Czechoslovakia, Alfred Goldschmied, wrote a report on the National Socialists' treatment of the Jews for the Office of Strategic Services (OSS), the precursor to the CIA. Goldschmied wrote:

> Of the 48,500 Jews still living in Prague before the occupation, approximately one half [were] deported [by] the day of my departure. Everything was carried through upon direct orders from Berlin, where they had had a good deal of practice before. From the small towns almost all Jews were deported, in Prague only those could remain who were married to an Aryan. Later transports went to Theresienstadt, a garrison about one hour from Prague.... Later on Theresienstadt was used only as a transit place. After three days the Jews were sent on to Poland.... Men and women were separated and many died of starvation. Reports coming in indirectly from Poland give heartbreaking details. If Hitler remains true to his program of destroying all European Jewry—he will

have achieved that goal soon and most countries will be depleted of Jews.[770]

On November 25, 1942, the *New York Times* reported, in a story that it published on page ten, that "old persons, children, infants and cripples among the Jewish population of Poland are being shot, killed by various other methods or forced to undergo hardships that inevitably cause death as a means of carrying out an order by Heinrich Himmler, Nazi Gestapo chief, that half the remaining Polish Jews must be exterminated by the end of this year, according to a report issued today by the Polish Government in London."[771]

The *Times* report noted that "as an instance of the rapidity with which the Jewish population had been cut down, either by evacuation to Nazi war factories, deaths from disease or by liquidation, the Polish officials said that only 40,000 October ration cards had been printed for the Jews in the Warsaw ghetto, where the population last March was 433,000."[772] This was just "the first step toward complete liquidation."[773] The report detailed the inhuman conditions of the trains transporting the Jews to the camps and added that "under the guise of resettlement in the east, the mass murder of the Jewish population is taking place."[774]

The *Times* inexcusably did not make this front-page news, but it could not be said to have buried the news altogether. Given the considerable reach and influence of what was and is widely known as the Paper of Record, a large segment of the Western world was informed

---

[770] "Thousands of Intelligence Documents Opened under the Nazi War Crimes Disclosure Act," National Archives, May 13, 2004, https://www.archives.gov/press/press-releases/2004/nr04-55.html.

[771] James MacDonald, "Himmler Program Kills Polish Jews," *New York Times*, November 25, 1942.

[772] Ibid.

[773] Ibid.

[774] Ibid.

that the National Socialists were busy committing mass murder of the Jews and planned to "liquidate" them altogether.

Hollywood screenwriter Ben Hecht, on March 9, 1943, presented a pageant at Madison Square Garden entitled *We Will Never Die*, which was designed to shed light on the plight of the Jews in Europe. During this production, the actor Jacob Ben-Ami stated: "We are here to say our prayers for the two million who have been killed in Europe."[775] In the final scene, a narrator intoned: "There will be no Jews left in Europe for representation when peace comes. The four million left to be killed are being killed."[776]

On April 7, 1944, two young men, Rudolf Vrba and Albert Wetzler, managed to escape from Auschwitz. They then wrote a detailed report about the camp and what was going on inside it. Vrba later recounted: "There was a place called the ramp where trains with Jews were coming in. They were coming day and night, sometimes one per day and sometimes five per day, from all sorts of places in the world. I worked there from August 18, 1942 to June 7, 1943. I saw those transports rolling one after another, and I have seen at least 200 of them in this position. Constantly, people from the heart of Europe were disappearing, and they were arriving to the same place, with the same ignorance of the fate of the previous transport. I knew that within a couple of hours after they arrived there 90 percent would be gassed."[777]

The Vrba/Wetzler report, according to historian Michael Berenbaum, "changed a June decision of the Jewish Agency in Jerusalem not to press for the bombing of Auschwitz since that would result in the death of innocent Jewish non-combatants incarcerated there. Yet one month later in London, Moshe Shertok (later Sharret) and

---

[775] "The 'We Will Never Die' Pageant," Holocaust Encyclopedia, US Holocaust Memorial Museum, https://encyclopedia.ushmm.org/content/en/article/the-we-will-never-die-pageant.

[776] Ibid.

[777] Michael Berenbaum, "Righteous Anger Fuels 'Auschwitz,'" *Jewish Journal*, October 14, 2004.

Chaim Weizmann were pressing for the bombing and secured the support of Winston Churchill who told Anthony Eden 'get what you can out of the Air Force and invoke my name if necessary.'"[778]

On August 9, 1944, A. Leon Kubowitzki of the World Jewish Congress wrote to US Undersecretary of War John J. McCloy, relaying to him a message from Ernest Frischer of the Czechoslovak State Council. Frischer wrote: "I believe that destruction of gas chambers and crematoria in Oswiecim [Auschwitz] by bombing would have a certain effect now. Germans are now exhuming and burning corpses in an effort to conceal their crimes. This could be prevented by destruction of crematoria and then Germans might possibly stop further mass exterminations especially since so little time is left to them. Bombing of railway communications in this same area would also be of importance and of military interest."[779]

McCloy replied on August 14, questioning "the practicability of this suggestion" that Auschwitz be bombed. "After a study," McCloy continued, "it became apparent that such an operation could be executed only by the diversion of considerable air support essential to the success of our forces now engaged in decisive operations elsewhere and would in any case be of such doubtful efficacy that it would not warrant the use of our resources. There has been considerable opinion to the effect that such an effort, even if practicable, might provoke even more vindictive action by the Germans."[780]

Auschwitz would not be bombed. No one, however, was as of yet denying that anything significant was happening there.

---

[778] Ibid.

[779] "Auschwitz Bombing Controversy: War Department Rejects World Jewish Congress Request to Bomb Auschwitz (August 9–14, 1944)," Jewish Virtual Library, https://www.jewishvirtuallibrary.org/war-department-rejects-world-jewish-congress-request-to-bomb-auschwitz-august-1944.

[780] Ibid.

ABU MAZEN'S DISSERTATION

As World War II was ending, the Supreme Allied Commander, General Dwight D. Eisenhower, visited a German camp and wrote this to his colleague, General George C. Marshall:

> On a recent tour of the forward areas in First and Third Armies, I stopped momentarily at the salt mines to take a look at the German treasure. There is a lot of it. But the most interesting—although horrible—sight that I encountered during the trip was a visit to a German internment camp near Gotha. The things I saw beggar description. While I was touring the camp I encountered three men who had been inmates and by one ruse or another had made their escape. I interviewed them through an interpreter. The visual evidence and the verbal testimony of starvation, cruelty and bestiality were so overpowering as to leave me a bit sick. In one room, where they were piled up twenty or thirty naked men, killed by starvation, George Patton would not even enter. He said he would get sick if he did so. I made the visit deliberately, in order to be in position to give first-hand evidence of these things if ever, in the future, there develops a tendency to charge these allegations merely to "propaganda."[781]

Now, the day when the facts of the Holocaust are dismissed as "propaganda" is upon us. False claims about the Holocaust proliferate

---

[781] Dwight D. Eisenhower, Letter to General George C. Marshall, April 18, 1945, https://www. eisenhowerlibrary.gov/sites/default/files/research/online-documents/holocaust/1945-04-15-dde-to-marshall.pdf.

on websites dedicated to revealing the alleged evils of the Jews. Much of this is low-level crackpottery, such as the claim that the gas chambers used to exterminate the Jews had wooden doors and were thus not airtight and could not have been employed for mass killing.[782] Yet the wooden door often pictured as evidence for this was actually a door to a washroom, not to the gas chamber.[783]

Some Holocaust revisionism, however, originates in quarters that are superficially more respectable. In 1982, in a tidy convergence of socialist and Islamic Jew-hatred, future Palestinian Authority President Mahmoud Abbas, a.k.a. Abu Mazen, successfully defended his doctoral dissertation, *The Relationship Between Zionists and Nazis, 1933–1945*, at the Institute of Oriental Studies of the Russian Academy of Sciences in Moscow. Abbas was a forty-six-year-old graduate student at the KGB's university, the Patrice Lumumba University of Peoples' Friendship.

In his dissertation, Abbas claimed that "there are no accurate statistical data or well-researched scientific findings regarding the number of these victims."[784] As this is supposed to be a scholarly investigation, Abbas includes what he presents as documentation of this claim: "According to data of the English researcher R. Hilberg, who specialized in the study of the Holocaust issue, the number of victims of Hitler's genocide among Jews during World War II was 896 thousand people."[785] Yet journalist Ariel Bulshtein, who examined Abbas's dissertation, notes: "A footnote he added at the bottom of the page purports to cite where Raul Hilberg wrote this: on page

---

[782] Jake Shields, X, April 3, 2024, https://twitter.com/jakeshieldsajj/status/1775417989267 124679.

[783] "Rebutting the 'Twitter Denial': The Most Popular Holocaust Denial Memes Debunked," Holocaust Controversies, May 21, 2017, https://holocaustcontroversies.blogspot.com/2017/05/rebutting-twitter-denial-most-popular.html#flimsydoor.

[784] Ariel Bulshtein, "PhD in Holocaust Denial: Abbas' Doctoral Dissertation Revealed in Full," *Israel Hayom*, April 12, 2024.

[785] Ibid.

670 of his book 'The Destruction of the European Jews'—a seminal work in Holocaust research. I did not hesitate and opened the book to the said page. There was no such number there. Not there, and not in any other source in the book."

Abbas was lying outright, and he did so by misrepresenting the views of a man who began an intensive study of the Holocaust because of minimizations of the number of people killed. Bulshstein adds: "Abu Mazen clearly wanted to convey to his readers the message that the number 6 million is inflated, and in order to lend this false message credibility—he fraudulently attributed it to an authoritative source. And not just any authority: Raul Hilberg, a Holocaust survivor born in Vienna, was one of the greatest historians of the Holocaust. 26 members of his immediate family were murdered by the Nazis. Hilberg himself admitted that this enormous number was one of the motivations for him to study the Holocaust in particular and not another historical topic."[786]

Four decades later, on August 24, 2023, Abbas made a speech before Fatah's Revolutionary Council, in which he made clear how such claims about the Holocaust could be used. While Bashar Assad, E. Michael Jones, and others claimed that the Holocaust had been fabricated in order to advance Jewish aims, Abbas demonstrated in his speech what the reality was: denial or minimization of the number of Jews murdered in the Holocaust, and of the National Socialist program against the Jews in general, was used as a weapon against the Jews of today.

Abbas claimed that the National Socialists killed Jews because of the Jews' crimes, not simply because they were Jews: "They say that Hitler killed the Jews for being Jews, and that Europe hated the Jews because they were Jews. Not true. It was clearly explained that [the Europeans] fought [the Jews] because of their social role, and not

---

[786]   Ibid.

their religion. Several authors wrote about this. Even Karl Marx said this was not true. He said that the enmity was not directed at Judaism as a religion, but to Judaism for is social role. The [Europeans] fought against these people because of their role in society, which had to do with usury, money, and so on and so forth. Even Hitler.... He said he fought the Jews because they were dealing with usury and money. In his view, they were engaged in sabotage, and this is why he hated them. We just want to make this point clear. This was not about Semitism and antisemitism."[787]

The goal of his speech was to shift the focus away from the victimization of the Jews of Europe and onto the alleged evils of the Jews that they were supposedly still committing. Those who deny that the National Socialists murdered six million Jews during World War II generally place themselves in the paradoxical position of saying that the Holocaust didn't happen, but it should have, as the Jews deserved it. And, of course, another one, presumably real this time, would be welcome. After October 7, this sentiment burst into full flower, with leftist and Muslim spokesmen all over the West claiming that the Hamas massacres were justified in view of the Israeli "occupation."

THE MUFTI AND THE HOLOCAUST

Abbas's Holocaust denial was ironic in light of the deep involvement in the Holocaust of the grand mufti of Jerusalem, Hajj Amin al-Husseini. After the war, Adolf Eichmann's assistant, Dieter Wisliczeny, testified that al-Husseini had been instrumental in the

---

[787] "Palestinian President Mahmoud Abbas: Hitler Fought the European Jews Because of Their Usury, Money Dealings; It Was Not about Antisemitism; Jews from Arab Countries Did Not Want to Emigrate, But Were Forced to Do So by Israel," MEMRI, September 3, 2023.

National Socialists' decision to commit a mass murder of the Jews rather than to exile them:

> The Grand Mufti has repeatedly suggested to the Nazi authorities—including Hitler, von Ribbentrop and Himmler—the extermination of European Jewry. He considered this a comfortable solution to the Palestine problem…. The Mufti was one of the initiators of the systematic extermination of European Jewry and had been a collaborator and adviser of Eichmann and Himmler in the execution of this plan. He was one of Eichmann's best friends and had constantly incited him to accelerate the extermination measures. I heard him say, accompanied by Eichmann, he had visited incognito the gas chambers of Auschwitz.[788]

Eichmann contradicted Wisliczeny's claim, but there is no question that al-Husseini wanted to see Jews killed en masse. On July 7, 1942, he said so:

> A large number of Jews residing in Egypt and a number of Poles, Greeks, Armenians and Free French, have been issued with revolvers and ammunition in order to help them against the Egyptians at the last moment, when Britain is forced to evacuate Egypt.
>
> In the face of this barbaric procedure by the British we think it best, if the life of the Egyptian nation is to be saved, that the Egyptians rise as one man to kill the Jews before they have a chance of betraying the

[788] Friedman, *A History of the Middle East*, op. cit., 243; David G. Dalin, "Hitler's Mufti," *First Things*, August 2005, https://www.firstthings.com/article/2005/08/hitlers-mufti.

Egyptian people. It is the duty of the Egyptians to annihilate the Jews and to destroy their property....

You must kill the Jews, before they open fire on you. Kill the Jews, who have appropriated your wealth and who are plotting against your security. Arabs of Syria, Iraq and Palestine, what are you waiting for? The Jews are planning to violate your women, to kill your children and to destroy you. According to the Muslim religion, the defense of your life is a duty which can only be fulfilled by annihilating the Jews. This is your best opportunity to get rid of this dirty race, which has usurped your rights and brought misfortune and destruction on your countries. Kill the Jews, burn their property, destroy their stores, annihilate these base supporters of British imperialism. Your sole hope of salvation lies in annihilating the Jews before they annihilate you.[789]

Al-Husseini lobbied the National Socialists not to allow Jews to leave Europe and emigrate to Palestine. In the eyes of his German friends, this left killing the Jews as the only viable option. In the summer of 1944, al-Husseini sent a series of letters to officials in Germany, Romania, Bulgaria, and Hungary, calling upon them to be more energetic in sending the Jews who were still in their territories to Poland, where the National Socialist death camps were operating.[790] On July 25, 1944, al-Husseini wrote to National Socialist Foreign Affairs Minister Joachim von Ribbentrop:

---

[789] Jeffrey Herf, *Nazi Propaganda for the Arab World* (New Haven, Connecticut: Yale University Press, 2009), 125–26.

[790] The Nation Associates, *The Arab Higher Committee: Its Origins, Personnel and Purposes, the Documentary Record Submitted to the United Nations, May, 1947* (New York: The Nation Associates, 1947).

I have previously called the attention of your Excellency to the constant attempts of the Jews to emigrate from Europe in order to reach Palestine and asked your Excellency to undertake the necessary steps so as to prevent the Jews from emigrating. I had also sent you a letter, under date of June 5, 1944, in regard to the plan for an exchange of Egyptians living in Germany with Palestinian Germans, in which I asked you to exclude the Jews from this plan of exchange. I have, however, learned that the Jews did depart on July 2, 1944, and I am afraid that further groups of Jews will leave for Palestine from Germany and France to be exchanged for Palestinian Germans.

This exchange on the part of the Germans would encourage the Balkan countries likewise to send their Jews to Palestine. This stop would be incomprehensible to the Arabs and Moslems after your Excellency's declaration of November 2, 1943 that "the destruction of the so-called Jewish national home in Palestine is an immutable part of the policy of the greater German Reich" and it would create in them a feeling of keen disappointment.

It is for this reason that I ask your Excellency to do all that is necessary to prohibit the emigration of Jews to Palestine, and in this way your Excellency would give a new practical example of the policy of the naturally allied and friendly Germany towards the Arab Nation.[791]

---

[791] Ibid.

Whatever the mufti's actual role in the establishment of the Nazi death camps, he certainly approved of their work, saying confidently: "The Arab nation awaits the solution of the world Jewish problem by its friends, the Axis powers."[792]

LOGICAL QUESTIONS

Abbas's claim that only 896,000 Jews, not six million, were killed in Europe during World War II doesn't stand up even to superficial scrutiny. On March 23, 1943, Adolf Eichmann's chief statistician, Richard Korherr, provided Heinrich Himmler with a document entitled "The Final Solution of the European Jewish Question," giving details of what had been done to the Jews up to December 31, 1942, to Himmler. On April 19, 1943, he provided Himmler's office with a short summary document that covered the period up to March 31, 1943.

Korherr reported that the National Socialists had deported around 2.6 million Jews from Western Europe to Eastern Europe and that even more had been eradicated from the continent. He concluded: "Since the seizure of power, the number of Jews in Europe, which was over ten million in 1933, has been halved; the decline of over four million is due to German influence."[793]

What happened to all these people? There is only one possibility: they were killed. If they had not been killed, there would be some indication of their being resettled somewhere in Eastern Europe, but there is no such record. Holocaust deniers Carlo Mattogno, Thomas Kues, and Jürgen Graf tried to find some trace of them but

---

[792] Friedman, *A History of the Middle East*, op. cit., 243.

[793] Roberto Muehlenkamp, "Richard 'I Didn't Know' Korherr," Holocaust Controversies, April 29, 2007, https://holocaustcontroversies.blogspot.com/2007/04/richard-i-didnt-know-korherr.html#more.

failed, admitting that "we are unable to produce German wartime documents about the destination and the fate of the deportees."[794] Holocaust researcher Hans Metzner points out that "according to contemporary German documents, the mass of the 'evacuated' Jews did not show up in the occupied Soviet areas under civilian administration, while the military governed areas were partisan populated/endangered and largely free of Jews."[795]

Some have suggested that this mass of people was resettled in the Pripet Marshes, a vast area of wetlands in what is today Belarus, while the region was under National Socialist occupation. Metzner notes, however, that the Pripet Marshes were the site of intense partisan activity, and "partisan areas were as a matter of course cleared of Jews rather than [being] a destination for deportations."[796] He states that on October 4, 1942, "the quartermaster of the rear army area 550 (West North-Caucasus region) ordered that '30 Jewish families from the partisan area...are to be deported to Armavir' (NARA, T501/R69). Now if already 30 Jewish families posed a problem for the Nazis—what would 2.3 Million of them be then?"[797]

Yet if these people were murdered, which is the only other alternative, Abbas's figure of 896,000 dead in the Holocaust is shown to be what it is: politically motivated propaganda. And the four million Jews Korherr mentions in 1943 were by no means the only ones who were killed before it was all over.

---

[794] Metzner, op. cit.
[795] Ibid.
[796] Ibid.
[797] Ibid.

PROVING THE OBVIOUS

The Holocaust took place over a period of years and over a massive expanse of Europe; the number of people who were involved, both participants and victims, who have provided testimony as to what happened is massive. Certainly, the Holocaust literature includes some fantasists, fabulists, and seekers of stolen valor. Those who traffic in "Holohoax" claims like to highlight accounts of fraudulent Holocaust survivors as if they demonstrate that every last person who spoke about suffering through World War II as a Jew in Europe was indulging in fakery. Yet the fact that some people lie doesn't come close to negating the huge abundance of records that establish that six million Jews were indeed killed in Europe during World War II.

According to the US Holocaust Memorial Museum, the evidence consists of "surviving Nazi German reports and records; prewar and postwar demographic studies; records created by Jews during and after the war; documentation created by resistance groups and underground activists; as well as other available, extant archival sources."[798] These records are available for anyone who wishes to examine them and is not so befuddled by hatred of Jews as to imagine that the mass of evidence involves forgery and fabrication on a scale that would be virtually inconceivable.

The claim that the Holocaust did not happen, or that significantly fewer than six million Jews were killed, and that the whole story was invented for political reasons is a classic instance of projection. Jews did not invent the Holocaust, as Assad claims, in order to create the pretext for the establishment of the state of Israel; the Zionist movement, which always had the creation of a Jewish state as

---

[798] "How Many People Did the Nazis Murder?," Holocaust Encyclopedia, US Holocaust Memorial Museum, https://encyclopedia.ushmm.org/content/en/article/documenting-numbers-of-victims-of-the-holocaust-and-nazi-persecution.

its goal, began in the nineteenth century, and the League of Nations awarded Britain the Mandate for Palestine with the express purpose of creating a Jewish National Home in 1922, when Adolf Hitler was a largely unknown Munich agitator.

The reality is that those who claim that the history of the Holocaust is largely or even wholly fictional are doing so in order to cast aspersions upon the state of Israel, as in the case of Assad and Abbas and others like them, or to buttress their claims about Jews being untrustworthy schemers who are bent on subverting and destroying Gentile society, as E. Michael Jones contends.

Were the Holocaust an event that did not involve Jews, a group that has been the object of suspicion from Christians, Muslims, and atheist socialist utopians both nationalist and internationalist, no one would think of questioning it, any more than there is any significant questioning of the idea that the United States dropped atomic bombs on Hiroshima and Nagasaki in 1945. Holocaust denial is born of hatred of the Jews and is designed to reinforce that hatred.

Chapter Eleven

THE JEWS CONTROL THE WORLD, AND MORE

THE JEWS CONTROL THE WORLD, CAPITALIST VERSION

"The Jews will sell you whatever dreams you wish for the tiniest copper coin," wrote the Roman poet and satirist Juvenal early in the second century CE, thereby creating the enduring image of the Jew as the crafty entrepreneur.[799] They are, however, selling these dreams for a pittance; in several passages, Juvenal mocks Jews for their abject

---

799   Juvenal, Satires, VI: 508–591, A. S. Kline, trans., https://www.poetryintranslation.com/PITBR/Latin/Juvenalhome.php.

poverty.[800] Augustine of Hippo, as we have seen, suggested that the dispersion and misery of the Jews was a sign of God's judgment on them and the truth of the Christian message.[801]

Yet as the Church forbade Christians to engage in usury, which was generally defined as any moneylending transaction at interest, while Jews had varying interpretations of the scriptures from which the prohibition was derived, Jews became distinguished as money-lenders and merchants. In Christian Europe, many professions were closed to them, with moneylending being one of the few exceptions. By 1714, the French historian and philosopher Montesquieu was summing up a commonly held view when he wrote: "You ask me whether there are Jews in France? Be sure that wherever there is money, there are Jews."[802]

Mark Twain explained what happened in an 1899 article: "Trade after trade was taken away from the Jew by statute till practically none was left. He was forbidden to engage in agriculture; he was forbidden to practice law; he was forbidden to practice medicine, except among Jews; he was forbidden the handicrafts. Even the seats of learning and the schools of science had to be closed against this tremendous antagonist."[803]

Twain continues: "Still, almost bereft of employments, he found ways to make money, even ways to get rich. Also ways to invest his takings well, for usury was not denied him."[804] As they were neither Christians nor Muslims, Jews were one of the only groups that could pass freely from Christian lands to Islamic lands and back again,

---

[800] Bernard Green, *Christianity in Ancient Rome: The First Three Centuries* (London: A & C Black, 2010), 12.

[801] See chapter two.

[802] Montesquieu, Letter 58, http://montesquieu.ens-lyon.fr/spip.php?article3437.

[803] Mark Twain, "Concerning the Jews," *Harper's Magazine*, March 1898, https://aish.com/48931627/.

[804] Ibid.

and this increased their possibilities for gathering wealth. Jews were adept at being middlemen between European countries and Islamic countries because many of them were multilingual. Yet the Jews' perseverance and ingenuity only fueled more hatred, as they came to be known as rich, grasping, and dishonest rather than poor and wretched, as well as disloyal to the society in which they resided.

In Mark Twain's view, this was why the Jews were expelled from various countries: "The Jew is being legislated out of Russia. The reason is not concealed. The movement was instituted because the Christian peasant and villager stood no chance against his commercial abilities. He was always ready to lend money on a crop, and sell vodka and other necessaries of life on credit while the crop was growing. When settlement day came he owned the crop; and next year or year after he owned the farm, like Joseph."[805] Likewise, "in the dull and ignorant England of John's time everybody got into debt to the Jew. He gathered all lucrative enterprises into his hands; he was the king of commerce; he was ready to be helpful in all profitable ways; he even financed crusades for the rescue of the Sepulchre. To wipe out his account with the nation and restore business to its natural and incompetent channels he had to be banished from the realm."[806]

And so on. Twain concluded: "I am persuaded that in Russia, Austria, and Germany nine-tenths of the hostility to the Jew comes from the average Christian's inability to compete successfully with the average Jew in business."[807] The identification of Jews with capitalism became common, albeit not universal; in 1905, the German sociologist Max Weber published a book entitled *The Protestant Ethic and the Spirit of Capitalism*, in which he argued that the Protestant idea of

---

[805]   Ibid.
[806]   Ibid.
[807]   Ibid.

the spiritual value of work had led to the cultivation of a work ethic that had resulted in the economic prosperity of Protestant societies.

Six years later, Weber's countryman and fellow sociologist Werner Sombart countered with a rival thesis in his own book, *The Jews and Modern Capitalism*. The guiding spirit of capitalism was not Protestantism, he argued, but Judaism: "Let me avow it right away: I think that the Jewish religion has the same leading ideas as Capitalism. I see the same spirit in the one as in the other."[808] He maintained that "the fundamental ideas of capitalism and those of the Jewish character show a singular similarity."[809]

This was, in essence, a positive restatement of Karl Marx's charge that the Jews' "worldly god" was "money," and that, therefore, "emancipation from usury and money, that is, from practical, real Judaism, would constitute the emancipation of our time."[810]

Jews were indeed well represented in the financial sphere, as was to be expected after centuries in which that arena was one of the only ones open to them. Marx and other Jew-haters, however, turned this example of making lemonade out of lemons into yet another indication of the Jews' malign intentions.

And so, the myths grew up that Jews control the banks and the entire global economic system. The infamous 1903 czarist forgery known as *The Protocols of the Elders of Zion* depicted the Jews plotting world domination through economic manipulation: "What we want is that industry should drain off from the land both labor and capital and by means of speculation transfer into our hands all the money of the world, and thereby throw all the goyim into the ranks of the

---

[808] Werner Sombart, *The Jews and Modern Capitalism*, M. Epstein, trans. (Kitchener, Ontario: Batoche Books, 2001), 143.

[809] Ibid., 191.

[810] Marx, *A World Without Jews*, op. cit., 37.

proletariat. Then the goyim will bow down before us, if for no other reason but to get the right to exist."[811]

The *Protocols* was, says economic historian Gerald Krefetz, "silly nonsense, but proving that was not easy. Finally, in 1921, a correspondent for the London Times pointed out its resemblance to a French satire and historians concluded that the *Protocols* was a forgery by the Russian secret police based on the French novel and other works. Subsequently, the *Protocols* was formally condemned in South African and Swiss Courts. But it had set the stage for hysterical anti-Semitism. Both the political right and left used the tract as proof of their theories about Jews."[812]

Automotive pioneer Henry Ford accepted *The Protocols* as fact. In *The International Jew*, his own work that is virtually as infamous as the *Protocols*, he expressed a certain perverse admiration for the fiendish Jews that he was convinced really were out for world domination. Of the *Protocols*, he wrote: "Whosoever was the mind that conceived them possessed a knowledge of human nature, of history and of statecraft which is dazzling in its brilliant completeness, and terrible in the objects to which it turns its powers. Neither a madman nor an intentional criminal, but more likely a super-mind mastered by devotion to a people and a faith could be the author, if indeed one mind alone conceived them. It is too terribly real for fiction, too well-sustained for speculation, too deep in its knowledge of the secret springs of life for forgery."[813]

[811] *The Protocols of the Learned Elders of Zion*, Victor E. Marsden, trans. (England: Mercian Free Press, 2014), 33.

[812] Gerald Krefetz, *Jews and Money: The Myths and the Reality* (New Haven: Ticknor & Fields, 1982), 48.

[813] Henry Ford, *The International Jew* (Aaargh Internet Edition, 2003), 46. https://archive.org/details/FordHenryTheInternationalJewTheWorldsForemostProblemEN2003496P./mode/2up?q=Protocols.

As with virtually all stereotypes, the idea that the Jews control "industry" to the extent that they can control "labor and capital" to their own advantage and the ruin of the "goyim" is based on hateful and unwarranted generalizations from some specific facts. There *is* a significant presence of Jews in banking and economics. Krefetz notes that "modern banking started in the nineteenth century with the rise of the House of Rothschild. They were not the only important Jewish bankers in Europe: indeed, a surprising number of continental banks were founded by Jews.... The new bankers floated state loans to finance emerging industries and railroads. While the five Rothschild brothers had banks in Frankfort, London, Paris, Vienna, and Naples, Bleichroder in Berlin, Warburg in Hamburg, Oppenheim in Cologne, and Speyer in Frankfort were operating their own banking houses. Individual Jews founded banks from London (Hambros) to Bombay (Sassoons) to St. Petersburg (Guenzburg), and a number of points in between."[814]

Yet this was not exactly the same thing as Jewish control of global financial systems: "Jewish bankers projected an image of concentrated power because they often acted in concert, collaborating on financial deals. But in size and power, they could not compare with the Protestant bankers—Morgan, Drexel, Gould, Fiske, Harriman, and Hill. Still, because of their clannishness and presumed power, they were objects of scorn among the Populists at the end of the nineteenth century."[815]

Not only was the alleged Jewish control of global finance not complete, but also, the Jew-haters' fundamental contention was based on assumptions that were, to put it gently, unproven. The fact that many titans of finance were Jewish was taken as ipso facto evidence that these financiers were in league with one another, were acting in

[814] Krefetz, op. cit., 46.
[815] Ibid., 47.

concert, and were working to fulfill Jewish aims of the subversion and destruction of Gentile society that were commanded in the Talmud. Yet as we have seen, the Talmud contains no such directives, and there is no reason to think that Jewish financiers were colluding any more than there was to assume that the Protestant bankers Krefetz mentions were doing so as well.

Nevertheless, Krefetz explains that "with the development of systematic anti-Semitism in Europe, and the rise of xenophobic nationalism, the wealthy Jew was seen as an alien financier, in collaboration with Jews abroad. The collection of Jewish bankers and banks in both Europe and America convinced many people that Jews were out to dominate and control the world."[816]

Among them was Adolf Hitler, who began a global war to end that supposed domination. Even in his final moments, with the world he had made in ruins and rubble all around him, he issued a final warning: "But before everything else I call upon the leadership of the nation and those who follow it to observe the racial laws most carefully, to fight mercilessly against the poisoners of all the peoples of the world, international Jewry."[817]

Yet while Hitler agreed that Jewish bankers were out to control the world, he simultaneously believed that they were the foremost enemies of the global economic system.

CONTRADICTIONS IN THE NARRATIVE

There is a contradiction inherent in Hitler's famous "prophecy" about the eradication of the Jews of Europe. He warns about "the

---

[816] Ibid.

[817] "From Hitler's Testament," Yad Vashem, The World Holocaust Remembrance Center, https://www.yadvashem.org/docs/hitler-testament.html.

international Jewish financiers" who supposedly wanted a world war that they evidently hoped would result in "the Bolshevization of the earth."[818] Yet as Karl Marx himself explained, financiers (Jewish or not) are the mortal enemies of Communism and thus have no interest in seeing, much less fostering, the Bolshevization of the earth.

In the various claims about Jews controlling global finance, and even controlling the world, Jew-haters entangle themselves in yet another contradiction: Jews supposedly control the world's money supply and the levers of international capital while simultaneously inventing Marxism in order to destroy capitalism. It appears as if those who hate the Jews are perfectly capable of believing in two (or more) contradictory ideas at once, as Anthony Julius has noted in his history of antisemitism in England:

> Jews are obtrusively, conspicuously Jewish *and* are adept at concealing their Jewish identity by name change, conversion, etc.; Jews seek the most luxurious, sensual style of life *and* are dirty, smelly, and unattractive; Jews stick together *and* take our jobs; Jews are economic parasites *and* our financial masters; Jews are capitalists *and* revolutionaries; Jews are nationalists *and* agents of national dissolution; and so on. The propositions of anti-Semitic anti-Zionism are similarly contradictory. Israel lacks the essential characteristics of a state, but it *also* has the power to assert itself as a strong nation; Israel could not survive without the United States, but *at the same time*, it has the power to manipulate the United States for its own

---

[818] *The Speeches of Adolf Hitler, April 1922–August 1939*, op. cit.

purposes; Israel is a cowardly, ephemeral entity but it *also* displays a 'Nazi' arrogance and cruelty.[819]

THE JEWS CONTROL THE WORLD, COMMUNIST VERSION

Hitler was not alone. Historian Paul Hanebrink names several "well-known modern antisemites, from Adolf Hitler to the Frenchman Charles Maurras to the Romanian Corneliu Codreanu," who present Communism and capitalism as "two faces of the same international (and antinational) Jewish evil. In their paranoid fantasies, Jewish Communists and Jewish financiers invariably worked together to pursue world domination, each feeding off the power of the other."[820]

This would subvert and destroy the other myth that often circulated (and still circulates) simultaneously along with this one: that the Jews constitute a monolithic group, marching in perfect unity to implement Talmudic commands. But here, it is clear how much Jew-hatred is an attempt to force reality to fit a procrustean bed of preconceived paradigms. Hanebrink also observes that "in many ways, the figure of the Jewish Bolshevik is a modern-day version of medieval fables about Jewish devils intent on subverting the Christian order."[821] To arrive at such a conclusion requires one to maintain a practically preternatural certainty about the intentions of others. It is hardly a rational assessment.

Yet the equation of Judaism with Communism seems at first glance to be based on a sober appraisal of the available data. No less

---

819   Anthony Julius, *Trials of the Diaspora: A History of Anti-Semitism in England* (Oxford: Oxford University Press, 2012), Kindle edition, 47.

820   Paul Hanebrink, *A Specter Haunting Europe: The Myth of Judeo-Bolshevism* (Cambridge, Belknap Press, 2018), Kindle edition, 119.

821   Ibid.

a luminary than Winston Churchill wrote in 1920 about a "sinister confederacy" of "International Jews," who were "mostly men reared up among the unhappy populations of countries where Jews are persecuted on account of their race."[822] He said that "most, if not all, of them have forsaken the faith of their forefathers, and divorced from their minds all spiritual hopes of the next world." He pointed out that among these "International Jews" were many of the most notorious revolutionaries of his day: "Trotsky (Russia), Bela Kun (Hungary), Rosa Luxembourg (Germany), and Emma Goldman (United States)."[823]

Churchill lamented that "this world-wide conspiracy for the overthrow of civilisation and for the reconstitution of society on the basis of arrested development, of envious malevolence, and impossible equality, has been steadily growing," and "now at last this band of extraordinary personalities from the underworld of the great cities of Europe and America have gripped the Russian people by the hair of their heads and have become practically the undisputed masters of that enormous empire."[824] This was, he maintained, a Jewish movement: "There is no need to exaggerate the part played in the creation of Bolshevism and in the actual bringing about of the Russian Revolution by these international and for the most part atheistical Jews."[825]

Churchill was simply expressing common assumptions of the time; the idea that Communism was a Jewish movement, and that those who engineered the Russian Revolution were all Jews, was widespread. Yet it was not accurate. In January 1919, posters circulated identifying the Catholic politician Matthias Erzberger as a Jew and

---

822 Winston Churchill, "Zionism versus Bolshevism: A Struggle for the Soul of the Jewish People," *Illustrated Sunday Herald*, February 8, 1920, 5, https://en.wikisource.org/wiki/Zionism_versus_Bolshevism.

823 Ibid.

824 Ibid.

825 Ibid.

lumping him together with actual Jews as part of a supposed Jewish conspiracy. Erzberger had earned the hatred of German nationalists by signing the armistice with the Allies on November 11, 1918. As the claim spread that Germany had lost the war because of Jewish subversion, Erzberger was "unmasked" as a secret Jew despite being a member of the Catholic Center Party.[826]

Likewise, in Russia, Alexander Kerensky, the first Russian prime minister after the fall of the Romanov dynasty, was widely identified as Jewish among those who believed that the toppling of the Romanovs was a crime against both God and man. Kerensky actually came from a Russian Orthodox family, and his father had been a teacher of Vladimir Ilych Ulyanov, another non-Jew, who later took the name Lenin and became Russia's first Communist leader.

In August 1919, the regime of one of the Jewish revolutionaries Churchill identified, Bela Kun, collapsed in Hungary. Profoundly worried that identification of his movement with Jews and Judaism would lead to persecution, a Hungarian Jewish congregation issued a public statement celebrating the fall of the Kun regime. The statement admitted that many key figures of that regime had been "men of Jewish origin," but stated that "almost without exception, [they] had betrayed first their religion and then their country."[827] They affirmed the loyalty of Jewish Hungarians and their rejection of Bolshevism: "Against every single Communist of Jewish origin stands at least 1000 Jewish Hungarian patriots, faithful to the Hungarian homeland and nation in peace and war...who stood as far from the teachings and mores of Communism as anyone else."[828]

This was a simple and direct affirmation of the truth that exploded virtually all of the central claims of antisemitism: Jews did

---

[826]   Hanebrink, op. cit., 271.
[827]   Ibid., 307.
[828]   Ibid.

not always march in lockstep, but like members of every other group, disagreed with one another, and could and did act in ways that did not accord with the dictates of their religion. Nor was this a matter of a small minority dissenting from the will of the overwhelming majority. Hanebrink observes that "*some* Jews embraced Bolshevism in particular places at particular times for particular reasons. How many were some? In the new Poland, for example, 20–40 percent of the members of the Polish Communist Party in the 1920s were individuals of Jewish origin. But only about 7 percent of Polish Jews voted for the Communist Party during this time. According to the most thorough analysis of the electoral data from this period, 'Jews were no more Communist than Catholic Poles.'"[829]

Facile believers in "Judeo-Bolshevism" or "Talmudic Bolshevism" should also consider an incident from a Jewish Congress that was convened in Kiev in May 1917. During these proceedings, Hanebrink says, "a rabbi asked all present to stand in honor of the Torah. Members of the socialist Bund refused. Shocked, the writer S. A. Ansky insisted that the Torah was not only a religious symbol but also a 'symbol of Jewish culture.' Soon thereafter, Zionists and leftists broke with each other."[830]

It must be granted that many Jews, particularly in Russia, did join the ranks of the Communists, hoping that they would create a society in which they would be relieved of the second-class status and periodic pogroms they had suffered under the rule of the czars. This was far, however, from establishing that Bolshevism was a Jewish movement, devised in order to advance Jewish aims, any more than the preponderance of black Americans in the National Basketball Association means that professional basketball is an inherently black enterprise. A culture that values learning and scholarship will fill the

---

[829] Ibid., 368.
[830] Ibid., 387.

ranks of movements that are intellectual in scope or that require intellectual labor, and that is true not just in politics, but in numerous other fields as well.

The ranks of the most important Marxists all over the world were filled with non-Jews, including such leading lights as Lenin, Mao Zedong, Pol Pot, Fidel Castro, and numerous others. No one has ever explained why these non-Jewish revolutionaries signed on to and became leaders of what was supposedly a Jewish enterprise. Marxism is aggressively atheistic, while Judaism is, in all its variants, quite obviously theistic. When confronted with this basic fact, Jew-haters tend to take refuge in the idea that it is all a clandestine plot to sweep away Christianity (and all other religions) in an atheistic tide. Global atheism will then reveal itself to have been in service of Jewish monotheism all along. At this point, however, those who sound the alarm about Jewish Bolshevism have departed entirely from any remotely rational discussion, and so rational responses are pointless.

THE JEWS CONTROL THE INTER-NATIONAL ORGANIZATIONS

A corollary of the idea of "Jewish Bolshevism" is the claim that the Jews are internationalists who want to subvert the nations of the world in order to solidify their hegemony. Antisemites ascribe efforts to break down the sovereignty of various nation-states, and subsume them into an international socialist megastate, to Jewish influence. They claim that this internationalist initiative arises from the Jews' supposed embrace, or even invention, of international socialism and Communism.

This is supposedly a longstanding imperative, such that the international apparatus of the post-World War II global order, particularly the United Nations, is also regarded as a tool of the Jews. The UN, after all, played a key role in the establishment of the modern state of Israel in 1947 when it proposed that Britain's Mandate for Palestine be divided into two states, a Jewish state and yet another Arab Muslim state. The Arabs turned down this proposal, but Israel declared its independence on May 14, 1948, and became a member state of the United Nations just short of a year later, on May 11, 1949. And on a larger plane, the UN is alleged to be just the first step toward achieving the Jews' internationalist goals.

Yet this claim is even more absurd than the others. The United Nations, despite its role in the founding of the state of Israel, has been unremittingly hostile to that state for decades. That hostility crystallized into a formal imperative with the creation of the UN Human Rights Council (UNHRC) in June 2006. In the nine years from its inception to August 2015, the UNHRC passed sixty-two condemnations of Israel and fifty-five for all the rest of the world combined.[831] In the same time period, despite the brutality of the mullahs' rule in the Islamic Republic of Iran, the UNHRC singled Iran out for condemnation only five times. The notorious human rights abuser North Korea was condemned only eight times. Turkey, despite its ongoing suppression and low-level persecution of the nation's indigenous Christians, leading to a drastic decline in their numbers, was never condemned at all. Bashar Assad's Syria was treated more roughly, receiving seventeen condemnations.

Was Israel really over twelve times worse a human rights abuser than Iran and nearly eight times worse than Communist North Korea? The idea was absurd. The condemnations of Israel generally came in the context of Israeli defensive actions after attacks from jihad groups. The UN did not, however, generally condemn the jihad attacks. And the pattern continued: in 2018, it condemned Israel twenty-one

---

[831] "Updated: Chart of all UNHRC Condemnations," UN Watch, August 11, 2015, https:// unwatch.org/2015/08/11/.

times; it didn't condemn Hamas at all.[832] From 2015 through 2022, the UN General Assembly passed 140 resolutions criticizing Israel and 68 regarding other countries. In 2022, the UN General Assembly passed fifteen resolutions criticizing Israel and thirteen on the entire rest of the world.[833]

Even the administration of US President Barack Obama, which was not friendly to Israel, took notice of this glaring double standard. On December 16, 2016, the US ambassador to the UN, Samantha Power, took the then-unprecedented step of declining to veto a UN resolution calling for an end to the construction of Israeli "settlements" on land over which Israel exercised sovereignty. In the course of this betrayal, however, Power acknowledged the UN's strong bias against the Jewish state:

> As long as Israel has been a member of this institution, Israel has been treated differently from other nations at the United Nations. And not only in decades past—such as in the infamous resolution that the General Assembly adopted in 1975, with the support of the majority of Member States, officially determining that, 'Zionism is a form of racism'—but also in 2016, this year. One need only look at the 18 resolutions against Israel adopted during the UN General Assembly in September; or the 12 Israel-specific resolutions adopted this year in the Human Rights Council—more than those focused on Syria, North Korea, Iran, and South Sudan put together—to see

---

[832]   Virginia Kruta, "UN Year in Review: 21 Condemnations for Israel, None for Hamas or China," *Daily Caller*, December 27, 2018.

[833]   "2022 UNGA Resolutions on Israel vs. Rest of the World," UN Watch, November 14, 2022, https://unwatch.org/2022-2023-unga-resolutions-on-israel-vs-rest-of-the-world/.

that in 2016 Israel continues to be treated differently from other Member States.[834]

If Israel controls the UN, it is doing a singularly poor job of it.

MASS MIGRATION

A corollary of the claim that the Jews control the international organizations is that they are using that control for nefarious ends, particularly in fostering the mass migration of Muslims into Europe in order to subvert and destroy Western civilization. In a 2010 interview, Barbara Lerner Spectre, an American who is the founding director of Paideia, the European Institute for Jewish Studies in Sweden, appeared to lend credence to this view when she said: "Europe has not yet learned how to be multicultural. And I think we are going to be part of the throes of that, of that transformation, which must take place. Europe is not going to be the monolithic, uh, uh, societies that they once were in the last century. Jews are going to be at the center of that. It's a huge transformation for Europe to make. They are now going into a multicultural mode, and Jews will be resented because of our leading role. But without that leading role, and without that transformation, Europe will not survive."[835]

Rabbi Baruch Efrati, a rabbi in Judea and Samaria, cast this mass migration as divine retribution. He was asked: "How do we fight the Islamization of Europe and return it to the hands of Christians and moderates?"[836] In response, Efrati declared: "Jews should rejoice at the fact that Christian Europe is losing its identity as a punishment

[834] "Full Text of US Envoy Samantha Power's Speech after Abstention on Anti-Settlement Vote," *Times of Israel*, December 24, 2016.

[835] IBA News Closeup, "The Jewish Community of Sweden," YouTube, July 9, 2020, https://www.youtube.com/watch?v=G7Z_CE7qTMU.

[836] Kobi Nahshoni, "'Islamization of Europe a Good Thing,'" *Ynet News*, November 11, 2012.

for what it did to us for the hundreds of years were in exile there. We will never forgive Europe's Christians for slaughtering millions of our children, women and elderly... Not just in the recent Holocaust, but throughout the generations, in a consistent manner which characterizes all factions of hypocritical Christianity.... A [sic] now, Europe is losing its identity in favor of another people and another religion, and there will be no remnants and survivors from the impurity of Christianity, which shed a lot of blood it won't be able to atone for."[837] *Ynet News* added that Efrati said, "Jews must pray that the Islamization of most of Europe will not harm the people of Israel."[838] A fond hope.

Another rabbi, David Touitou, who was born in France and now lives in Israel, saw the mass migration as a positive development that hastened the coming of the Messiah. Touitou said in 2013: "The Messiah will come only when Edom, Europe, Christianity has totally fallen. So I ask you, is it good news that Muslims are invading Europe? It's excellent news! It means the coming of the Messiah! Excellent news!"[839]

The statement of a handful of individuals, however, does not make for a Jewish conspiracy. Here again, there is no agreement within the Jewish community that the Islamization of Europe is a positive development. Rabbi David Rosen, an internationally prominent rabbi, warned in 2010 that if Europe didn't recover its Christian roots, it would be "overrun" by Islam, and he did not see this as a remotely positive development.[840] In the heads-I-win-tails-you-lose world of antisemitism, however, Spectre, Efrati, and Touitou are often quoted. Rosen never is.

---

[837] Ibid.

[838] Ibid.

[839] "The Jewish Messiah Will Only Appear Once Edom, Europe, and Christianity Will Be Totally Destroyed," YouTube, May 11, 2024.

[840] Andrew Rettman, "Leading Rabbi Says Europe Risks Being 'Overrun' by Islam," *EU Observer*, November 30, 2010.

Likewise left unquoted are the leading non-Jews who favor the mass migration of Muslims into Europe. The enterprise of mass migration has gained support from a large variety of organizations. The Roman Catholic Church has been among the foremost of these. In 2017, Pope Francis acknowledged that "massive migrant flows" into Europe had "thrown into crisis migratory policies held up to now."[841] He denounced, however, the idea that Catholics or anyone else in Europe should be concerned about preserving the cultural and religious identity of the continent: "I won't hide my concern in the face of the signs of intolerance, discrimination and xenophobia that have arisen in different regions of Europe."[842]

Pope Francis claimed that this intolerance was "often fueled by reticence and fear of the other, the one who is different, the foreigner. I am worried still more by the sad awareness that our Catholic communities in Europe are not exempt from these reactions of defensiveness and rejection, justified by an unspecified 'moral duty' to conserve one's original cultural and religious identity."[843]

In May 2024, the pontiff railed against efforts to close a Catholic charity, Annunciation House, that aids migrants crossing the US Southern border into the United States. The border, he insisted, must remain open. "That is madness," Francis insisted. "Sheer madness. To close the border and leave them there, that is madness. The migrant has to be received."[844]

Francis consistently framed the acceptance of mass migration policies, with no regard for the cultural identity or integrity, much less the security, of the host nation, as a core aspect of the Christian

---

[841] Thomas D. Williams, "Pope Francis Says Concern for 'Cultural Identity' Doesn't Justify Opposition to Mass Migration," *Breitbart*, September 22, 2017.

[842] Ibid.

[843] Ibid.

[844] Nick Robertson, "Pope Francis Denounces Attempts to Close Southern Border as 'Madness,'" *The Hill*, May 19, 2024.

commitment. In his 2018 apostolic exhortation *Gaudete et Exsultate* (Rejoice and Exult), he asked rhetorically whether welcoming migrants was "exactly what Jesus demands of us, when he tells us that in welcoming the stranger we welcome him (cf. *Mt* 25:35)? Saint Benedict did so readily, and though it might have 'complicated' the life of his monks, he ordered that all guests who knocked at the monastery door be welcomed 'like Christ,' with a gesture of veneration; the poor and pilgrims were to be met with 'the greatest care and solicitude.'"[845]

The Greek Orthodox Church was likewise invested in the migrant project. In December 2023, Ecumenical Patriarch Bartholomew of Constantinople implied that opposition to mass migration stemmed from racism or religious bigotry. He echoed Francis in framing support for the migrant issue as simply an outgrowth of the Christian identity: "Let us look beyond the terminology, refugees-migrants-asylum-seekers-internally displaced peoples; let us look beyond the color of their skin, the creed or faith they adhere to; and let us see the eyes of God's human creation, transforming these crises to an opportunity for building bridges, for practicing solidarity, for changing hearts."[846]

So, is the mass migration of Muslims into Europe a Christian plot? The idea that bringing massive numbers of Muslims into Europe, which has already led to sweeping cultural changes in Britain and on the continent, is a Jewish project ignores the central role of major Christian churches in fostering this migration. The real perpetrators of this crisis are the internationalist leftist elites that hold political power in Europe and North America. Antisemites will claim that those elites are made up of Jews or controlled by Jews, but this once again ignores the significant presence of non-Jews among them.

[845] Pope Francis, Apostolic Exhortation *Gaudete et Exsultate*, March 19, 2018, https://www.vatican.va/content/francesco/en/apost_exhortations/documents/papa-francesco_esortazione-ap_20180319_gaudete-et-exsultate.html.

[846] "Address by His All-Holiness Ecumenical Patriarch Bartholomew at the Global Refugee Forum," World Council of Churches, December 14, 2023.

If some Jews believe that the mass migration of Muslims into Europe will be beneficial for the Jews for various reasons (a belief that looks increasingly fanciful as Islamic antisemitism has made the lives of Jews across Europe considerably more precarious), so also some Christians, as well as atheists and others, believe that the mass migration of Muslims into Europe will be beneficial for them as well. For opponents of this mass migration and defenders of Europe's historical identity to single out the Jews for particular blame in this regard is short-sighted.

The mass migration of Muslims into Europe has not benefited the Jews at all. Rabbi Menachem Margolin, the chairman of the European Jewish Association, said several weeks after October 7: "We do get a lot of information, a lot of calls, a lot of emails from Jewish people from Europe, both individuals in the institutions, synagogues, schools. People see in the street that they get much more remarks, many more bad looks, hatred, looks and call for death and physical incitement."[847]

This is largely the result of the huge influx of Muslims into Europe. Political analyst David P. Goldman pointed out in 2018 that Muslim migrants were "the sole source of violent attacks on Jews" in Europe.[848] Noting that Hungary had resisted this migration, Goldman added: "Whatever residual anti-Semitism remains among Hungarians, it doesn't interfere with the open embrace of Jewish life. There are no risks to Jews because there are very few Muslim migrants."[849]

[847] Maria Psara, "Antisemitism in Europe Reaching Levels Unseen in Decades, Says Top Rabbi," *EuroNews*, October 25, 2023.
[848] David P. Goldman, "The Safest Country for European Jews? Try Hungary," *PJ Media*, May 28, 2018.
[849] Ibid.

If the mass migration of Muslims into Europe is a Jewish initiative, it is the handiwork of Jews who are either terminally ignorant of Islamic antisemitism or are nurturing some sort of suicidal impulse.

THE JEWS CONTROL THE MEDIA

Filmmaker Oliver Stone explained it in 2010: "The Jewish domination of the media…There's a major lobby in the United States. They are hard workers. They stay on top of every comment, the most powerful lobby in Washington. Israel has fucked up United States foreign policy for years."[850]

In an October 2022 interview, rapper Kanye West showed that he believed it as well, blaming "Jewish Zionists" for salacious stories about his ex-wife Kim Kardashian: "It's Jewish Zionists that [are] about that life. That's telling this Christian woman that has four black children to put that out as a message in the media."[851] He took for granted that what "Jewish Zionists" wanted out in the media would get there. West added: "You get used to paparazzi taking a picture of you, and you don't get money off it. You just get used to being screwed by the Jewish media. The Jewish media blocked me out. This shit lit right?"[852] He complained of being canceled by "the left, the Jewish media and the Chinese."[853]

The idea that the Jews control the media is much older than both Stone and West. Like the claim that the Jews control the banking industry and global finance, the roots of any plausibility this idea has can be found in the fact that there is such a large number of

---

850   Ben Child, "Oliver Stone Apologises for 'Antisemitic' Remarks," *Guardian*, July 27, 2010.
851   Gadi Zaig, "Kanye Says 'Jewish Zionists' Control the Media, Jews Own the Black Voice," *Jerusalem Post*, October 17, 2022.
852   Ibid.
853   Ibid.

Jews in the establishment media. The *New York Times*, which is still generally considered the leading newspaper in the United States, has been owned by a Jewish family since 1896. David Sarnoff of NBC and William Paley of CBS, as well as Jeff Zucker of CNN somewhat later, lent credence to the idea that the media was a Jewish enterprise.

As in the case of the banking industry, however, the presence of Jews at the helm of major media companies doesn't even come close to establishing that the industry exists in order to further Jewish aims, or even that it represents a Jewish perspective on the news. Comedian Jon Stewart, who is Jewish, put it succinctly in 2005: "If Jews control the media, why don't we give ourselves better press?"[854]

Indeed. In 2006, the Committee for Accuracy in Middle East Reporting and Analysis (CAMERA) pointed out that "in the early years of the Zionist movement, the longtime publisher of the *Guardian*, C.P. Scott, had a close relationship with Zionist Chaim Weizman, and the left leaning paper was considered highly sensitive to the plight of the Jews and their desire for a homeland."[855] That was a long time ago: "But after Israel's victories in the 1967 war much of the Left turned against the Jewish state. As a media standard bearer for highbrow left of center politics in Britain, the *Guardian* followed suit becoming increasingly critical of Israel."[856]

The Left, not the Jews, controls the media, and so when the Left turned against the Jewish state, more than just the *Guardian* fell into line. This is continued up to today. In December 2022, as Benjamin Netanyahu was poised to return as Israeli prime minister, the *New York Times* ran an editorial entitled "The Ideal of Democracy in a Jewish State is in Jeopardy," stating that even though Netanyahu had

---

[854]   Henry Bial, "Jew Media: Performance and Technology for the 58th Century," *TDR*, Vol. 55, No. 3, Jewish American Performance, Fall 2011, 134.

[855]   Steven Stotsky, "Partisanship in The Guardian's Middle East Coverage," CAMERA, January 23, 2006.

[856]   Ibid.

won the recent election, "his coalition's victory was narrow and cannot be seen as a broad mandate to make concessions to ultrareligious and ultranationalist parties that are putting the ideal of a democratic Jewish state in jeopardy."[857]

Netanyahu responded acidly on X with a reference to the *Times's* inglorious history: "After burying the Holocaust for years on its back pages and demonizing Israel for decades on its front pages, the New York Times now shamefully calls for undermining Israel's elected incoming government. While the NYT continues to delegitimize the one true democracy in the Middle East and America's best ally in the region, I will continue to ignore its ill-founded advice and instead focus on building a stronger and more prosperous country, strengthening ties with America, expanding peace with our neighbors, and securing the future of the one and only Jewish state."[858]

Netanyahu was right. *Times* critic Ashley Rindsberg, in a revealing book about the *Times's* biases, observes: "Of all the major failures of the New York Times, its coverage of the Holocaust is the most bitter and difficult to digest."[859] That coverage was just short of nonexistent, and the *Times* wasn't alone in giving scant coverage to one of the most important stories of the twentieth century: "The New York Times was only one of many newspapers that failed in its duty, not just to the Jews interned in death camps, but also to the newly established concepts of international justice and to their own journalistic standards of unwavering truth-telling."[860]

---

[857] *New York Times* Editorial Board, "The Ideal of Democracy in a Jewish State Is in Jeopardy," *New York Times*, December 17, 2022.

[858] Benjamin Netanyahu, X, December 18, 2022, https://twitter.com/netanyahu/status/1604595303230889991.

[859] Ashley Rindsberg, *The Gray Lady Winked: How the New York Times's Misreporting, Distortions and Fabrications Radically Alter History* (Midnight Oil Publishers, 2021), 111.

[860] Ibid., 112.

By the time of Netanyahu's complaint, little or nothing had changed. In a piece about the *Times*'s slanted coverage and Netanyahu's riposte, the media watchdog HonestReporting noted that "a study of The New York Times' coverage of Israel from earlier this year found that the 'newspaper of record' had focused more stories on Israel than on any other Middle Eastern country. Of these stories, 53% were negative in their portrayal of the Jewish state, 34% were neutral, and only 13% were positive."[861]

The *Times* also made it a regular practice to lionize Israel's foes: "In recent years, The New York Times has published an opinion piece that whitewashed the anti-Israel BDS movement, as well as a guest essay that effectively undermined the Israeli fight against Hamas terror by accusing the Jewish state of wantonly and cruelly destroying Gazan infrastructure that has no strategic value. It also ran a guest essay that claimed that the campaign against antisemitism has become a 'threat to freedom.'"[862]

Nothing changed after October 7. Two weeks after the massacre, HonestReporting ran a piece with the headline "OUTRAGE: New York Times Defends Rehiring Pro-Hitler, Pro-Terror Freelancer in Gaza."[863]

Once again, the *Times* was not alone in its anti-Israel bias. HonestReporting stated in January 2024 that "despite The Washington Post espousing principles of 'truth' and 'fairness,' its expansive coverage of the Israel-Hamas war since October 7 has been marred by its bias against Israel's defensive actions and conduct in the region."[864]

---

[861] "Netanyahu Calls Out New York Times in Response to 'Democracy Doomsday' Piece; Palestinians Open Fire at Bus Carrying Knesset Member," HonestReporting, December 19, 2022.

[862] Ibid.

[863] Simon Plosker, "OUTRAGE: New York Times Defends Rehiring Pro-Hitler, Pro-Terror Freelancer in Gaza," HonestReporting, October 21, 2023.

[864] Chaim Lax, "The Washington Post Abandons 'Truth' and 'Fairness' in Its Israel-Hamas War Coverage," HonestReporting, January 29, 2024.

CNN was no better, as HonestReporting noted in April 2024: "CNN recently published articles by two journalists who are better described as anti-Israel mouthpieces. Tamara Qiblawi, a Senior Investigations Writer, and Khader Al Za'anoun, a Gaza-based journalist are both platformed despite CNN being aware of the former's anti-Israel social media posts and the latter's position as a staffer for Wafa, the official Palestinian news agency."[865]

The situation was the same in Britain. CAMERA stated on October 16, 2023, that it had "long challenged BBC editors on their grievous lack of objectivity and double standards in news reporting about the Jewish state."[866] After October 7, CAMERA reported that the BBC had "received considerable pushback for refusing to term the perpetrators of the shocking atrocities 'terrorists.'"[867]

BBC's World Affairs Editor John Simpson tried to justify this as a byproduct of journalistic objectivity: "Terrorism is a loaded word, which people use about an outfit they disapprove of morally. It's simply not the BBC's job to tell people who to support and who to condemn—who are the good guys and who are the bad guys."[868] CAMERA, however, pointed out that "such moral judgements have been made repeatedly by BBC editors when the 'bad guys'—the terrorists—are not-Palestinians and the 'good guys'—the victims—are not Jews. Reporting on terrorist attacks in London, Kuwait, France, Tunisia, Norway and Northern Island, BBC has employed the term 'terror' or 'terrorists' to refer to the attacks and/or to the perpetrators."[869]

---

865   "CNN Platforms Biased Journalists in Coverage of Iran, Gaza," HonestReporting, April 15, 2024.

866   Ricki Hollander, "BBC and CBC Refuse to Call Hamas 'Terrorists' or Refer to Their Actions as 'Terrorism,'" CAMERA, October 16, 2023.

867   Ibid.

868   John Simpson, "Why BBC Doesn't Call Hamas Militants 'Terrorists,'" BBC, October 11, 2023.

869   Hollander, "BBC and CBC Refuse...," op. cit.

Such examples could be multiplied endlessly. One would, in fact, be hard-pressed to find a major establishment media print or broadcast media outlet that was favorable to Israel, or that even provided the Jewish state with consistently fair coverage. And so, the question must be asked of those who still believe that the Jews control the media, even after the entire world has ganged up against Israel in the wake of the October 7 massacre: why are they so bad at it? As Jon Stewart asked, why have they been so singularly inept in exercising this control? In 2021, 80 percent of Jews in the United States said that they supported Israel and that Israel was important to them.[870] If Jews controlled the media, one could reasonably expect that this overwhelming support would have translated to favorable or at least objective and fair coverage of Israel. It has not.

Yet the myth that Jews control the media, and that the media is a mouthpiece for Jewish causes and concerns, has been as persistent as other antisemitic fabrications. This illustrates yet again that hatred and suspicion of the Jews is not a distaste based upon rational evaluation and honest consideration of the available evidence. This is an irrational hatred that is frequently presented in the dress of reasoned conclusions in order to fool the unwary.

THE JEWS CONTROL THE PORN OGRAPHY INDUSTRY?

The Talmud is charged, as we have seen, with commanding Jews to subvert and destroy Gentile society. Christian antisemites claim that by rejecting Christ, Jews became the everlasting enemies of Christian

---

[870] "7. U.S. Jews' Connections with and Attitudes toward Israel," Pew Research Center, May 11, 2021, https://www.pewresearch.org/religion/2021/05/11/u-s-jews-connections-with-and-attitudes-toward-israel/.

society, and even of civilization in general. What more effective way to accomplish the destruction of the hated society than by sapping its moral strength and destroying its character, rendering it weak, selfish, hedonistic, and so addicted to pleasures that it would be both unwilling and unable to summon the will to make the sacrifices necessary to defend itself in a time of crisis? This is, antisemites claim, the purpose of the Jews' involvement in the pornography industry.

This is not a new charge. Adolf Hitler believed that the Jewish effort to poison society was in full swing in his day. In *Mein Kampf*, he wrote: "The fact that nine tenths of all literary filth, artistic trash, and theatrical idiocy can be set to the account of a people, constituting hardly one hundredth of all the country's inhabitants, could simply not be talked away; it was the plain truth."[871] Today, one of the main forms that filth, trash, and idiocy take is pornography, and if Hitler were among us today, he would readily assert that pornography, too, was a Jewish plot.

Reality is more prosaic. There are some people from Jewish backgrounds who are involved in the pornography industry. But there are also people from Christian backgrounds, and yet no one claims that pornography is a Christian plot. Pornography is also a worldwide industry. Antisemites point to a number of Jews who are involved in pornography in the US and the West in general, but pornography is also produced in areas of the world where few Jews live, and they don't have any significant involvement in the pornography industry. Pornography is a global phenomenon, and Jews only make up a small percentage of those who are involved in it.

Just as Jews became bankers and financiers when the Roman Catholic Church's prohibition on usury closed those fields to Catholics, so also the wider society's disdain for pornography tended to make it a field to which those who were marginalized and often treated as

---

[871] Hitler, op. cit., 58.

outcasts gravitated, and so some Jews got involved in it. This is, once again, a tremendous distance from seeing the pornography industry as a massive and insidious Jewish plot. Luke Ford, an Australian-born convert to Judaism, porn industry gossip, and anti-porn crusader with an ongoing fascination for it, sees the problem from the other side: the Jews' culturally cultivated creativity and dynamism lead to their being despised and relegated to the margins of society. When non-religious Jews rebel against the values of their own community, they sometimes embrace businesses, such as pornography, that historically have existed at those margins:

> That's part of the reason that Jews are hated. The world doesn't want to be changed. Rooted in nothing, radical Jews frequently seek to make others equally rootless by tearing down their religious, national, communal and traditional allegiances. Such Jews carry on the traditional Jewish hatred of false gods but without offering anything to replace the scorned allegiances…. Rather, the most important result of the domination of non-Jewish Jews in these fields is their war on traditional values. Porn is just one expression of this rebellion against standards, against the disciplined life of obedience to Torah that marks a Jew living Judaism.[872]

In his 2004 memoir, a chronicle of ambivalence entitled *XXX-Communicated: A Rebel Without a Shul*, Luke Ford recounts his meeting with Al Goldstein, who was described in his *New York Times* obituary as "the scabrous publisher whose *Screw* magazine pushed

---

[872] E. Michael Jones, *The Jewish Revolutionary Spirit and Its Impact on World History* (South Bend, Indiana: Fidelity Press, 2015), 1024.

hard-core pornography into the cultural mainstream."[873] In a quotation that circulates widely among Jew-haters to this day, Goldstein appears to confirm the worst antisemitic charges. Ford recounts that "at the insistence of *Weekly Standard* journalist Matt Labash, I explain to Al my theory about why porn attracts so many Jews."[874] Ford doesn't remind the reader of his theory at that point, and it doesn't seem to be coherently delineated elsewhere in his book, either, but it is likely akin to his statements about non-religious Jews being at war with traditional values.

E. Michael Jones, who believes that Jews fabricated the Holocaust in order to gain world sympathy for the creation of the state of Israel, says that Goldstein's response "got to what one might call the theological heart of the matter."[875] Goldstein interrupts Luke Ford's retelling of his theory to ask him: "Now where were you born, Luke? Australia? You don't know a flying fuck about anything. You're an ex-felon. If you weren't, your father was. You're a bunch of refugees from a penal colony. The only reason that Jews are in pornography is that we think that Christ sucks. Catholicism sucks. We don't believe in authoritarianism. We know that the anti-porn stuff is a bunch of claptrap to make us feel guilty. We have a clean slate when we look at the world. We see opportunities."[876]

Despite his contradiction of Luke Ford, Goldstein seems to be confirming the idea that he is at war with traditional values. He also appears to be confirming the antisemitic claim that pornography is a Jewish weapon against Gentile society. Jones asserts that "the conversation got progressively more theological, at least in the Goldstein

---

[873] Andy Newman, "Al Goldstein, a Publisher Who Took the Romance Out of Sex, Dies at 77," *New York Times*, December 19, 2013.

[874] Luke Ford, *XXX-Communicated: A Rebel Without a Shul* (Lincoln, Nebraska: iUniverse, 2004), 69.

[875] Jones, *Jewish Revolutionary Spirit*, op. cit.

[876] Ford, op. cit., 69.

mode."[877] Goldstein is, however, poorly cast in the role of theologian that Jones so very much wants him to play. When Ford asks him if he believes in God, Goldstein replies: "I believe in me. I'm God. Fuck God. God is your need to believe in some super being. I am the super being. I am your God, admit it. We're random. We're the flea on the ass of the dog."[878] When asked what being Jewish means to him, Goldstein is once again stingingly blunt: "It doesn't mean shit. It means that I'm called a kike."[879]

For Jones, Goldstein's response carries extraordinary significance. "Being Jewish," Jones claims, "provides Goldstein with a rationalization for being in an unsavory business."[880] Goldstein, Jones adds, "can hide behind centuries old Jewish antipathy to Christianity as the justification for what he is doing. Jews like Goldstein have become so habituated to defining themselves as the antithesis of things Christian that they start to define themselves in opposition to things which both Judaism and Christianity hold in common as well, namely, the moral law in general and sexual prohibitions in particular."[881]

Yet Jones's analysis of Goldstein's words was heavily influenced by his own presuppositions. Goldstein does not actually use being Jewish as a rationalization for being in an unsavory business. He rejects being Jewish and says it means nothing to him except that it makes him a victim of bigotry; Jones quotes this but passes over Goldstein's disavowal of Judaism without comment. In reality, Goldstein identifies Christ and Catholicism with authoritarianism and Jews in pornography as fighting against that authoritarianism, presumably in the name of the freedom of expression. He sees himself as a victim of

---

877   Jones, *Jewish Revolutionary Spirit*, op. cit., 1025.
878   Ford, op. cit.
879   Ibid.
880   Jones, *Jewish Revolutionary Spirit*, op. cit., 1024.
881   Ibid., 1024–5.

anti-Jewish prejudice and sees working in pornography as a way to strike back against those who treated him unjustly.

But that is all. Quite aside from the question of whether this was a rational, prudent, fruitful, or productive path for Goldstein to have taken, his words cannot be taken as evidence of pornography being part of a Jewish plot of subversion without ignoring key elements of what he said. He does not say he was motivated to go into pornography because of Jewish (or "Talmudic") principles. He does not say that he sees Judaism as playing any role in his life at all. He mentions it, and his antipathy to Christ and Catholicism, in the context of his rejection of authoritarianism and bigotry, with which he identifies them.

Jones, however, contends that Goldstein's stated goal of subversion is derived from Judaism's antipathy to Christ and that Goldstein, although an unbeliever who is contemptuous of theism, has somehow imbibed what he characterizes as the subversive and revolutionary aspects of Judaism without accepting any of the rest of it, including its traditional sexual morality.

Jones would contend that this is precisely how secular Jews operate: having lost the idea of God and the spiritual realm, they aim to transform this world in accordance with their vision of the perfect society. This supposedly leads to Marxism as well as to the materialistic hedonism of which the acceptance of pornography is a part. In this scenario, Judaism is inescapable, and not only for Jews. Even the Jews who discard it find themselves implementing its agenda, even in spite of themselves, as in the case of Goldstein. And thus, any movement of any kind in which Jews are involved becomes a Jewish movement with nefarious ends. Jones also approvingly quotes Ford as saying:

> Virtually all movements to change the world come
> from the Jews—Christianity, secular humanism,

Marxism, Socialism and Communism, feminism, and
the labor movement.[882]

Jones clearly endorses this view, but he believes that Jews and
Judaism are at perpetual war with Christianity, while embracing secular humanism, Marxism, Socialism and Communism, feminism, and
the labor movement without any hesitation. For Jones, there is apparently no possibility of a Jew living as a Jew without being consumed
with a hatred for Christianity and a desire to destroy it.

Meanwhile, whatever the merits of Luke Ford's argument may
be, he is not actually supporting Jones's case at all. While Ford contends that there is significant Jewish involvement in pornography,
he posits the "obedience to Torah that marks a Jew living Judaism"
as the alternative to the war on traditional values that he says that
"non-Jewish Jews," that is, Jews who aren't religious or observant, are
pursuing. Yet in Jones's world, a "Jew living Judaism" will end up
being just as subversive and hostile to Gentile society as Al Goldstein
was, and Goldstein's subversive impulse can itself be traced back to
Jewish principles.

This is a classic example of someone trying to have his cake and
eat it, too, or playing the game of "heads I win, tails you lose." Jones's
argument is superficial and ultimately incoherent. He has set up a
scenario in which practically anything he dislikes can be ascribed to
Judaism if any Jews can be found to be involved in it. If they're religious, they're raging with hatred of Christ and determined to destroy
Christian societies. If they are not religious, they're subversives and
revolutionaries who are likewise determined to destroy Christian
societies, because that determination is all that remains of their Jewish identity.

---

[882]   Ibid., 1024.

In reality, if Goldstein was not an observant Jew, or even someone with any interest in Judaism, his actions cannot be ascribed to Judaism. If there are Jews at high levels of the pornography industry, this is not because they are Jews executing some subversive Jewish agenda, but because in that field, as in so many others, people who are intelligent, capable, motivated, and driven—all qualities that Jewish culture generally encourages—tend to rise to the top.

Jones does the same thing with many other secular Jews. He describes the twentieth-century psychiatrist Wilhelm Reich, one of the intellectual pioneers of the sexual revolution (indeed, he coined the phrase and published the book *The Sexual Revolution* in 1945), as a "Jewish cultural subversive."[883] Yet Reich's biographer Myron Sharaf notes that Reich objected to his father having been identified as "Jewish-born" in a publication about Reich.[884] Reich, says Sharaf, "acknowledged this but described at length how his father had moved away from 'Jewish chauvinism' and reared his children in a progressive, international way. Reich himself did not follow Jewish customs or beliefs and he did not wish to be categorized as a Jew despite the conventional practice in this matter."[885]

It may have been the absence of Judaism, and of an appreciation for traditional values, that led Reich down the path that he took. For Jones and others who share his perspective, however, there is no escape: one is always a Jew, no matter what one believes. If one does anything that can be construed or portrayed as subversive, this is yet more evidence of Jewish perfidy.

---

[883] Ibid., 724.
[884] Myron Sharaf, *Fury on Earth: A Biography of Wilhelm Reich* (London: André Deutsch, 1983), 463.
[885] Ibid.

PORNHUB

Another target of this approach has been a Canadian Jewish attorney named Solomon Friedman. Friedman is vice president of compliance at Ethical Capital Partners, a private equity firm that bought MindGeek (now Aylo), the parent company of PornHub, in 2023. Friedman studied Talmudic law in Jerusalem but later studied law at the University of Ottawa. Although he is widely identified as a rabbi, he is actually a practicing attorney. His involvement in the ownership of the leading pornography site on the Internet has made him a lightning rod for those who claim that the dissemination of pornography itself is a gigantic Jewish plot.

Yet the way Friedman is portrayed in antisemitic material flies in the face of the facts. There is no actual evidence anywhere that his actions regarding Aylo were motivated or guided by Talmudic or Jewish principles. Human beings, including Jews, can and do act from a variety of motives, while antisemitism sees Jews who do things to which they object as wholly and solely motivated by Jewish principles calling for the destruction of the larger society.

For his part, Friedman does not appear to see his efforts as destructive at all. While many take for granted that pornography is corrosive to society and that anyone involved in it is either a corruptor or someone who has been corrupted, the idea of ridding the pornography industry, or at least PornHub, of exploitation and coercion while continuing to present pornographic content is based on several undeniable facts: pornography is legal in Western societies and isn't going to disappear, so it is better regulated than consigned to the shadows, where illegal activity can go on under cover of darkness. Friedman has instituted an elaborate system of regulation at PornHub that is designed to eliminate exploitation as much as possible. The *Washington Post* said in an April 2024 article that Friedman "wants to reform Pornhub, he said, with plans to compensate performers more fairly, keep nonconsensual material off the site, and vet studios and performers more closely."[886]

Friedman says that Pornhub's executives "share the very same values of the general public. We want to respect people's bodily autonomy. We want to protect young people. We cherish freedom of expression, individuality and sexuality. There's a reason why adult content is constitutionally protected in every single Western liberal democracy."[887] He has detailed safeguards that he and his team have implemented in order to minimize the damage that pornography can do, including age restrictions and stringent requirements of consent from all the performers.[888]

In February 2024, Aylo began working with Crime Stoppers International in order to police the content on PornHub more efficiently. Crime Stoppers deputy CEO Hayley Van Loon said: "We can either partner with the adult entertainment industry, which is going to produce content regardless, or we can ignore it," she said. "So why not partner? Why not be involved in making the space safer?"[889] Friedman observed: "I think it's a real turning point not only for the company, but also the industry. We would like to lead by example in the adult industry. We want this to be the norm."[890]

One may not agree with the contention that pornography is better regulated than banned outright. It is hard to see, however, Aylo's efforts to make the industry safer for everyone involved as evidence of an effort to destroy society, much less a Talmudic one. Of course, those who cast Solomon Friedman in that role in the first place will

---

[886] Hallie Lieberman, "Can PornHub Be Ethical?," *Washington Post*, April 20, 2024.
[887] Ibid.
[888] Ibid.
[889] Andrew Duffy, "Pornhub's Ottawa Owners Join Forces with Crime Stoppers International," *Ottawa Citizen*, February 19, 2024.
[890] Ibid.

not be deterred by anything he says or anything Aylo or PornHub does. Like E. Michael Jones, if they see a Jew involved in something they can use to portray Jews and Judaism in a negative light, they will use it, and the evidence be damned.

Chapter Twelve

THE MOST
HATED STATE

GENOCIDE IN GAZA?

On November 3, 2023, Rep. Rashida Tlaib (D-Michigan) published a video in which she accused US President Joe Biden of supporting "the genocide of the Palestinian people."[891] On March 22, 2024, Rep. Alexandria Ocasio-Cortez (D-New York) said on the floor of the House of Representatives: "If you want to know what an unfolding genocide looks like, open your eyes. It looks like the forced famine of 1.1 million innocents. It looks like thousands of children eating grass as their bodies consume themselves, while trucks of food are

---

[891] Zoë Richards, "Rep. Rashida Tlaib Accuses Biden of Supporting 'Genocide' of Palestinian People," *NBC News*, November 3, 2023.

slowed and halted just miles away."[892] Late in April 2024, Rep. Ilhan Omar (D-Minnesota) suggested that some Jewish students were "pro-genocide."[893]

Tlaib, Ocasio-Cortez, and Omar, the founding members of the far-left "Squad," were considered radical. But many others who were thought to be more mainstream agreed that Israel's defensive action in Gaza was a massive humanitarian crisis that had to be curtailed before it attained its goal of completely destroying Hamas, or else an unprecedented catastrophe would ensue.

"The United States is unequivocal; international humanitarian law must be respected. Too many innocent Palestinians have been killed," declared Vice President Kamala Harris on December 2, 2023.[894] "Frankly, the scale of civilian suffering and the images and videos coming from Gaza are devastating."[895] Two days later, the Associated Press (AP) reported that Sen. Bernie Sanders (I-Vermont) and what it called "a robust group of Democratic senators" were "done 'asking nicely' for Israel to do more to reduce civilian casualties in Gaza."[896]

These senators "warned President Joe Biden's national security team that planned US aid to Israel must be met with assurances of concrete steps from Israeli Prime Minister Benjamin Netanyahu's hard-right government."[897] Sanders thundered, "The truth is that if asking nicely worked, we wouldn't be in the position we are today."

892   Nicholas Fandos, "Ocasio-Cortez, in House Speech, Accuses Israel of 'Genocide,'" *New York Times*, March 22, 2024.

893   Maggie Astor, "Omar Draws Criticism for Suggesting Some Jewish Students Are 'Pro-Genocide,'" *New York Times*, April 29, 2024.

894   Josh Meyer, "VP Harris Calls on Israel to Respect International Law, Stop Killing Innocent Palestinians," *USA Today*, December 2, 2023.

895   Ibid.

896   Ellen Knickmeyer and Lisa Mascaro, "Democratic Senators Demand Israel Reduce Civilian Casualties in Gaza as Part of Aid Package," Associated Press, December 4, 2023.

897   Ibid.

AP added, "It was time for the United States to use its 'substantial leverage' with its ally, the Vermont senator said."[898]

Worried about losing their far-left base, Biden and his handlers heeded their warning. After a few months of steadily increasing pressure, the American delegation at the United Nations allowed the Security Council to pass a resolution calling for an immediate ceasefire in Gaza, knowing that this would enable Hamas to survive and regroup.[899] Shortly thereafter, the White House announced that during a phone conversation on April 4, 2024, Biden told Israeli Prime Minister Benjamin Netanyahu "to announce and implement a series of specific, concrete, and measurable steps to address civilian harm, humanitarian suffering, and the safety of aid workers. He made clear that U.S. policy with respect to Gaza will be determined by our assessment of Israel's immediate action on these steps."[900] Secretary of State Antony Blinken added: "Look, I'll just say this: if we don't see the changes that we need to see, there will be changes in our policy."[901]

There were. On April 22, 2024, the State Department published its 2023 Country Reports on Human Rights Practices.[902] Fox News noted that the Biden State Department report "highlighted Israel prominently, featuring concerns over the country's precautions to minimize the civilian toll of Palestinians on the first page, which is normally reserved for the most egregious of human rights abusers."[903]

---

[898] Ibid.

[899] Richard Roth, Ivana Kottasová, Lauren Izso, and Jeremy Diamond, "Israel Cancels Washington Visit after US Allows UN Gaza Ceasefire Resolution to Pass," *CNN*, March 25, 2024.

[900] Arshad Mohammed, Matt Spetalnick, and Steve Holland, "Biden Ultimatum to Netanyahu: Protect Gaza Civilians, or Else," *New York Times*, April 5, 2024.

[901] Ibid.

[902] "2023 Country Reports on Human Rights Practices," US State Department Bureau of Democracy, Human Rights and Labor, April 22, 2024, https://www.state.gov/reports/2023-country-reports-on-human-rights-practices/.

[903] Julia Johnson, "Biden Admin Notes 'Urgent' Concern over Israel in Gaza Human Rights Report," *Fox News*, April 22, 2024.

Not only did the report include Israel among the most barbaric human rights abusers—China, Putin's Russia, the Taliban, and Iran—but "Israel was mentioned before the Biden administration's State Department addressed 'ongoing and brutal human rights abuses in Iran' or 'the Taliban's systemic mistreatment of and discrimination against Afghanistan's women and girls.'"[904] In Iran, they chant "Death to America" and have been waging war against their own people, brutally suppressing nationwide riots that broke out after Sharia police murdered a young woman, Mahsa Amini, who had been arrested for not wearing her hijab properly.[905] In Afghanistan, girls have been denied the right to an education, and the Taliban regime's Supreme Leader announced in late March: "We will flog women in public, we will stone them to death in public."[906] The State Department offered no comparable quotes from Israel's leaders because, of course, there were none to be had.

Nevertheless, as far as the State Department is concerned, Israel's alleged human rights violations were so egregious that they warranted discussion immediately after the report mentions "the Kremlin's disregard and contempt for human rights," which were "on full display in its war against Ukraine," and the "horrific violence, death, and destruction, including mass killings, unjust detentions, rape, and other forms of gender-based violence" that the Sudanese Armed Forces had unleashed in that country.[907]

The United Nations threw the full weight of its moral authority behind these claims. On October 27, 2023, the UN Office for the Coordination of Humanitarian Affairs (OCHA) began keeping

[904]   Ibid.
[905]   Tzvi Joffre, "Iranian Activist: Desperate Regime Waging All-Out War against Women," *Jerusalem Post*, April 21, 2024.
[906]   John Simpson, X, March 25, 2024, https://twitter.com/JohnSimpsonNews/status/1772400 270896508990.
[907]   "2023 Country Reports on Human Rights Practices," op. cit.

a running tally of casualties among Palestinians and Israelis. As of that day, OCHA stated, 7,028 Palestinians had been killed, including 1,709 women and 2,913 children, constituting a startling 69 percent of the fatalities.[908]

Such figures not only aroused the righteous indignation of numerous political and media figures; they also moved Jew-haters to the heights of hysteria. In late November 2023, the antisemitic Unz Review wrote: "Over 14,000 Gazans have died from the relentless Israeli bombardment of the last few weeks, two-thirds of them women and children and almost none of them members of Hamas. That total represents the official figures of identified bodies, and with most of the local medical system destroyed and so many thousands more missing, buried under the rubble of the tens of thousands of demolished buildings, the true death toll probably already exceeds 20,000."[909] Unz claimed that this constituted a genocide of world-historical proportions: "We are certainly witnessing the greatest televised slaughter of helpless civilians in the history of the world, with nothing even remotely comparable coming to mind."[910]

The Unz Review article included a link on "official figures of identified bodies" that led to an article in *The Economist* that cited figures from Gaza's Ministry of Health. *The Economist* did have the residual decency to note that Gaza's Health Ministry was "run by Hamas," although it did not spell out for its readers why Hamas would want to exaggerate, or even fabricate outright, its casualty figures in order to garner sympathy and demonize Israel.[911] Nor did

---

[908] "Hostilities in the Gaza Strip and Israel - Reported Impact | Day 20," OCHA, October 27, 2023, https://www.ochaopt.org/content/hostilities-gaza-strip-and-israel-reported-impact-day-20.

[909] Ron Unz, "American Pravda: Gaza and the Antisemitism Hoax," Unz Review, November 27, 2023. https://www.unz.com/runz/american-pravda-gaza-and-the-anti-semitism-hoax/.

[910] Ibid.

[911] "Deaths in Gaza Surpass 14,000, According to Its Authorities," *The Economist*, November 23, 2023.

it say anything about Hamas's practice of launching attacks from civilian areas in order to draw retaliatory fire that could be used for propaganda purposes.

The Unz Review and the far-left *Economist* were one thing, but it could have been reasonably expected that the UN would rely on more accurate sources. Yet it did not. From the first day it reported casualties in Gaza, OCHA admitted in fine print that its figures came from "the Palestinian Ministry of Health in Gaza."[912] These figures were generally accepted and widely repeated in the establishment media, with only occasional reminders that they actually came from Hamas.

The small-print notation that the figures came from the Gaza Health Ministry could be found on each day's OCHA casualty report through Day 48, November 23, 2023.[913] OCHA then stopped publishing the daily reports until Day 57, December 2, 2023; when they returned, the previous double notation "Soruces [sic]: Ministry of Health, Government Media Office" and "According to the Ministry of Health in Gaza" had been changed to the single notice, "Soruces [sic]: Ministry of Health, Government Media Office," with no indication of exactly which government or health ministry was meant.[914]

Two days after the OCHA report reappeared, Salo Aizenberg, a board member of the media watchdog HonestReporting, took a close look at OCHA's day-to-day casualty figures and found a large number of significant anomalies. "It is immediately obvious," he noted, "that Hamas does not report ANY combatant deaths & the numbers amazingly seem to indicate that IDF bombs & bullets disproportionately

912   "Hostilities in the Gaza Strip and Israel - Reported Impact | Day 20," op. cit.
913   "Hostilities in the Gaza Strip and Israel - Reported Impact | Day 48," OCHA, November 23, 2023, https://www.ochaopt.org/content/hostilities-gaza-strip-and-israel-reported-impact-day-48.
914   "Hostilities in the Gaza Strip and Israel - Reported Impact | Day 57," OCHA December 2, 2023, https://www.ochaopt.org/content/hostilities-gaza-strip-and-israel-reported-impact-day-57.

hit women, children & elderly. The IDF CANNOT seem to hit too many fighting age men."[915] But also, "the numbers are faked."[916]

A close look at those numbers makes that fact undeniable. On October 19, 2023, the total casualty number increased by 307, from 3,478 to 3,785. Yet at the same time, the total number of children killed went from 853 to 1,524, an increase of 671.[917] Nor was that the only time such a thing happened. On October 26, 2023, the total number of casualties increased by 481, while the number of children casualties went up by 626.[918] Clearly, the Hamas Ministry of Health in Gaza was not concerned that people would study the numbers it supplied particularly closely; the idea was simply to shock and appall people with Israel's alleged inhumanity, and that was working well enough.

By April 8, 2024, Day 184 of the conflict, OCHA was reporting, still via the Gaza Ministry of Health, that 33,207 Palestinians had been killed, including "more than 9,500 women" and "~14,500 children."[919] That was, however, the last day of OCHA's daily casualty reports, although it maintained on the front page of its website a running tally of the "Reported Impact Since 7 October 2023."[920] OCHA did not announce why it discontinued the daily reports, but it may have had something to do with another news item that appeared shortly before the reports stopped. On April 6, 2024, the Gaza Ministry of Health actually admitted in a statement on its Tele-

---

[915] Salo Aizenberg, X, December 4, 2023, https://twitter.com/Aizenberg55/status/1731753066 402115900.

[916] Ibid.

[917] Salo Aizenberg, X, December 4, 2023, https://twitter.com/Aizenberg55/status/1731753068 738326846.

[918] Salo Aizenberg, X, December 4, 2023, https://twitter.com/Aizenberg55/status/1731753071 972106356.

[919] "Hostilities in the Gaza Strip and Israel - Reported Impact | Day 184," OCHA, April 8, 2024, https://www.ochaopt.org/content/hostilities-gaza-strip-and-israel-reported-impact-day-184.

[920] "Reported Impact Since 7 October 2023," OCHA, https://www.ochaopt.org/.

gram channel that it had "incomplete data" for over a third of the casualties it was claiming to have counted: 11,371 out of 33,091.[921]

The Foundation for the Defense of Democracies also pointed out that the Hamas-controlled health ministry had "released a report on April 3 that acknowledged the presence of incomplete data but did not define what it meant by 'incomplete.' In that earlier report, the ministry acknowledged the incompleteness of 12,263 records. It is unclear why, after just three more days, the number fell to 11,371—a decrease of more than 900 records. Prior to its admissions of incomplete data, the health ministry asserted that the information in more than 15,000 fatality records had stemmed from 'reliable media sources.' However, the ministry never identified the sources in question and Gaza has no independent media."[922] Yet OCHA continued to report the Hamas figures without noting this "incomplete data" in any way.

There were other anomalies as well. Chaim Lax of HonestReporting noted in April 2024 that there were also discrepancies between "the different casualty counts released by the Hamas government organs."[923] A study published in *Fathom Journal* in March 2024, "Statistically Impossible: A Critical Analysis of Hamas's Women and Children Casualty Figures," explained one of these instances: "Perhaps the most bizarre examples of disinformation occurred in early December, when the GMO [Hamas' Government Media Office] was the leading provider of Gazan casualty statistics. Between 1 December and 8 December the recorded number of dead men *declined* from

[921] "Hamas-Run Gaza Health Ministry Admits to Flaws in Casualty Data," Foundation for the Defense of Democracies, April 9, 2024, https://www.fdd.org/analysis/2024/04/09/hamas-run-gaza-health-ministry-admits-to-flaws-in-casualty-data/.

[922] Ibid.

[923] Chaim Lax, "Skewed Statistics: A Look at the Numbers Behind Gaza's Civilian Casualties," HonestReporting, April 2, 2024, https://honestreporting.com/skewed-statistics-a-look-at-the-numbers-behind-gazas-civilian-casualties/.

4,850 to 3,499, with multiple individual declines occurring over the period (2 December, 5 December, 8 December). It was the statistical equivalent of the resurrection of over a thousand men!"[924]

Another study found that "according to the media reports methodology, only 1,192 men had been killed in northern and central Gaza as of March 18, despite four and a half months of heavy ground fighting.... Five days later, that number inexplicably *decreased* to 1,170—a feat that would have required 22 men to somehow come back to life by March 23 in order to reconcile the central collection system data with the overall claim."[925]

Finally, in May 2024, the UN tacitly admitted that its data, which had gone around the world, was faulty. On May 6, it claimed that the Israelis had killed over 9,500 women and over 14,500 children. Two days later, however, it was reporting that only 4,959 women and 7,797 children had been killed.[926] No explanation was given for the discrepancy, but it was likely that the UN had found it impossible to ignore the growing number of studies proving that the Hamas figures it was endorsing were fabricated.

The charge of genocide was never anything more than an obscene libel. John Spencer, chair of urban warfare studies at the Modern War Institute (MWI) at West Point, analyzed the IDF's actions in Gaza and reported in late March 2024 that "Israel has implemented more precautions to prevent civilian harm than any military in history—above and beyond what international law requires and more than the

---

[924] Tom Simpson, Lewi Stone, and Gregory Rose, "Statistically Impossible: A Critical Analysis of Hamas's Women and Children Casualty Figures," *Fathom Journal*, March 2024, https://fathomjournal.org/statistically-impossible-a-critical-analysis-of-hamass-women-and-children-casualty-figures/.

[925] Gabriel Epstein, "Gaza Fatality Data Has Become Completely Unreliable," Washington Institute for Near East Policy, March 26, 2024.

[926] Yuval Barnea, "UN Seemingly Halves Estimate of Gazan Women, Children Killed," *Jerusalem Post*, May 11, 2024.

U.S. did in its wars in Iraq and Afghanistan."[927] Likewise, the British Colonel Richard Kemp stated in early April 2024 that in Gaza, "the ratio of deaths of civilians to military personnel was far lower than in other wars where armies had not been accused of war crimes, adding that he was 'not aware of any war crimes [committed by the IDF].'"[928]

The ancient antisemitic charges are repurposed against Israel, and new ones added. Yet upon examination, they have no more substance than any of the others.

STOLEN LAND?

Any college or university student living in a pro-Palestinian encampment after October 7 can tell you that he or she is struggling for the rights of the indigenous people of the land, the Palestinians.

This assumption coincides with claims that the Palestinians themselves make. Palestinian Authority President Mahmoud Abbas declared in 2016: "Our narrative says that we were in this land since before Abraham. I am not saying it. The Bible says it. The Bible says, in these words, that the Palestinians existed before Abraham. So why don't you recognize my right?"[929] One reason why not is because the Bible doesn't actually mention "the Palestinians" at all, much less state that they existed before Abraham.

Abbas may have been thinking of the Canaanites. A spokesman for the aged Palestinian president stated: "The nation of Palestine upon the land of Canaan had a 7,000-year history B.C.E. This is the

[927] John Spencer, "Israel Has Created a New Standard for Urban Warfare. Why Will No One Admit It?," *Newsweek*, March 25, 2024.

[928] Gaby Wine, "Hundreds Show Solidarity with Israel at 6-month Vigil in St John's Wood," *The Jewish Chronicle*, April 7, 2024.

[929] Itamar Marcus, "Abbas Falsely Claims 6,000-year-old Palestinian Nation," Palestinian Media Watch, June 6, 2016.

truth, which must be understood, and we have to note it, in order to say: 'Netanyahu, you are incidental in history. We are the people of history. We are the owners of history.'"[930] A member of Fatah's Revolutionary Council, Dimitri Diliani, said: "The Palestinian people [are] descended from the Canaanite tribe of the Jebusites that inhabited the ancient site of Jerusalem as early as 3200 BCE."[931]

Such claims may impress students at Columbia University or UCLA, but there is no substance to them and no archaeological or historical evidence for any continuity between the ancient Canaanites or Jebusites and today's Palestinians.[932] There is, however, a clear continuity between the ancient Israelites and the Jews who inhabit modern Israel. The State of Israel is on land that never was an independent Arab state of Palestine, but that was known in ancient times as Judea (that is, the land of the Jews), as well as Samaria, Idumea, and Galilee, which were also all inhabited by Jews. The Romans conquered Judea in 63 BCE, but the Jews never fully reconciled themselves to that fact and embarked upon a series of revolts that led to the destruction of the Temple in 70 CE and their official expulsion from the land in 134 CE.

In order to rub salt into the Jews' wounds, as well as to try to erase their links to the land, the Romans gave a new name to Jerusalem: Aelia Capitolina. This did not catch on, but the new name they gave to Judea did: Palestine. As we have seen, they found this name in the Bible; it was adapted from the name of the ancient and long-extinct enemy of the Jews in the Hebrew scriptures, the extinct Philistines. "Palestine," however, was not the name of any people or the marker of any ethnicity or nationality. Instead, it was akin to "Staten Island":

---

[930] Matthew Gindin, "Are Both Jews and Palestinians Indigenous to Israel?," *Forward,* May 24, 2017.

[931] Caroline Glick, "Yes, Palestinians Are an Invented People," *Real Clear World,* December 13, 2011.

[932] Ibid.

the name of a region, never of a people or a nation. That region remained part of the Roman Empire until the Arabs conquered it in the seventh century. The Turks supplanted the Arabs late in the eleventh century and ruled the area all the way until the first two decades of the twentieth century.

Yet throughout all these centuries, some Jews remained in what they maintained was their ancestral homeland. Occasionally, the authorities were favorable to this claim: in 438 CE, the Roman Empress Eudocia removed a prohibition that had been in place for three hundred years, forbidding Jews to pray on the Temple Mount. At this news, Jews in Galilee sent a message to "the great and mighty people of the Jews," stating happily: "Know then that the end of the exile of our people has come."[933]

This was premature. Seven centuries later, Palestinian Jews once again issued a call to Jews who were in exile to return home.[934] There were, however, always inducements not to do so. On July 15, 1099, crusaders from Western Europe entered Jerusalem and attacked Jews along with Muslims. The twelfth-century Syrian Muslim chronicler al-Azimi noted laconically that these crusaders "burned the Church of the Jews."[935] Al-Azimi's contemporary and fellow chronicler, Ibn al-Qalanisi, provided more details: "The Franks stormed the town and gained possession of it. A number of the townsfolk fled to the sanctuary and a great host were killed. The Jews assembled in the synagogue, and the Franks burned it over their heads. The sanctuary was surrendered to them on guarantee of safety on 22 Sha'ban [14 July] of this year, and they destroyed the shrines and the tomb of Abraham."[936]

[933] Samuel Katz, *Battleground: Facts and Fantasy in Palestine* (New York: Taylor Productions, revised edition 2002), 89.
[934] Ibid., 97.
[935] Carole Hillenbrand, *The Crusades: Islamic Perspectives* (Routledge, 2000), 64–65.
[936] Ibid.

The crusaders revived the old Roman prohibition on Jews entering Palestine, but this new prohibition was no more effective than the first one. In 1140, while the crusaders were still occupying Jerusalem, a Jewish philosopher and poet, Yehudah Halevi, wrote a book with the enduring title *Kuzari*, or *Book of Refutation and Proof in Support of the Despised Religion*. Halevi maintained that it was essential for Jews to return to the land of Israel, as that was the one place where they could be closest to the God who had led them out of slavery in Egypt and given them the land of Israel. When he tried to act upon his own words, Halevi, however, ran afoul of an Arab in Jerusalem who murdered him as he sang an elegy he had written, "Zion ha-lo Tish'ali."[937]

Despite such incidents, Jews continued to stream into the Holy Land, which some Jews had never left. The noted philosopher Maimonides returned in the thirteenth century. Toward the end of the fifteenth century, a Czech traveler named Martin Kabátnik encountered Jews in Jerusalem and wrote of their plight: "The heathens [that is, the Muslim rulers] oppress them at their pleasure. They know that the Jews think and say that this is the Holy Land that was promised to them. Those of them who live here are regarded as holy by the other Jews, for in spite of all the tribulations and the agonies that they suffer at the hands of the heathen, they refuse to leave the place."[938] There were, at that time, around thirty Jewish communities in the region.[939]

The growth of these communities faced numerous impediments. Because Jews were known as capable businessmen, the Ottoman Sultan Murad III, in 1576, ordered a thousand Jews to be deported from Safed in Palestine to Cyprus. The deportees had done nothing

---

[937] Richard Gottheil, Max Schloessinger, and Isaac Broydé, "Judah Ha-Levi (Arabic, Abu al-Hasan al-Lawi), *Jewish Encyclopedia*, 1906, http://www.jewishencyclopedia.com/articles/9005-judah-ha-levi#2223.

[938] Katz, 92.

[939] Ibid.

wrong. Murad just wanted to strengthen Cyprus's economy.[940] It is unclear whether those who had been ordered deported actually left for Cyprus. But if they did, they might have been able to establish a more comfortable existence than they enjoyed in Palestine. Early in the seventeenth century, two travelers in Safed said that for the Jews there, "life here is the poorest and most miserable that one can imagine.... They pay for the very air they breathe."[941] Yet they remained there, for it was their homeland.

The Turks took full advantage of the Jews' economic acumen. A Jesuit priest, Father Michael Naud, wrote in 1674 that the Jews in Jerusalem were resigned to "paying heavily to the Turk for their right to stay here.... They prefer being prisoners in Jerusalem to enjoying the freedom they could acquire elsewhere.... The love of the Jews for the Holy Land, which they lost through their betrayal [of Christ], is unbelievable."[942] Naud noted that other Jews were joining them: "Many of them come from Europe to find a little comfort, though the yoke is heavy."[943]

In 1695, the Dutch Orientalist Adrian Reland embarked upon an extensive tour of Palestine, visiting places that were mentioned in the Bible, Mishnah, and Talmud. In 1716, he published his findings as a book, *Palaestina, ex monumentis veteribus illustrate* (Palestine, Illustrated from Ancient Monuments). Reland made a map of the entire region and related every place he visited to its mention in the scriptures or Jewish tradition, if there was one. For each place, he gave the original source of its name, whether it was from Hebrew, Greek, or Latin sources. He didn't give the Arabic source of place names because there were no such place names.

---

[940] Ibid., 94.
[941] Ibid., 94–5.
[942] Ibid., 95.
[943] Ibid.

Contrary to the modern-day claims that the indigenous people of the land are the Palestinian Arabs, Reland found not a single settlement in the entire region at that time that had a name of Arabic origin. Some places were renamed later, but their Arabic names are of relatively recent vintage. Like many other travelers, Reland found the area generally empty and desolate. Most of the people he did encounter living there were Jews; the rest were Christians. Reland encountered very few Arab Muslims; most of those whom he did meet were nomadic Bedouins. The "indigenous Palestinians" were nowhere in evidence. In Nazareth of Galilee, Reland found around seven hundred Christians. In Jerusalem, he said that there were around five thousand people, most of whom were Jews, along with some Christians. In Gaza, he found around 550 people, half of them Jews and the other half Christians.[944]

In 1810, Jews who were disciples of the Vilna Gaon, a renowned Talmudic scholar, arrived in Palestine and rejoiced, although it was no more populated than it had been during Reland's time: "Truly, how marvelous it is to live in the good country. Truly, how wonderful it is to love our country.... Even in her ruin there is none to compare with her, even in her desolation she is unequaled, in her silence there is none like her. Good are her ashes and her stones."[945]

Nearly four decades later, an American navy commander, William F. Lynch, visited Palestine and wrote in Tiberias, "we had letters to the chief rabbi of the Jews, who came to meet us, and escorted us through a labyrinth of streets to the house of Heim Weisman, a brother Israel ite."[946] In that city, Lynch said, the Jews had "two synagogues, the

[944] Avi Goldreich, "A Tour of Palestine; The Year is 1695," Nurit Greenger, trans., Think-Israel, August 4, 2007, http://www.think-israel.org/goldreich.palestina.html.

[945] Katz, 100–101.

[946] William F. Lynch, *Narrative of the United States' Expedition to the River Jordan and the Dead Sea* (Philadelphia: Lea and Blanchard, 1850), 89.

Sephardim and Askeniazim, but lived harmoniously together."[947] Some were relatively new arrivals: "There are many Polish Jews, with light complexions, among them. They describe themselves as very poor, and maintained by the charitable contributions of Jews abroad, mostly in Europe."[948]

Lynch noted that there were more Jews in Tiberias than any other group: "There are about three hundred families, or one thousand Jews, in this town. The sanhedrim consists of seventy rabbis, of whom thirty are natives and forty Franks, mostly from Poland, with a few from Spain. The rabbis stated that controversial matters of discipline among Jews, all over the world, are referred to this sanhedrim. Besides the Jews, there are in Tiberias from three to four hundred Muslims and two or three Latins, from Nazareth."[949]

Lynch took a dim view of the ruling power, the Ottoman Empire: "It needs but the destruction of that power which, for so many centuries, has rested like an incubus upon the eastern world, to ensure the restoration of the Jews to Palestine."[950]

ANTISEMITISM AND ANTI-ZIONISM

As Zionism took hold and Jews began returning to Palestine in large numbers, the Ottomans proved Lynch's words correct as they moved to stop the burgeoning movement. In November 1881, the Ottoman Council of Ministers announced that Jewish immigrants would "be able to settle as scattered groups throughout Turkey, excluding

---

947   Ibid.
948   Ibid., 92.
949   Ibid., 93.
950   Ibid., 280.

Palestine."[951] As the Jews kept applying for visas to enter Palestine, the Ottoman consul-general at Odessa posted this notice outside his office on April 28, 1882: "The Ottoman Government informs all [Jews] wishing to immigrate into Turkey that they are not permitted to settle in Palestine. They may immigrate into the other provinces of [the Empire] and settle as they wish, provided only that they become Ottoman subjects and accept the obligation to fulfil the laws of the Empire."[952] Nevertheless, Jews continued to brave deportation or worse by making their way to Palestine.

On June 28, 1891, the Ottoman Sultan Abdulhamid II reiterated the empire's absolute opposition to Zionism: "It is not permissible to take a course which, by accepting [into the empire] those who are expelled from every place, may in the future result in the creation of a Jewish government in Jerusalem. Since it is necessary that they should be sent to America, they and their like should not be accepted, and should be put aboard ships immediately and sent to America."[953]

The Ottomans compelled Muslim Arabs to move into Palestine to counter the Jewish immigration. Arabs also began moving there voluntarily, thinking they would be able to get jobs in the businesses the Jews started. Eli E. Hertz of Myths and Facts, an organization that dispels myths about Israel, points out that "family names of many Palestinians attest to their non-Palestinian origins. Just as Jews bear names like Berliner, Warsaw and Toledano, modern phone books in the Territories are filled with families named Elmisri (Egyptian), Chalabi (Syrian), Mugrabi (North Africa). Even George Habash—the arch-terrorist and head of Black September—bears a

---

[951]   Neville J. Mandel, Ottoman Policy and Restrictions on Jewish Settlement in Palestine: 1881–1908-Part I, *Middle Eastern Studies*, Vol. 10, No. 3 (October 1974), 312–3.
[952]   Ibid., 313.
[953]   Ibid., 323.

name with origins in Abyssinia or Ethiopia, *Habash* in both Arabic and Hebrew."[954]

Christian antisemites, meanwhile, also tried to head off the establishment of a Jewish state. In 1905, a Maronite Catholic named Négib Azoury published a book in French entitled *Le Réveil dela Nation Arabe dans l'Asie Turque* (The Awakening of the Arab Nation in Turkish Asia) in which he called upon Muslims and Christians, including the Vatican and all the Churches, to work together prevent the reestablishment of a Jewish state. Azoury noted that the burgeoning Arab nationalist movement, which brought together Muslims with Christians, "comes just at the moment when Israel is so close to succeeding, in order to destroy its [Israel's] plans for universal domination."[955] Azoury says that he wrote his book "with the aim of facilitating understanding of the *Jewish Peril*."[956]

The historian Bat Ye'or notes that in order to try to prevent the creation of a Jewish state, "foreign missionaries from the Syrian Protestant College, the Jesuits, the religious missions of the Vatican, and the Orthodox Churches linked to Moscow" distributed antisemitic pamphlets in Arabic among Muslims.[957]

This enterprise, however, did not proceed unopposed. A year after Azoury's book appeared, a Lebanese Greek Orthodox Christian, Farid Kassab, defended the Jews, saying that they were reviving the land and were not foreigners to that land "morally or politically."[958] Kassab criticized Azoury's vision of an "Arab nation" and reserved his strongest attacks for Azoury himself. According to Kassab, Azoury

---

[954] Eli E. Hertz, "Palestinians 'Peoplehood' Based on a Big Lie," Myths and Facts, March 31, 2008, https://israelbehindthenews.com/2018/10/23/palestinians-peoplehood-based-on-a-big-lie/.

[955] Bat Ye'or, *Islam and Dhimmitude* (Teaneck, New Jersey: Fairleigh Dickinson University Press, 2002), 143.

[956] Ibid.

[957] Bat Ye'or, Élie: Al-Kahira, 1913–1942 (Paris: Provinciales, 2021), 47.

[958] Neville J. Mandel, *The Arabs and Zionism before World War I* (Berkeley, California: University of California Press, 1976), 51.

was a "Catholic bigot, a member of the Society of Jesus," who hated the Jews because he believed that they killed Christ.[959] Azoury, he said, was "not only anti-Jewish from the religious point of view, but also anti-Semitic."[960] Kassab charged that the Vatican had its own plans for the territory:

> What is extremely interesting and likely is that the Roman Curia, loyal to its principles and traditions, and with its shaven-headed groups, is working to bring about the emergence of a Muslim kingdom. Solely to this end, and in an amicable way, it [the Curia] will continue to recruit bands of sympathetic monks in Europe, send them to the East in order to help its establishment [the Muslim kingdom], and to prepare the hearts of Christians, instilling in them [Arab] national feeling and bring them closer to Muslims from whom they have been estranged.[961]

At the time he wrote this, Kassab most likely did not know of the pioneering Zionist Theodor Herzl's audience with Pope Pius X on January 26, 1904. But during that meeting, the pontiff told Herzl something similar. When Herzl told him about Zionism and asked for his support, the pope replied firmly: "We cannot give approval to this movement. We cannot prevent the Jews from going to Jerusalem—but we could never sanction it. The soil of Jerusalem, if it was not always sacred, has been sanctified by the life of Jesus Christ. As the head of the Church, I cannot tell you anything different. The

---

[959] Ibid.
[960] Ibid.
[961] Bat Ye'or, *Islam and Dhimmitude*, op. cit., 144.

Jews have not recognized our Lord, therefore we cannot recognize the Jewish people."[962]

Jerusalem, Pius insisted, "must not get into the hands of the Jews."[963] To that, Herzl responded: "And its present status, Holy Father?"[964] The pope said: "I know, it is not pleasant to see the Turks in possession of our Holy Places. We simply have to put up with that. But to support the Jews in the acquisition of the Holy Places, that we cannot do."[965] Thus, Kassab was correct: the Vatican had no problem with a Muslim kingdom ruling the region but would not stand for a Jewish state there.

World War I upset these plans. A new Muslim kingdom would not be established. The old one was collapsing. At the dawn of the twentieth century, the Ottoman Empire was known as "The Sick Man of Europe," but it still had sovereignty over the territory that is now Israel and the supposedly occupied land as well. By the end of the war, however, the empire, which had backed Germany and Austria, was doomed. In the early 1920s, just before the empire fell altogether, it ceded control of its Middle Eastern holdings, including the territory that would later become the State of Israel, to the League of Nations.

A Jewish state would ultimately be established. But the antisemitic Muslim-Christian collaboration of which Azoury dreamed still persisted and continues to be a fond hope of many to this day, although, as always, the outreach and gestures of goodwill come entirely from the Christian side and not from the Muslim one. After the October 7 Hamas attack, the Vatican threw its moral authority behind the

---

[962] "Theodor Herzl: Audience with Pope Pius X (1904)," Council of Centers on Jewish-Christian Relations, https://ccjr.us/dialogika-resources/primary-texts-from-the-history-of-the-relationship/herzl1904.

[963] Ibid.

[964] Ibid.

[965] Ibid.

Palestinian jihadis. Despite its irenic renunciations of antisemitism at the Second Vatican Council and thereafter, it began to sound like the Vatican of old.

On May 7, 2024, the Vatican daily *L'Osservatore Romano* published an article entitled "Antisemitismo e Palestina" (Anti-Semitism and Palestine). The author, a Jesuit priest named David Neuhaus, ascribed the post-October 7 rise in Jew-hatred to Israel's "ruthless war against the Palestinians."[966] Neuhaus, according to journalist Jules Gomes, even "equated fighting antisemitism with struggling for Palestinian liberation, and drew a moral equivalence between the Shoah (Holocaust) and the Nakba (Catastrophe), which he defined as Israel's 'destruction of Palestinian society in 1948.'"[967] Neuhaus said nothing about the war that the neighboring Arab states had waged in order to destroy the nascent state of Israel or about the Arab Higher Committee's calls to the local Arabs to leave the area of the new state until it could be annihilated.

Neuhaus followed this up with a lengthy essay in the Vatican's other main publication, *Civiltà Cattolica*, in which he publicly advised Pope Francis not to take sides in the conflict between Israel and Hamas. Gomes notes that Neuhaus "parroted Palestinian talking points to claim that most of the Jews arriving in Israel 'were fleeing European anti-Semitism.' He failed to mention that there were more Jewish refugees expelled from Arab countries (850,000 to one million) than Palestinians who became refugees in 1948 (the UN estimated 726,000). Iran later expelled 70,000 Jews following the Islamic Revolution in in 1979–80."[968]

---

[966] Gomes, "The Vatican's Mouthpieces," op. cit.
[967] Ibid.
[968] Ibid.

MANDATORY PALESTINE

On July 24, 1922, the League granted administrative control over Palestine to Britain, in view of "the declaration originally made on November 2nd, 1917, by the Government of His Britannic Majesty, and adopted by the said Powers, in favor of the establishment in Palestine of a national home for the Jewish people, it being clearly understood that nothing should be done which might prejudice the civil and religious rights of existing non-Jewish communities in Palestine, or the rights and political status enjoyed by Jews in any other country; and whereas recognition has thereby been given to the historical connection of the Jewish people with Palestine and to the grounds for reconstituting their national home in that country."[969]

Britain immediately turned over 77 percent of the Mandate for Palestine, which was supposed to be the site of the Jewish National Home, to the Arabs to create Jordan. Nevertheless, the British remained generally committed to establishing a Jewish national home in the remainder. Leftists sometimes point to Mandatory Palestine as the Palestinian state that supposedly predated Israel. But this claim relies on the ignorance of the fact that this British territory had been explicitly set aside for Jewish settlement. Nine years before the founding of the modern state of Israel, a 1939 flag of "Palestine" sports a star of David.[970]

When the state of Israel was founded in 1948, it immediately had to fight a war for its survival against the surrounding Arab nations that had vowed to destroy it. Then there was finally an occupation—in fact, two: Egypt occupied Gaza, and Jordan occupied Judea and Samaria (which it renamed the West Bank in 1950). Israel won back

---

[969] "League of Nations Mandate for Palestine as a Jewish State," The Israel Forever Foundation, July 24, 1922, https://israelforever.org/state/Mandate_for_Palestine_Jewish_State/.

[970] Robert Spencer, "The Flag of Palestine, 1939," Jihad Watch, November 15, 2014.

those territories in the Six-Day War of 1967, but that was actually ending an occupation, not starting one: the only international law governing sovereignty over those territories stipulated that they were to be part of a national home for the Jewish people.

So, from whom was the land stolen? Not from the Ottomans, who had ceded it to the League of Nations. Not from the League of Nations, which had granted administrative powers over it to the British. Not from the British, who only had it in order to help create a Jewish state there. And not from the Palestinians, who didn't even exist until the 1960s.

STOLEN IDENTITY?

In April 2024, students at George Washington University's pro-Palestinian encampment posted a handwritten sign: "Students will leave when Israelis leave. Students will go back home when Israelis go back to Europe, US, etc. (their Real homes.)"[971] Whoever wrote this is apparently unaware of the Jews' historical connections to and unbroken continuity in the land of Israel, and that is not surprising, given the low quality and propagandistic nature of American education today.

Yet the assumption is common and endlessly repeated among Palestinian propagandists and their allies that the "Zionist Jews," and all Ashkenazi Jews (Jews who settled in Europe) are actually ethnic Europeans who have no actual historical or ethnic connection to the land of Israel at all. This would substantiate the claim that the Israelis

---

[971] "Scratch the Surface of 'Anti-Zionism' and You Find Antisemitism," Elder of Ziyon, April 28, 2024, https://elderofziyon.blogspot.com/2024/04/scratch-surface-of-anti-zionism-and-you.html.

are just "colonizers" in the Middle East and that Israel is a "settler-colonialist" state.

Many of the Jews who were forced to leave Israel did, of course, settle in various parts of Europe, but the claim that is made is that they are native Europeans with no background in the Middle East. The objective here is obvious: if the Jews of today have no ethnic connection to the ancient Jews of the land of Israel, then they have no right to return and claim to be the indigenous people of the land.

Some Jewish historians have inadvertently lent credence to this claim. In 1913, the rabbi and historian Jacob S. Raisin noted that a rabbi, Isaac Baer Levinsohn (1788–1860), "was the first to express the opinion that the Russian Jews hailed, not from Germany, as is commonly supposed, but from the banks of the Volga. This hypothesis, corroborated by tradition, Harkavy established as a fact."[972] Abraham Harkavy was a Lithuanian Jewish historian who died in 1919. Neither Levinson nor Harkavy, or Raisin for that matter, intended to say that the Jews of Russia were native Russians or to deny that they had originated in the land of Israel; they were remarking on much more recent movements of people.

Nevertheless, the idea that the Jews had no actual connection to Judea began to gain ground. In 1883, the French historian Ernest Renan said in a lecture: "This conversion of the kingdom of the Khazars has considerable importance in the question of the origin of the Jews who inhabit the Danubian countries and the south of Russia. These regions contain large masses of Jewish populations who probably have nothing or almost nothing ethnographically Jewish."[973]

It took twenty-first-century genetic testing to put this claim to rest. In December 2012, an Israeli geneticist, Eran Elhaik, published

---

[972] Jacob S. Raisin, *The Haskalah Movement in Russia* (Philadelphia: The Jewish Publication Society of America, 1913), 18.

[973] Louis Vivien de Saint-Martin, *Juifs: extrait du Dictionnaire universel de géographie de Vivien de Saint-Martin* (Paris: A. Lahure, 1884), 36.

a study in which he announced, to the joy of antisemites everywhere: "Our findings support the Khazarian hypothesis depicting a large Near Eastern–Caucasus ancestry along with Southern European, Middle Eastern, and Eastern European ancestries, in agreement with recent studies and oral and written traditions."[974] Yet even Elhaik's study did not claim to establish that Ashkenazi Jews had no Middle Eastern ancestry. Elhaik explained: "We conclude that the genome of European Jews is a tapestry of ancient populations including Judaized Khazars, Greco–Roman Jews, Mesopotamian Jews, and Judeans and that their population structure was formed in the Caucasus and the banks of the Volga with roots stretching to Canaan and the banks of the Jordan."[975]

One year later, thirty geneticists published an in-depth study that sharply criticized Elhaik's study. Elhaik, the geneticists wrote, "relied on the provocative assumption that the Armenians and Georgians of the South Caucasus could serve as appropriate proxies for Khazar descendants, This assumption is problematic for a number of reasons."[976] Chief among these was the fact that "because of great variety of populations in the Caucasus region and the fact that no specific population in the region is known to represent Khazar descendants, evidence for ancestry among Caucasus populations need not reflect Khazar ancestry."[977]

The geneticists conducted their own study that refuted Elhaik's findings. It included 1,774 genetic samples "from 106 Jewish and non-Jewish populations that span the possible regions of potential Ashkenazi ancestry: Europe, the Middle East, and the region

---

[974] Eran Elhaik, "The Missing Link of Jewish European Ancestry: Contrasting the Rhineland and the Khazarian Hypotheses," *Genome Biology and Evolution*, Vol. 5, Issue 1, January 2013, 61.

[975] Ibid.

[976] Doron M. Behar et al., "No Evidence from Genome-wide Data of a Khazar Origin for the Ashkenazi Jews," *Human Biology*, December 2013, 85(6): 859–900.

[977] Ibid.

historically associated with the Khazar Khaganate."[978] The study "found that Ashkenazi Jews share the greatest genetic ancestry with other Jewish populations and, among non-Jewish populations, with groups from Europe and the Middle East. No particular similarity of Ashkenazi Jews to populations from the Caucasus is evident, particularly populations that most closely represent the Khazar region."

On top of that, Ashkenazi Jews don't make up a majority of Israel's population. Most of the Jews in Israel are Sephardis, Jews of Middle Eastern origin.

IS ISRAEL REALLY AN "APARTHEID STATE"?

As pro-Palestinian demonstrations take place on campuses all across the nation, the idea is persistent and pervasive: yes, the Hamas attacks on October 7 were terrible, but Israel had it coming because it is an oppressive apartheid state. The "apartheid" word gets thrown around quite a lot in connection with Israel. Yet like so many other charges leveled at the Jewish state, there is nothing to it.

The term "apartheid" comes from South Africa, which institutionalized a system of racial segregation and discrimination that was in place from 1948 to 1991. The word itself means "separateness," and South Africa enforced numerous laws to keep the races apart in schools, workplaces, and areas where the public gathered, such as beaches.

There is absolutely nothing like this in Israel. As political analyst Hugh Fitzgerald has explained: "In Israel, Arabs sit on the Supreme Court, serve in the Knesset, go abroad as ambassadors. The chairman of Israel's largest bank, Bank Leumi, is an Arab. Jews and Arabs work in the same factories and offices, play on the same sports teams and

---

[978] Ibid.

in the same orchestras, act in the same films, are treated in the same hospitals by both Jewish and Arab medical personnel, attend the same classes in the same universities. Jews and Arabs own restaurants and start high-tech businesses together. The only difference in their treatment is that Jews *must*, while Arabs *may*, serve in the military."[979]

There are no legal restrictions upon Arabs in Israel. The media watchdog HonestReporting points out that "the legal, state-sanctioned discrimination that is the definition of apartheid is not only absent from Israel, it is furiously combatted by its laws and independent judiciary. Israel's basic laws serve as legal safeguards, providing protection of life, body, and dignity in a democratic state with equal rights for all, including ethnic minorities."[980]

In September 2023, Mosiuoa Lekota, who had been an anti-apartheid activist from South Africa, said: "I was in Israel, my brother. In Israel, you won't find the same divisions between Jews and non-Jews that we used to witness during apartheid. There are no segregated buses for different ethnic groups, like Jews and Arabs. In Israel, everyone boards the same bus, travels wherever they need to, and disembarks as they wish. There is no apartheid in Israel, not even within their schools."[981]

Why, then, has the "apartheid" smear become so common among haters of Israel? Because it plays on Western traumas about racism and serves as a shorthand way to demonize the Jewish state without having to bother with actual evidence. The primary evidence that those who claim Israel implements apartheid policies offer, when they offer any evidence at all, is that Israel has built fences between Israel

---

[979] Hugh Fitzgerald, "Marc Lamont Hill Appointed 'Presidential Professor' at CUNY, No One Objects," *Jihad Watch*, August 28, 2023.

[980] Gidon Ben-Zvi, "The 'Apartheid' Myth: The Improper Use of False and Misleading Claims Regarding Israel," HonestReporting, March 9, 2023.

[981] Zvika Klein, "Israel Is Not an Apartheid State, Former South African Defense Minister Says," *Jerusalem Post*, September 24, 2023.

proper and the areas under Palestinian Authority control. Palestinians who work in Israel have to pass through checkpoints, some of which involve long lines, to get to and from work.

These measures are in place, however, not because of racism on Israel's part, but because so many Palestinians have victimized Israelis in jihad attacks. The leftists who denounce Israel for being an apartheid state would see it rendered defenseless against those who have repeatedly vowed to destroy it.

That's likely the whole idea. The deck is stacked against Israel, as it has been against Jews ever since Apion claimed that they carried out human sacrifices of non-Jews in the Temple. Old lies never die, and new lies build on old ones. Any action that a Jew takes in any field, even if the Jew in question is not religious, can be used as evidence of a vast Jewish plot against the non-Jewish world.

Yet whenever these charges are exposed to rational evaluation, they fall apart. While no group is sinless or entirely above reproach, the record of Jews throughout history is of a people far more sinned against than sinning. After October 7, hating Jews has once again become fashionable and accepted. Yet it is no more rational or justified in the America of today than it was in Berlin in 1933 or in medieval Baghdad or Paris. And it carries the same lethal possibilities that it did in the past, of innocent people being liable to be brutalized and killed.

As such, it is one of the world's longest-standing and foremost injustices.

Epilogue

A SOCIAL CONTAGION

The Russian dissident Aleksander Solzhenitsyn wrote: "Gradually it was disclosed to me that the line separating good and evil passes not through states, nor between classes, nor between political parties either—but right through every human heart—and through all human hearts."[982]

Indeed. The line separating good and evil doesn't pass between people of one ethnicity and another, nor between people of one religion and another. There are Jews who do good and Jews who do evil, just as there are Christians who do good and Christians who do evil, and the same can be said of people of every group. Only when Jews are involved in some enterprise or another, however, does their presence become evidence that the enterprise itself is a massive Jewish conspiracy. People have been captivated by this delusion throughout history, and it is on the rise again now.

---

[982] Aleksandr Solzhenitsyn, *The Gulag Archipelago*, Part 4, Chapter 1, "The Ascent," The Aleksandr Solzhenitsyn Center, https://www.solzhenitsyncenter.org/notable-quotations.

This is an age of social contagions. There have been occasions of mass hysteria throughout the ages: the Salem witch trials, the COVID-19 panic, and many more. It is apparently an impulse deep within human nature: to be susceptible to suggestion that overpowers the ability to reason and leads to a stampede. Hatred of Jews is a persistent and recurring social contagion that is now cresting again, after people of goodwill around the world thought that it had been definitively laid to rest in the ashes of National Socialist Germany in 1945.

Against social contagions, rational argumentation is only of limited value. In this book, I have tried to show the fundamental irrationality and wrongheadedness of some of the principal charges against Jews, but I'm well aware that attempting to argue rationally against those who insist that people are acting clandestinely on the basis of secret teachings is an unwinnable proposition. There is a sucker born every minute, said P. T. Barnum, and he could have said the same thing about antisemites and their theories. Since I began writing this book, new antisemitic conspiracy theories have been born, and some people will always be willing or even happy to be convinced.

The everlasting wellsprings of antisemitism that we have examined, in Christianity, Islam, and national and international socialism, are still active today and will continue to nourish bitter fruit. Imams are preaching about how the "genocidal" Jews are acting according to their nature in Gaza. Christians are claiming that the Jews secretly control US foreign policy (they apparently haven't noticed the Biden administration's comprehensive and multifaceted betrayal of Israel) and are manipulating the Gentile leaders of the world like so many puppets on a string. All over the world, people believe, in line with the United Nations, that Israel is uniquely evil and deserving of far more attention and condemnation than North Korea, the Islamic Republic of Iran, and other violators of human rights. Jew-hatred is as old as Judaism itself. It has persisted for centuries. It will not end.

Nevertheless, people of goodwill recall with horror where Jew-hatred has led, and where it is quite obviously leading today if the present circumstances continue. There are many who are working to prevent it from leading there again. Most people can never be entirely irrational any more than they can be entirely rational, and some who have fallen prey to this particular social contagion will eventually wake up and realize that they have embraced irrationality and hatred. While Jew-hatred is fashionable again, we can only hope that this most pernicious of social contagions will soon pass as did the others and leave in its wake minimal damage.

In the meantime, amid the ongoing barrage of propaganda, factionalism, chauvinism, prejudice, and blindness, the truth still shines forth as clearly as ever from scapegoating, prejudice, and propaganda. It is always available for that small number of people who still, as quaint as it is to do so these days, hold the truth dear.

Acknowledgments

The idea for this book arose from discussions with two people I had respected and admired, but not in the usual way. After the October 7 massacre, they stunned me with their open avowals of age-old antisemitic myths that I thought no sane and rational individual took seriously anymore—the Jews control the media, the Jews control the international organizations, and so forth. They know who they are, and I dedicate this book, in particular, to them, in the somewhat quixotic hope that it will move them to reconsider their positions.

Many people kindly helped me with this project. Some explained the nature of the Talmud and clarified some of the proof texts that antisemites use. Others offered me valuable information on other topics and helpfully pointed out typographical errors and other infelicities in the manuscript. As with all my books, however, virtually all of these people preferred not to be named here so as not to become a target. Thus, I will not strain the reader's patience with a long list of names, most of which will be unknown to him. Suffice it to say that I am deeply grateful to all those who offered help, great and small, with this book, and once again affirm the truth that whatever good is in it comes from them, and whatever weaknesses in it from me.

David S. Bernstein at Bombardier Books has been extraordinarily supportive and helpful over the years, and I am grateful to him that he saw the need for this book. I appreciate also Aleigha Koss's invaluable aid with the book's production, as well as that of all the people who were involved in various ways. May we all live to see saner times.